AN OLD TESTAMENT CC

THE BOOK OF
EZEKIEL

KEVIN J. CONNER

AN OLD TESTAMENT COMMENTARY

THE BOOK OF
EZEKIEL

KEVIN J. CONNER

Published by Conner Ministries Ltd

CONNER
MINISTRIES

Email: kevin.conner321@gmail.com

Web: www.kevinconner.org

TABLE OF CONTENTS

FOREWORD

My dad loved the Bible. He read it, studied it, memorised it, and taught it as often as there was opportunity. He enjoyed digging beneath the surface of a text as well as discovering, then following the many themes though-out the various books of the Bible. In due course, he became recognised as a leading Bible teacher within the wider church world, known for his insights and ability to unpack the meaning of God's Word.

Before passing away at the age of 92, in February 2019, my dad had written and published over 60 books. However, many of his personal Bible study notes had yet to be published. The book of Ezekiel is one such commentary.

The prophet Ezekiel lived in the ancient city of Babylon during a critical time in Israel's history. This Old Testament commentary contains many seed thoughts and insights from this intriguing book. It will be of assistance to pastors, teachers and Bible students everywhere.

May this book be an encouragement to you in your own journey of faith and your ministry to others.

Mark Conner
Melbourne, Australia
August 2020

INTRODUCTION TO EZEKIEL

THE RELEVANCE OF EZEKIEL

The New Testament writers continually appealed to the Old Testament writings, especially the Prophets, for the validity and relevancy of all that God was doing in their generation.

The Prophets, though men and women of their own generation, spoke truths and gave principles of living that are appropriate for each and every generation.

1. God spoke to the fathers by the prophets – Heb.1:1. Amp. NT.
2. The Prophets foretold the coming of Christ and spoke on His Church – Luke 24:26-27, 44-46; Matt.5:17-18; 11:12-13; Rom.16:25-26.
3. The prophets experienced revelation, inspiration, interpretation and application of many of the things God revealed to them – 1Pet.1:9-12.

Although the Prophets were written originally and primarily to natural and national Israel the truths are applicable prophetically and spiritually to the Church, the spiritual Israel of God (Gal.6:15,16).

If Ezekiel were alive today, what word would he have to say to the church - it's people and its leaders? Note: Acts 13:27. "…the voices of the prophets…"

THE HISTORICAL SETTING OF EZEKIEL

Ezekiel's name means: " He will be strengthened of God", or, "the Strength of God." As a young man, of the priestly line, he lived to see the desolation of the Temple, the house of the Lord at Jerusalem, under the King of Babylon – Nebuchadnezzar. He had seen visions of the Glory of God departing reluctantly from the Temple because of the various abominations of Israel and t he leaders which had brought such into the Temple of God.

Judah had been carried away captive, and both Daniel and Ezekiel were taken among the captives to Babylon (2Kgs.24:11-16; 2Chron.36:5-6; Dan.1:1-3; Ezek.1:1-2). Ezekiel is about 25 years of age. He lived to hear Jeremiah's prophecy that the Babylonian Captivity would last for 70 years (Jer.29:5-7).

"Babylon" means, "Confusion". Babel began in rebellion and ended up in confusion by the judgment of God (Gen.11). River Euphrates river. Confusion generation today. But God has His hand on the Jeremiah's, the Daniel's, the Ezekiel's of today in this Babylonian situation. Prophetic voices speaking today! My people have gone into captivity because they have no knowledge (Isa.5:13). My people destroyed for lack of knowledge. Captivity. Reject knowledge, reject you as being priest to Me.

Babylonian Captivity situation today: confusion politically, culturally, governmentally, ideologically, family, morally, economically, ecclesiastically – founded on rebellion again God's laws. Rejection of Biblical absolutes, and Biblical knowledge and understanding.

But though these Prophets were in Babylonian situation, they did not it get into them. In Babylon but Babylon not in them! In the world, not of the world. Have heart to understand what God is saying to the Church in these days. Understand the times we are living in.

The golden lamp-stand of the Church shines over against the wall and speaks in unknown tongue (writing): Babylon is about to fall (Dan.5).

GENERAL ANALYSIS OF EZEKIEL

1. **JERUSALEM - Chapters 1-24**
   A. Call and Charge of Ezekiel.   1 – 3
   B. Signs of the Siege. 4 – 5
   C. Death and Desolation. Judgments on Judah.   6 – 7
   D. Sinful Conditions – Visions. 8 – 16
      1. Idolatry. Chambers of Imagery. Ch. 8.
         a. Idols. Chambers of Imagery. 8
         b. Discrimination. Sealing of the Faithful. 9.
         c. Cherubim and Glory. 10.
         d. Rulers. 11-12.
         e. Rejection of the Prophets. 13.
         f. People. 14.

      2. Abominations. 15 – 16.

   E. Suffering for sin. 17 – 19.
      1. Judgment. 17.
      2. Justice. 18.
      3. Lamentations. 19.

   F. Last Warnings. 20 – 23.
      1. Rebellious. 20.
      2. Sword. 21.
      3. Sins. 22-23.

   G. Final Destruction. 24.

2. **FOREIGN NATIONS – GENTILES – 25 – 32, 35.**
   H. Ammon, Moab, Edom, Philistia. 25
   I. Tyre and Sidon. 26-28.
   J. Egypt. 29-32.

3. **RESTORATION AND MESSIANIC.** – 33 – 34, 36 – 38.
    K. Watchman. 33.
    L. Shepherds. 34.
    M. Mount Seir. 35
    N. Moral Restoration. 36.
    O. Corporate Restoration – Valley of Bones and Two Sticks. 37.
    P. Gog and Magog. 38-39.
    Q. The Temple itself. 40-42.
    The Glory. 43.
    The Ordinances. 44-46.
    The Temple River. 47.
    The City and the Land. 48.

OUTLINE OF EZEKIEL: THE BOOK OF VISIONS

Judgment on Judah and Jerusalem	Judgment on Gentile Nations	Restoration under Messiah
Pre – Siege Chapters 1-24	Mid – Siege Chapters 25-32, 35	Post – Siege Chapters 33-48
The Old Temple Glory Departs	The Gentiles	The New Temple Glory Returns
1. Glory leaves old material Temple (Ch.1-12) 2. Judgment on Princes, Prophets, Priests, Elders and Nation (Ch.12-23) 3. The Siege of Jerusalem in finality (Ch.23) • 5th yr of Captivity - 1-7 • 6th yr of Captivity - 8-19 • 7th yr of Captivity - 20-23 • 9th yr of Captivity - 24	Seven Nations under the Judgments of God Refer also to Isaiah 13-23, Jeremiah 46-51, Ezekiel 25-32, 35 1. Ammonites 2. Moabites 3. Edomites 4. Philistines 5. Tyrus 6. Zidon 7. Egypt	1. Restoration of Judah through the Messiah (Ch.33-36) 2. Valley of Dry Bones and the Two Sticks (Ch.37) 3. Gog and Magog (Ch.38-39) 4. The New Temple, the River, and the Glory Returns (Ch.40-48)

ALTERNATIVE OUTLINE:

I. **EZEKIEL'S CALL AND COMMISSION** – Ch. 1-3.

II. **EZEKIEL'S MESSAGE** – Ch. 4-24.
  A. It's Contents – Predictions concerning Jerusalem, Ch. 4-7.
    1. Seige – 4:1-3.
    2. Famine – 5:8-10.
    3. Pestilence – 6:11-12.
    4. Desolation – 7:3, 27.

  B. It's Cause – Why must God judge? Ch. 8.
    Ezekiel had a vision of the immorality of Jerusalem – 8:3.
    1. The image of jealousy – vs 3)
       At the Gate of the Altar – vs 5)
    2. The abominable acts – vs 9   ) Immoral acts of men
       At the Door of the Temple court – vs 7)
    3. Women weeping of Babylonian gods – vs 13-14
       Idolatry of women
    4. In the inner court of the Lord's House
       Sun-worship – vs 16. Heathen sun-worship. Creature instead
       of the Creator.
       Result was that God could only deal in judgment. Vs 18.

  C. It's Course – How would God judge? Ch. 9-11.
    1. Outward – Ch. 9. The death-penalty. Ch. 9-11. Ch. 9:1, 2, 6.
    2. Inward – Ch. 10-11. Commencing with God's House.
       God removed His glorious presence and abandoned both City
       and Temple. Refer 10:4, 18-19; 11:23.
       God will not share His temple with rival gods. If sin comes
       in, the glory is driven out.

  D. It's Character – Whom God would judge. Ch. 12-24. Here
     prophecies are interspersed with pictures.
     Prophecies – 12-14; Picture – 15.
     Prophecies – 16; Picture – 17.
     Prophecies – 18-22; Picture – 23-24.

III. **PARENTHESIS – JUDGMENT ON FOREIGN NATIONS** – Ch.
     25-32, 35.
     A. Ammon – Ch. 25.   Key vs 3-4.
     B. Moab – Ch. 25.   Key vs 8-9.
     C. Edom – Ch 25.   Key vs 12-13.
     D. Philistia – Ch 25. Key vs 15-16.
     E. Tyre – Ch. 26-28. Key vs 26:2-3.

F.   Egypt – Ch. 29-32. Key vs 29:3-7.
       Israel's enemies are also God's enemies.
G.   Mt Seir. Ch. 35.

IV.   **PREDICTION OF RESTORATION** – Ch. 33-39.
    A.   Call to Prayer – Ch. 33-36. Key vs 36:37.
    B.   The message of hope. Ch. 37. Key vs 37:11-12.
    C.   The summons to prepare. Ch. 38-39. Key vs 38:7-8.
    So Israel buried as a nation, was to have a national resurrection, and Northern and Southern Kingdoms were to be re-united under one King, the Messiah.

V.   **THE VISION OF THE REBUILT TEMPLE.** Ch. 40-48.
Key verses 43:1-5; 48:35. The vision was given to keep fresh in the minds of the Exiles the duty of returning to Palestine and rebuilding God's Temple.

EZEKIEL CHAPTER ONE

1. **TIME OF EZEKIEL'S CALL** – vs 1-3.

    Vs 1.   Time – 30th year, 4th month, 5th day of the Captivity. BC. 595
            about. Ezekiel among the captives by the River Chebar, in the
            land of the Chaldeans. Babylonia or Chaldea. Chaldea
            "as demons".

    Vs 2.   The 5th year of Jehoiachin's captivity. Ezekiel carried away
            captive about BC, 598.

    Vs 3.   Ezekiel – "Strength of God."
            A Prophet-Priest.
            As Prophet – Outward. Speak from God to man. His
            spokesman.
            As Priest – Inward.   Speaks for Man to God, spokesman.
            Son of Buzi or "Despised". So he was among his fellow
            captives.
            The call to the prophetic office came about the 5th year of
            Ezekiel's captivity, thus he was about 30 years of age. As was
            Joseph, David, Priests to ministry, and Jesus. Cf. Num 4:3 etc.

            Note the experiences and expressive clauses of the Call of the
            Prophet of God.
            1. Heavens were opened to him. Clear vision, Heaven's
                viewpoint.
            2. Visions of God seen. Need clear vision.
            3. Word of the Lord came expressly to him. God's word.
                Hear from Him. Not man.
            4. The Hand of the Lord was upon him.

2. **THE VISION OF THE LIVING CREATURES AND THE
    THRONE OF GOD.** - vs 4-28.
    There is no doubt about the fact that the vision is symbolic. Such
    creatures as described here not in God's creations.   But they do
    symbolise real spirit beings. Ezekiel is a prophet of vision.

    This chapter (chapters 1, 10) should be compared where the Living
    Creatures are seen again. It will be noted that Ezekiel 1:4-28 uses the
    words "Living Creatures" about 14 times, with 3:13; 10:15, 17, 20.

    Ezekiel 10:1-22 uses the words "Cherub" or "Cherubim" mostly, used
    about 22 times, with 11:22; 9:3 and thus area really the same beings.

Note the list of symbolics used and their significance, or the truth symbolised therein. Vs 4.

A. The Cloud of Glory – vs 4.
  1. A whirlwind – Divine agitation, movement.
  2. Out of the North – place of God's throne. Psalm 75; Isa 14:12-14. Judgment also.
  3. A great Cloud – the Shekinah Glory cloud, cf. Ex 14. The Pillar of Cloud led Israel, and the cloud on the mercy seat of the Ark of God. Num 7.
  4. A fire enfolding itself – Fire, symbol of holiness of God. Burning Bush, Tongues of fire, etc. Heb. 12:29. God a consuming fire.
  5. Brightness about it – Majesty, light, brightness of God's being. Unapproachable light. 1 Tim. 6:16. Dwells in light, is Light.
  6. Out of midst colour of amber – Yellowish combination of gold and silver. Light of God.
  7. Out of the midst of the fire.
     The whole description is symbolic of the SHEKINAH GLORY of God, the Glory Cloud and the Pillar of Fire.
     Clouds are used as Divine transport and His chariots.
     Cloud descended on Mt Sinai, and God in action and manifestation. Ex 19:9.
     Cloudy Pillar led Israel.
     Cloud over the blood-stained mercy seat and the Cherubim on Ark of the Covenant.

  So this will be seen here also. The heavenly archetype of earthly throne of God.

B. The Living Creatures or Cherubim – vs 4-14.
  1. Their Number – vs 5.
     The likeness of 4 Living Creatures.
     Four – number of earth, worldwide, universal ministry.
     Living Creatures – alive, active, not dead. Creatures – created beings therefore.

  2. Their Appearance – vs 5.
     All had the appearance of a Man. Man – highest of God's creatures, the Masterpiece of creation, the image of God, king of creation under God. Gen 1:26-27.

  3. Their Faces – vs 6, 8.
     Refer to vs 10. Each had four faces. Possibly the 4 Standards of Tribes of Israel also.

12

Likeness of their faces:
1. Face of a Man – King of Creation
2. Face of a Lion – King of Beasts. Carnivorous.
3. Face of an Ox – King of Domestic Animals.
4. Face of an Eagle – King of the Birds.

Thus each speaks of Kingship, Royalty. Typical of Christ and the Church too.

Note: Angelic spirit beings never likened to these things, though sometimes angels did appear as men. However, Christ and the saints are likened to each of these creatures.
Matthew – King. Mark – Ox. Luke – Man. John – Eagle. The four Gospels present a Face of Christ.

4. Their Wings – vs 6, 8, 9, 11, 23, 24, 25.
Two wings – used to fly, stretched upwards. Supernatural transport.
Two wings – used to cover their bodies. Covering needed in the Divine presence.
Wings – symbolic of Divine transport. The wings of the Almighty. The wings of the Cherubim.

Note the important significance of wings in the Tabernacle and Temple. Wings of the Cherubim inwrought in the Veil, the Temple doors, the curtains of the Tabernacle of Moses, and the walls of the Temple, etc.

The protection of the wings of the Almighty. Eagle's wings. Shadowing protection and security under His wings. Refer to Psalm 63; Rev 12:6, 14. Church receives wings also. Isa 40:30-31. Wait on Lord and mount up on wings like an eagle.

5. Their Hands – vs 8.
Symbolic of service. Ministry of holy hands. Psalm 24. Clean hands needed in His presence.

6. Their Feed – vs 7.
   a. Their feet were straight – not crooked walk.
   b. Sole of a calf's foot – clean animal. Divided hoof and chews the cud. Two signs of clean creatures. Lev. 11.
   Note divided tongues of fire at Pentecost also. Acts 2:1-4.
   c. Feet sparkled like colour of burnished brass – Brass, symbolic of burning judgment against sin. Cf. Feet of Christ. Dan 10:6; Rev 1:15; 2:18.
   Note brass in the Tabernacle and Temple.

i.e. Brazen Altar, Brazen Laver, Sea, etc   Zion – Hoofs of brass.

7. <u>Their Walk</u> – vs 7, 9, 10.
They went straight forward. Turned not as they went, cf. Lk 9:62.   Not turning to the right hand or the left hand, but keeping central in the path of God.   Isa 30:20-21; Psalm 1; Josh 1:9-12.

8. <u>Their Brightness</u> – vs 13, 14.
Likeness of the Living Creatures, their appearance – as burning coals of fire, bright fire, and lightning sent forth from the fire, as appearance of lamps.

He makes His ministers as flames of fire.   Psalm 104:4. Symbolic also of the flashing brightness and holiness of God on His ministers.

9. <u>Their Speed</u> – vs 14.
Ran and returned as the appearance of a flash of lightning, cf Mt24:27; Lk 17:24. Rapidity of movement. As the lightning, so shall the coming of the Son of Man be.

10. <u>Their Four Wheels</u> – vs 15-21.
Cf. The Wheels in Solomon's Temple. The Living Creatures had 4 wheels in all.   Symbolic of the Chariot of the Lord. Colour like beryl.   Wheels to transport the throne of God. The wheels were like wheels in the middle of a wheel. When on earth or in the firmament, the wheels turned not as they went.

The Living Creatures were one with the wheels.

The Cherubim of Olive wood in Solomon's Temple were apparently on Chariot wheels in the Holiest of All. 1 Kgs 5-7.

11. <u>Their Rims</u> – vs 18.
Their rings, high and dreadful. Speaks of the circumferences of God. The complete circle and cycle of things. God sees the complete thing, beginning to end, eternity to eternity.

12. <u>Their Eyes</u> - - vs 18.
The rings (rims) of the wheels were full of eyes round about. Eyes speak of sight, insight, perception and perfection of sight. Full discernment into the purposes of God. Know and

understand and see where they are going in relation to eternal things.

13. The Spirit in Them – vs 12, 20.
    Note: Their spirit was so one with the Holy Spirit. Where the Spirit would go, they would go. 1 Cor 6:17. Joined to the Lord in one spirit.

    The Spirit of life of the 4 Living Creatures was in the wheels. One spirit and one life with them. Speaks of union with the Lord in that one Spirit. Unity of Spirit. Oneness of spirit in purpose, attitudes and direction.

    John 3:3-5; Rom 8:14-17. Spirit bears witness with our spirit.

14. The Firmament – vs 22.
    Likeness of a firmament above them, and above the heads of the Living Creatures was as the colour of terrible crystal. Crystal clear – symbolic of absolute transparency. Cf. The City of God. Rev 21:11.

    All things are crystal clear. Crystal clear covering the expanse. Heaven open. Not closed as through sin. Open Heavens – theme.

15. Their Obedience – vs 23-25.
    Sound of wings like the noise of waters – majestic flow. Like the voice of the Almighty which was the voice above the firmament, which governed all their movements. At the sound of the voice, they stood and let down their wings.

    Adam heard the voice in the Garden. Cf Gen 3:8.

    Elijah heard the still small voice. 1 Kgs 19.

    The Living Creatures give instant and immediate and unquestioning obedience to the voice of the Lord. This voice speaks to Ezekiel in vs 28.

16. The Likeness of the Throne – vs 26.
    a. Likeness of a Throne, cf. Isa 6:1. The throne of God.
    b. Appearance of sapphire – cf. Ex 24. Sapphire associated with throne of God.

    Suggested to be a light blue gem, next to the diamond in hardness. Ex 24:10. Second stone in the Breastplate of the

15

High Priest. Ex 28:18. Foundation stone in the City of God. Rev 21:19.

17. <u>The Man in the Throne</u> – vs 26.
No doubt, the Lord Jesus Christ in theophany. A theophany is a pre-cross manifestation and revelation of the Lord Jesus Christ before His incarnation. Cf. Rev 1:13; Zech 3; 6:12; Phil 2:5-8; Psalm 2 etc

    a. The colour of amber, cf 8:2; 1:4. Lustre as if it were glowing metal. Amp. OT.
    b. The appearance of fire. Round about the throne and glowing from the Man in the throne. Brightness of a halo round Him. Amp. OT.

18. <u>The Rainbow</u> – vs 28.
The brightness around the throne was like the rainbow in all its beauty colour. God is light. Symbolic of broken light, light which passes through a prism, in its number and colour. One light, yet multiple colour from 3 major and 7 minor colours.

Revelations of the Rainbow in Scripture show:
    a. Gen 9:11-17. Rainbow sign and seal of the Noahic Covenant of God to creatures, man and beasts and earth. Comes after the storm.
    b. Rev 4:3. The rainbow encircling the throne of God and the 4 Living Ones also.
    c. Rev 10:1. The rainbow around the head of the Son of Man, the Jehovah Angel with the little open Book.
    d. Ezekiel 1:28. The rainbow around the throne with the Living Creatures. Thus the Covenant keeping God is here. The Covenant Man also.

19. <u>The Appearance of the likeness of the Glory of the Lord</u> – vs 28.
Draw diagram to suit. Diagram of the Tabernacle of Moses, and the 4 Standards of Israel under which the 12 tribes gather together, in relation to the Ark of God and the Cherubim and Glory Cloud in the midst of the Camp. Num 1-2-3.

3.   **EZEKIEL OVERCAME BY THE LORD'S GLORY** – vs 28.
When the prophet saw the symbolic vision of the glory of the Lord, he fell on his face. No man can see God and live. All flesh must die in His presence. Ex 33.

The voice of the Lord called to him. Rev 4:3.

<u>SUMMARY</u>
The vision consists of:

a. A Throne above the firmament.
b. The throne encircled by the rainbow.
c. The Man in the throne in all brightness and glory.
d. The 4 Living Creatures as the guardians and transporters of the throne.
e. The Chariot of the Cherubim.

The prophet Ezekiel, being a Priest before the Temple of the Lord, although probably not ministering until the age of 30 years, but in training, saw this vision. Before the Temple was destroyed by Babylon, his mind would be saturated no doubt with the concepts of the Cherubim. Within the Sanctuary, the Cherubim were figures carved in the walls of the Temple. Then within the Holiest of All, there were the two great cherubim with the chariot wheels and their wings stretching out across from wall to wall in the Most Holy Place. Then beneath the wings was the Ark of the Covenant with its Cherubimed Mercy-seat. Though the earthly Temple would be destroyed, yet the heavenly remains unchanged and eternal.

Note the comparison between this vision and Johns in Revelation. Ezekiel 1 – Rev 4.

<u>Ezekiel</u>		<u>John</u>
1. Opened heavens	-	Opened heavens
2. A throne	-	A throne
3. A Rainbow	-	A rainbow
4. The voice of the Lord	-	The voice of the Lord
5. The 4 Living Creatures	-	The 4 Living Ones
6. Four faces each	-	One face each
Man/Eagle/Lion/Ox		Man/Ox/Lion/Eagle
7. Four wings each	-	Six wings each
8. The Glory of the Lord	-	The Glory of God
9. Appearance of the Man	-	The Lamb of God

EZEKIEL CHAPTER TWO

1.   **EZEKIEL'S COMMISSION BY THE LORD** – vs 1-5.

Vs 1.   Son of Man – used about 100 times in the Book.
Messianic Title. Psalm 8:1-4. Ezekiel, type of the Son of Man, Jesus Christ.
Shadows His humanity, His incarnation.
Stand of thy feet – cf. 1:28. Prostrated before the Glory of the Lord.
I will speak to thee – no use Ezekiel speaking to man unless God has first spoken to him.

Vs 2.   The Spirit entered into me – cf. 1:12, 20, 21.   The same quickening, energising Spirit.
Set me on my feet – enabling Ezekiel to do what he was commanded. Divine energy. As in Vs 1.
Heard Him that spoke to me – the voice.   Thus enabling Ezekiel to hear what would be so spoken to him. Vs. 1.

Vs 3.   Ezekiel sent to a REBELLIOUS Nation, cf 12:2. One of the key words in the Book is "rebellious people".
Rebellion as the sin of witchcraft. 1 Sam 16:22-23. Rebellion means "armed, open resistance to the government", "defiance of any control". A rebel is one who resists and opposes any authority.
Transgressions of them and their fathers.   Ex 20:5. To go across a given boundary.   Sin is transgression of the Law. 1 John 3:4.

Vs 4.   Impudent – not to feel shame, bold, insolent, shameless.
Stiff-hearted – hard to bend, rigid, firm; hard to move. Stubborn, obstinate.
Such was the type of people Ezekiel was sent to minister to. What a call!

Vs 5.   The nation to know, whether they will listen or not, that God did send a prophet amongst them.
Note the words used to describe the spiritual condition and attitude of the nation.
1.   Rebellious – vs 3, 5, 6, 8.
2.   Transgressors – vs 3.
3.   Impudent – vs 4.
4.   Hard-hearted – vs 4.

2.　　**WORD OF ENCOURAGEMENT TO THE PROPHET** – vs 6-8.

Vs 6.　Ezekiel not to be afraid of:
  a.　Their persons – the people.
  b.　Their words – what they say,
  c.　Their looks.

  All true ministers generally afraid of these three things as they minister to people.
  Symbolics used to describe the rebels:
  1.　Briers – rebels
  2.　Thorns –
  3.　Scorpions –

  Descriptive of that which is cursed and Satanic. People are likened to that symbolised here. Most rebellious, cf. Judges 9:14-21; 11:12; Rev 9:10, 19.

Vs 7.　Ezekiel to speak God's word to them however, whether they will hear or not hear. Cf. "Their words" and "God's words". Vs 6, vs 7.

Vs 8.　Ezekiel to hear what God says to him – not to be like the nation who will not hear what God says to them through Ezekiel. Told to open his mouth and eat the Book.

3.　　**THE ROLE OF THE BOOK** – vs 9-10.

Vs 9.　The hand of the Lord. The Scroll of the Book in the hand, cf Rev 10. John has a such experience also, similar to Ezekiel's.

Vs 10.　The Scroll written within and without. Both sides. No room for additions, subtractions, or alterations. God's Word.
  The message or contents:
  1.　Lamentations –
  2.　Mourning –
  3.　Woe –

  All speak of further judgments coming on the rebellious nation.

EZEKIEL CHAPTER THREE

1. **EZEKIEL EATS THE ROLL OF THE BOOK** – vs 1-3.

Vs 1.   Ezekiel told to eat the roll that he found in the hand of the Lord, then go and speak. Principle is always – Eat the Word first, chew, digest; and then speak. Jeremiah 25:17. Zech 5:1; Mt 4:4; Mt 10:7. Not to speak unless we eat first.

Vs 2.   Open mouth. Caused to eat the roll. Spiritual receptivity for Prophets. The Word is the food of prophets.

Vs 3.   Ezekiel caused to eat, inwardly digest. Belly and bowels. Jeremiah 6:11; 15:16. Only give out what is digested within. Word sweet as honey – Psalm 119:47; Rev 10.
Bitter in the belly. The Word has both the sweetest and bitterest things in it. Sweet in the mouth in reception (theory), but bitter in experience (practice). Thus reception, responsibility in the Word.

2. **EZEKIEL'S FURTHER COMMISSION** – vs 4-14.

Vs 4.   Ezekiel commanded to go to the House of Israel and speak God's Word to them. Cf. Num 16:28. Note now – "The House of Judah" is spoken of many times in this Book as "the House of Israel", for they are what is left of the Nation of Israel. Although BOTH Houses are spoken of at times, cf Ezekiel 37.

Vs 5.   The prophet sent not to a Foreign nation, as Jonah was, where there was a language or communication gap, cf Jonah 1:2; Acts 14:11.

Vs 6.   The Lord tells Ezekiel that the Gentiles would have heard if God had sent a prophet to them. Even as Assyria and Nineveh repented at Jonah's preaching, and as the other Gentiles in Acts. Cf. Mt 12:21, 39-39-40; Acts 10:45.

Vs 7.   The House of Israel will not hear Ezekiel even as they would not hear the Lord.
They would be deaf to the prophet as to the Lord.
They were impudent and hard-hearted, cf 2:4.
Stiff of forehead and hard of heart (Marginal).

Vs 8. God would give the prophet spiritual resistance and strength. His face would be against their faces. His forehead against their foreheads.
Cf. Jeremiah 1 also. Jeremiah had similar prophecies, as a brazen wall, and pillar who would be against the people, and able to withstand their words and looks.

Vs 9. Ezekiel's forehead made as an adamant (flint).
Not to fear them or their rebellious looks, cf 2:6. Jeremiah 1:18; Deuteronomy 1:17.

Vs 10. Ezekiel to receive God's word, all of them to be spoken in his heart and ears.

Vs 11. Sent to the people of the Babylonian Captivity, whether they will hear or forebear.

Vs 12. The Spirit take shim up. Cf 1:12, 20, 21; 2:2. Dependance upon the Spirit. Zech 4:6; Acts 1:5,8. Book of Acts – Not by might, or power, but by the Spirit.
Acts 8:39; 2:2; Rev 1:10. The Spirit of the Lord came ...
The voice like the rushing of waters – Blessed be the GLORY of the Lord from His Place. Cf 1:28. Vision of the Glory. His Place – Heaven. In Earth – The Holiest of All in the Temple.

Vs 13. The noise of movements of the Cherubim/wings/wheels/ movement, cf. 1:14; 10:9.

Vs 14. Ezekiel transported to the Captivity. Spirit lifted him up, cf. Vs 12.
Ezekiel goes in the heat and bitterness of his own spirit. The Divine pressure on him, cf Jeremiah 6:11.
Hand of the Lord strong on him, cf 1:9; 3:22.

3. **EZEKIEL WARNED AS A WATCHMAN** – vs 5-21. Cf. Ezek 18: Ezek 33.

Vs 15. The Prophet to those of the Captivity at Tel-Abib, that were living by the River Chebar. Refer to Map.
SAT where they sat – in silent astonishment. Job 2:13. So must all Ministry learn to "sit where the people sit" before they speak.
Perhaps the prophet was too overcome with the vision as yet to speak also. Waited 7 days before he spoke – one week!

Vs 16. The word of the Lord comes to him after 7 days. God's rule concerning prophecy.

Vs 17. Ezekiel charged to be a WATCHMAN to the House of Israel. Therefore he must speak and give the warning from the Lord. Cf. Heb 13:17; Acts 5:20.
Responsibility of the Watchman is twofold:
1. To WATCH the enemy for all that is without,
2. To WARN the people within of that which is without and coming. Cf. Isa 21:5-10; Hab 2:1-4.

Vs 18. When God takes the prophet and tells him to warn the wicked of coming death for his wicked way, in order that his life may be saved – if the man dies in his iniquity, the blood will be on the prophet's head. Responsibility of the prophet to warn. Cf Isa 56:10; Ezekiel 33:9.

Vs 19. If the prophet does warn the wicked and he heed not and die in his iniquity, the prophet's soul is delivered, cf Acts 18:6.

Vs 20. If a righteous man turns from his righteousness and commits iniquity, God will place a stumbling block (Rock of offence, Isa 8:14) before him. The purpose? To trip the person up so he does not fall headlong into hell. Backslider, spiritual lapse need warnings.
The prophet must warn the righteous as well as the wicked, or else blood of both is on his hands. Not be neglectful of his duty. If the righteous die in his sin, his righteousness shall not be remembered.

Vs 21. If the righteous is warned, accepts it, and stops his sinning, he shall live and the soul of the prophet is delivered. Thus we have the responsibility of the Watchman of God.

<u>GOD</u>
WATCHMAN
WORD OF THE LORD
WARN

The Wicked   The Righteous
Wicked way/Warned/   Turn from right/warned/die/
Die in sin/Blood on head   blood

UNWARNED
Blood on Prophet's head
Turned and Live   Turn and Live
Prophet Delivered

23

4.   **GOD'S WORD TO THE PROPHET IN THE PLAIN** – vs 22-27.

Vs 22.   Hand of the Lord on the prophet. Sends him forth to the plain
          to speak with him.
          That spoken in secret to be spoken in the open. Mt 14:23.
          Alone with God for the Spirit to communicate.

Vs 23.   Ezekiel's obedience. Goes into the plain and sees the Glory
          of God again. The Shekinah Glory, cf 1:28; 3:12. As seen in
          vision previously.
          Prostration and reverence before God.

Vs 24.   The Spirit enters him again, setting him on his feet, speaking
          to him. Thus we have Divine energy, quickening of the Spirit
          of God, cf. 2:2; 1:28.

Vs 25.   Ezekiel would be bound with bands and fetters by the people,
          so as to hinder the movement of the prophet among them.
          Cf. Mt 23:2-32; 21:33-46. So they treated the prophets.

Vs 26.   Ezekiel to be made dumb. His tongue to cleave to the roof of
          his mouth. Not to say anything to the rebellious house.
          Silences of God. Psalm 39:2; Lk 1:20-22; Josh 6:10; Hos
          4:17; Amos 8:11, 12. Unable to say anything to them.
          Nothing to say unless God speaks.

Vs 27.   When God speaks, then his mouth will be opened. Divine
          utterance.
          "He that hears, let him hear" -   cf. Son of Man in Mt
          13:10-17.
          "He that forebears, let him forbear."
          Cf. 12:2; Mt 13:34-35. Prov 20:12; Acts 28:27; Rev 1-2-3.
          Thus spiritual dullness, and blindness and hardness of heart.

EZEKIEL CHAPTER FOUR

1.   **THE SEIGE AGAINST JERUSALEM** – vs 1-8.

Note: It is interesting to note how Jeremiah and Ezekiel correspond so much. Jeremiah in Jerusalem, with clear prophetic utterances, and Ezekiel paralleling in Babylon with enigmatic prophetic pictures and signs, etc. Yet at the same time, many times.
In this passage, the prophet is called to take a tile and demonstrate with it the siege that is going on up at Jerusalem, miles away. Illustrated sermon indeed!

Vs 1.   Ezekiel commanded to take a tile, portray upon it the City of Jerusalem. 1 Kgs 14:25.

Vs 2.   The tile is laid siege against. A fort and a mount of battering rams is set up, as well as the enemy camp about it. "Toy soldiers" – cf. 21:22.
         Note the five-fold "against" in this verse.

Vs 3.   The prophet to take an iron plate and set it as a wall between himself and the city and press the siege. This would be A SIGN to the House of Israel.

Vs 4.   Then the prophet was to lay on his LEFT side (and North. Amp OT) to bear symbolically the iniquities of the House of Israel, the 10 Tribes, for so many days. The NORTHERN Kingdom.

Vs 5.   A day for a year of Israel's sins and iniquities. Thus 390 days on his left side, symbolic of 390 years.
         Thus about 13 months if 30 days per month, or a whole year of so doing. The Son of Man, the Priest-Prophet, bearing the iniquities of God's people. So does the ministry and shadows forth Christ, cf. Ex 32-33. Moses making an atonement for Israel's sins.
         Paul – Rom 9:1-4. Jesus – Mt 26. Covenant of blessing of Elijah to Jeroboam, BC 977-390 = 587.
         Thus 13 x 30 = 390 days. Or 360 + 30 = 390. (Perhaps dates back to the close of Solomon's reign.) BC.985 – 309 = BC 595, or about the time of this siege-sign.
         Note "the day for a year" in prophetic time-element. Ex 12:40; Gen 15:12; Num 13:34 etc

Vs 6.   The prophet to do the same for the House of Judah, and their iniquities. Lay on right side (South. Amp OT) and bear their sins. SOUTHERN Kingdom.
A day for a year also; 40 days = 40 years. Prophetic time piece, cf. Num 14:33-34; Jonah 3:4. Refer to 40 years in the Wilderness also. Temptation.
Forty – number of probation, ending with victory or failure.
40 years in the Wilderness – failure.
40 years to AD 70 – failure to accept the Messiah and Outpoured Spirit.
Then Jerusalem destroyed. Perhaps here, 40 years probation from BC629-590, when Jeremiah begins his ministry, under Josiah's reign, unto the destruction of the City and the Temple. 13th Josiah (BC627) to 11th Zedekiah (BC567).

Vs 7.   Ezekiel to set the siege against the Jerusalem tile and prophesy against it. Num 11:25; Ezekiel 3:25. His arm to be uncovered, ready for battle.

Vs 8.   The Lord would bind the prophet so that he would not move from one side to the other until the days of the siege were fulfilled.

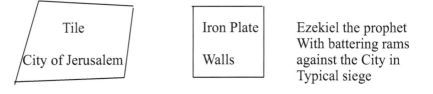

Tile

City of Jerusalem

Iron Plate

Walls

Ezekiel the prophet
With battering rams
against the City in
Typical siege

Thus enacting what Nebuchadnezzar was doing at Jerusalem.

2.   **THE FAMINE IN THE SEIGE SYMBOLISED** – vs 9-17.

Vs 9.   The prophet takes a) Wheat, b) Barley, c) Beans, d) Lentils, e) Millet, and f) Fitches, in one vessel to make bread for the 390 days.

Vs 10.   Meals to be eaten by weight. Food rationing at 20 shekels a day in his various meals.

Vs 11.   Water measured out also, 6th part of an hin. Daily needs.

Vs 12.   Eat the bread as barley cakes, baked with mans dung, in their sight. Cf Isa 36:12.
Defiled bread.

Vs 13. The interpretation of the symbolics.
Israel among the nations of the Gentiles would eat defiled bread. Hos 9:3.

Vs 14. The prophet professes his separation to his Lord from his youth. As a Priest, he has not eaten or touched abominable things. Hos 9:3; Lev 7:21; Acts 10:14; Deut 14:3; Isa 65:4; Gen 9:4.

Vs 15. God permitted the prophet to use cows dung instead of mans dung to prepare his bread.
Possibly dry cow's dung.

Vs 16. The staff of bread to be broken in the siege of Jerusalem. They would eat bread with weight and care and drink waters by measure and astonishment. The prophet enacts and experiences symbolically the Jerusalem siege.

Vs 17. Bread and water, 5:12, scarcity in the siege. Pine away and be consumed because of iniquity. Cf 24:23.

EZEKIEL CHAPTER FIVE

1. **THE SYMBOLIC MESSAGE IN EZEKIEL'S HAIR** – vs 1-4
   Vs 1.   Ezekiel commanded to take a barber's razor and shave his hair off his head and his beard.
   After this he is to weigh his hair in the balances, cf Dan 5:27; Lev 21:5; Ezekiel 44:20.
   The hair is divided into three portions.

   Vs 2.   Hair divided into three parts:
   1. A 3rd part burnt in the fire in the midst of the city, after days of siege ended.
   2. A 3rd part smitten about with the knife.
   3. A 3rd part scattered to the wind, with a sword drawn after them, cf vs 12 also.
   Note also Zech 13:8-9. Theme of "the third".

   Vs 3.   A few hairs in number bound in his skirts. Symbolic of the very small remnant. Cf vs 10.

   Vs 4.   Some of these also to be taken and cast into the fire. Fire of judgment to come on all of the House of Israel.

2. **THE BARBER'S RAZOR INTERPRETED** – vs 5-11.
   Vs 5.   Jerusalem, set in the midst of nations and countries about her.

   Vs 6.   Jerusalem, became worse in wickedness than the surrounding nations.
   1. Changed God's statutes and judgments.
   2. Refused to walk in them.

   Vs 7.   Because of the sins of Jerusalem of vs 6, in disobedience to the Law.

   Vs 8.   God will execute judgments on Jerusalem in the sight of the surrounding nations, i.e. the Barber's razor to come on His own people and their glory.

   Vs 9.   God will do judgment the like of which has never been because of her abominations.

   Vs 10. Fathers and sons to devour each other, cf Deut 28:53; Jeremiah 19:9. Judgment on the city. Whole remnant scattered to all winds, like hair is. Vs 2, 12.

Vs 11. Because of defiling God's sanctuary with detestable things and abominations, God will diminish them.
God will not spare or have pity.
Symbolic of shaving the people.

3.   THE INTERPRETATION OF THE THIRD PART – vs 12-17

Vs 12. The three parts of the hair interpreted. Cf vs 12.
1. A 3rd part to die with the pestilence and great famine – The fire.
2. A 3rd part to fall by the sword round about – The knife.
3. A 3rd part to be scattered to the winds with a sword after them – scattered hair.

Vs 13. God's anger and fury thus accomplished would be comforted. Divine judgment must judge un-repented of sin.   Otherwise His Holiness is outraged. God is zealous over the Word He has spoken and He will accomplish it.

Vs 14. Israel to be a waste and reproach among nations round about.

Vs 15. Their punishment to be a lesson to others also.   God has spoken it. Lam 2:15.
1. A reproach
2. A taunt
3. An instruction
4. An astonishment

God's anger, judgments and furious rebukes – a lesson to all nations. God who is perfect love dealing with His own people illustrates He must judge those not His own also.

Vs 16. Famine – the evil arrows of famine sent on Jerusalem, cf 4:9-17; Deut 32:23, 24.
Famine to increase until it destroys them.

Vs 17. Evil Beasts – also to destroy them. Note vs 16-17 with 6:11; 14:21. God's FOUR sore judgments.

1. Famine	Correspond what happens in
2. Evil Beasts	Jerusalem under Jeremiah
3. Pestilence and blood	with the 3rd and "remnant"
4. Sword	and "remnant of a remnant".

The Lord Himself has spoken it – not man.

EZEKIEL CHAPTER SIX

1. **JUDGMENT ON THE ALTARS OF ISRAEL** – vs 1-7.

Vs 1.   Word of the Lord, cf 1:3.

Vs 2.   The prophet called to set his house and face towards the Mountains (ie, Kingdoms) of Israel. Mountains, hills, rivers, valleys – cf Isa 40:1-4.

Vs 3.   Symbolic here of high and low, rich and poor, etc.
Word of the Lord in judgment on the HIGH PLACES of idolatry. The sword to come to them. War. 5:17; 21:12.

Vs 4.   ALTARS to be destroyed.
IMAGES to be desolated and broken. Lev 26:30.
Slain men cast down before their idols.

Vs 5.   Dead carcasses and scattered bones round about the altars. The things they worship, powerless to help them with the true God judges.

Vs 6.   In all houses in the cities, the High Places, altars, idols and images to be broken, ceased, cut down and their idolatrous works to be abolished. Ex 32:30.

Vs 7.   The slain in their midst will be evidence that the Lord alone is the true God. Israel had ONE TRUE ALTAR and ONE TRUE GOD. In the Temple was God's place for worship. All other places became idolatrous. Violation of the Commandments of the Lord to have any altars and other gods and make graven images to bow down to. Ex20; Deut 12; Deut 16.

2. **INSTRUMENTS OF DIVINE JUDGMENT** – vs 11-14.

Vs 11.   The prophet is told to MAKE SMITING with his HAND and STAMP with his FOOT. Lamenting the evil abominations of the House of Israel. Cf 9:4; 25:6.
To fall by:
1.   The sword
2.   The Famine
3.   The Pestilence - cf 5:16-17; 14:21.

Vs 12. Interpretation of the threefold judgments of vs 11.
1. He that is far off dies by pestilence.
2. He that is near dies by the sword.
3. He that remains in the besieged city shall die by the famine. Fury of God done.

Vs 13. Israel will know that God is the Lord when they see the slain in the places of idolatry.
1. Idols
2. Altars
3. High Hills
4. Tops of the Mountains
5. Under green trees and thick oaks

Places where they offered sweet savour to their idols!

Vs 14. God's hand of judgment to bring all to desolation, more than desolate Wilderness towards Diblath. Desolation in the land and habitations. Know the Lord is God.

EZEKIEL CHAPTER SEVEN

1. **THE TIME AND END IS COME** - vs 1-15.

    Note the theme of this passage is that the END is at hand, THE TIME is come for the final judgments on Jerusalem.

    Note the word "end" – vs 2, 3, 6, 7, 10, 12.

    Should be kept in mind that Jeremiah and Ezekiel are "flowing together" in the same prophetic stream. Jeremiah – clear prophecy; Ezekiel, enigmatic and symbolic prophecy.

    Vs 1.   The Word of the Lord. Prophetic formula.

    Vs 2.   The end is come upon the 4 corners of the land.
            Cf. Mt 24:3, 6, 13, 14; 13:39. Type of the END of the age.

    Vs 3.   God's anger, judgment, recompense to come on Israel for her abominations, cf Rom 11:21; 2 Pet 2:4; 1 Pet 4:17. Judgment begins at the House of God.

    Vs 4.   No mercy or pity. Their ways and abominations to come back on their own heads, cf. 5:11; 12:20, Know the Lord is the Lord.

    Vs 5.   Only evil is come. 2 Kgs 21:12-13.

    Vs 6.   The end is come. Watching and coming on Israel.

    Vs 7.   Morning of judgment is come. Day of trouble. Sound of it on the mountains. Cf vs 10; Zeph 1:14-15; Mal 4:6; Isa 22:5; Joel 2:1, 11.

    Vs 8.   Fury, anger, judgments of God, cf vs 3; 20:8, 21.
            Judgment according to their works.

    Vs 9.   Refer again to vs 4. Lord smites, cf 6:11.

    Vs 10. The day is come, cf vs 7. ROD Blossomed, and PRIDE buds. Cf Aaron budding and blossoming rod. Num 17.

    Vs 11. Violence as told of wickedness. Jeremiah 7:6; 16:5, 6.
            All to be cut off, neither shall any wail for them. Unlamented dead. Tumultuous person. Ezekiel 24:16, 22.

Vs 12. Time is come, day draws ever near, cf vs 6, 10. 1 Cor 7:30. Buyer or seller not rejoice or mourn. Wrath of God on all.

Vs 13. Seller not return to that sold, though alive. The vision touches the whole multitude. None be able to strengthen himself in the life of iniquity.

Vs 14. The TRUMPET of preparation for battle has been blown, to call all to war. None respond to it. God's wrath is on all.

Vs 15. The threefold instrument on all, cf vs 11, 12 and notes. Deut 32:25; Lam 1:20.
1. The sword without
2. The pestilence within
3. The Famine within also.

2. **THOSE THAT ESCAPE** – vs 16-19

Vs 16. The ones who escape shall be as mourning doves in the mountains; mourning for their iniquity.

Vs 17. Hands feeble and knees as weak as water. Isa 3:7; Jer. 6:24.

Vs 18. Sackcloth, horror, shame, baldness on all faces and heads. Isa 3:24; Amos 8:10.

Vs 19. Silver and gold to be cast out into the street. Not able to deliver them in the day of the Lord's wrath. Cannot buy life. Not satisfy their dead souls – materialism. Not fill their bowels. Their iniquity is their STUMBLING BLOCK (Margin). Prov 11:4; Zeph 1:18.

3. **THE LAND AND THE SANCTUARY DEFILED** – vs 20-22.

Vs 20. The beauty of his ornament, ie. The Land, and The Temple. Set in majesty. Images of abominations and detestable things therein. God makes it an unclean thing. Jeremiah 7:20.

Vs 21. To be given into the hand of strangers and wicked. They shall spoil and pollute it.

Vs 22. The secret place of God polluted by burglars. Psalm 91:1-2. Ie., The Temple polluted by the enemy.

4.　**JUDGMENT ON THE LAND AND CITY** – vs 23-27.

Vs 23.　Make a chain.　The land and the city full of crimes and violence. 2 Kgs 21:16.

Vs 24.　Worst of the heathen to come and possess the houses of the people. Pomp of proud and strong to cease.　So the Post-Samaritans possessed the houses of Israel also.
The Holy Places to be defiled, ie. The Temple and the sacred places of Israel.

Vs 25.　Cutting off come.　Peace sought and not to be found.

Vs 26.　Mischief on mischief.
Rumour on rumour.
People seek:
1.　A vision of the prophet
2.　The law of the priest
3.　The counsel from the ancients (elders).
Deut 32:23;　Jer 4:20;　Psa 74:9;　Ezek 20:1, 3.

Vs 27.　The King and Prince to mourn, clothed in desolation. People of the land troubled. God will judge according to their way and what they deserve.　Know that He is the Lord.

EZEKIEL CHAPTER EIGHT

1. **THE GLORY OF GOD APPEARS IN VISION** - vs 1-4.

Vs 1. Dated prophecy. The 6th year, 6th month and 5th day of the Captivity.
Ezekiel in his house. The Elders of Judah before him.
Evidently the prophet's house a meeting place for the Word of the Lord in Babylon, cf 14:1; 20:1; 33:31.

The hand of the Lord upon him. 1:3; 3:22.

Vs 2. The appearance and likeness of the Lord as FIRE. Symbol of holiness. Heb 12:29. His whole Being radiant with fire, brightness, colour of amber. 1:26, 27: 1:4.
A theophany of the Lord Jesus before His incarnation. As in Ezekiel 1.
Cf. Daniel's vision also and Isaiah 6 with John 12:41. Dan 10.

Vs 3. The hand of the Lord takes the prophet by a lock of his head and the Spirit takes him in vision of God to Jerusalem.
Cf Dan 5:5; Ezekiel 3:14; 11:1, 24; 40:2; Num 12:6-8.
Ezekiel a prophet of vision.
Brought to the Inner Gate of the Court that faced North.
Seat of the Image of Jealousy. Our God a Jealous God. 2 Kgs 16:10-16; 21:4, 5. Deut 32:16, 21. God will have no rivals.
He alone is the true God, the Living God.

Vs 4. The Glory of God there as seen in the earlier vision, cf 1:28; 3:22, 23.

2. **THE IMAGE OF JEALOUSY** – vs 5-6.

Vs 5. The prophet is told to lift up his eyes and look towards the North. At the Gate of the ALTAR stood the Image of Jealousy, cf. Ex 20.
Violation of the Commandments. It was bad enough for them to have idols and images in every high place, etc., but this was right in the very dwelling places of God. At His sacred Altar. Idol altars! One for God, and other for the other gods. These abominations caused God to go far from His Sanctuary.

The prophet is told to see greater abominations. An abomination is anything that is detestable, a stench in the nostrils of God.

3.	**FURTHER ABOMINATIONS** – vs 7-12.

Vs 7.	Ezekiel is brought to the door of the court (the Outer Court possibly, cf vs 16), and as he looked he saw a hole in the wall.

Vs 8.	The prophet is told to dig into the wall, which he did, and as he did, he looked and saw a door.

Vs 9.	He is commanded to enter in and behold the wicked abominations that were being done.

Vs 10.	After he entered, he saw all forms of creeping things, abominable beasts and idols of the House of Israel portrayed on the wall round about.

Vs 11.	The 70 Elders or Ancients stood there, all of them with the censer in their hand.
Ja-azaniah, the son of Shaphan (the scribe) stood in the midst of them. A thick cloud of incense arose. Burning incense to their idols, in prayer to their gods.

Vs 12.	Idolatry done in the dark, in the chambers of his imagery. Naturally, and also spiritually in the heart.
1.	In the Priestly chambers, probably, surrounding the Temple.
2.	In the Chambers of the mind, in the imaginations.

The 70 plus 1 = the Sanhedrin and the Scribes, possibly here. They felt the Lord did not see, as He had forsaken the earth. Believers in an "absentee God". This was a repudiation of the Divine attributes of Omniscience (He sees all) and Omnipresence (He is everywhere present at all times). Cf 9:9.

4.	**GREATER ABOMINATIONS** - vs 13-14.

Vs 13.	The prophet called to turn again and see greater abominations. Was this not a great and terrible VISION?

Vs 14.	Brought to the Door of the Gate of the Lord's House which was towards the North.
There he sees women weeping for TAMMUZ, or "Sprout". A Syrian idol corresponding to the Greek Adonis. Also "Abstruse, conceded" – name of a pagan deity.
Amp. OT Tammuz – "A Babylonian god, who was supposed to due annually and subsequently be resurrected."

Alexander Hislop traces it all back to the Tower of Babel, and Nimrod and his wife in the worship of the "Mother and Child" doctrine.

Thus counterfeit of the Death and Resurrection of the Lord Jesus in the fulness of time. Some equate her with the Queen of Heaven of Jeremiah 7:18; 44:17-25. Refer to notes on Jeremiah.

5. GREATER ABOMINATIONS – vs 15-16.

Vs 15. The prophet called to see greater abominations.

Vs 16. Brought to the Inner Court of the Lord's House, and at the Door of the Temple, between the Porch and the Altar (cf Joel 12:17; Mt 23) there were 25 men with their back towards the Lord. Cf 11:1.

With their faces towards the East, they worshipped the SUN. Thus 24 plus 1 of the Priestly Courses, no doubt involved here.

Thus Sun-worshippers in the Tempe Court. Jeremiah 2:27; 32:33; Deut 4:19; 2 Kgs 23:5, 11; Job 31:26; Jeremiah 44:17.

Worship of the heavenly bodies forbidden. Violation of the commandments of the Lord.

Jeremiah's reproving them in Jerusalem for the same sins.

6. JUDGMENT PRONOUNCED – vs 17-18

Vs 17. God asks the prophet if it was a light thing that he had seen here, with these various abominations.

The land was filled with violence.

God is provoked to jealousy. They put branch to the nose, ie. Symbolic of doing despite to God. Cf 9:9. Amp OT. Actually, before their mouths, in superstitious worship.

Vs 18. God will deal with them in His fury. He will not pity or take heed to their crying for their punishments, cf. 5:13; 16:42; 24:13; 5:11; 7:4, 9; 9:5, 10; Prov 1:28; Isa 1:15; Jeremiah 11:11; 14:12; Mic 3:4; Zeph 7:13.

As a father punishes his children and does not heed their crying, so the Lord here.

SUMMARY:

1. The image of jealousy – idol altars. Vs 5-6, 3. Rom 1:19-32. Worship of creatures or creation. IMAGE of jealousy. Ash-toroth, goddess of love, fertility, judgment and war.

2. The abominable paintings on the wall – vs 7-12. The 70 + 1 worshipping and burning incense to such.
3. The women weeping for Tammuz at the Door of the Gate of the Lord's House. Vs 13-14. "Sprout, vegetation". Agriculture god. Life and light. Death and Resurrection – goddess.
4. The 24 + 1 Sun-worshippers towards the East between Porch and Altar – vs 15-16. Looking beyond the blood.

All these things find their source in the true God – not false gods. Thus we see the progression to perversion in idolatry.

Note Romans 1:19-32.
A. Rom 1:21-23. Idols of birds, beasts etc.
B. Rom 1:24-25. The image of jealousy. Worship creature more than Creator. Base and debase worship here. Woman and beast, cf Diana of Ephesus. Acts 19. Temple prostitutes. Uncleanness.
C. Rom 1:27. Tammuz – also means "Burning one", or men and women burning in their lust towards one another.
B. End state is Rom 1:28. Reprobate mind. A mind given over to a state of continued depravity. Idolatry leads to immorality, which leads to perversion, which leads to reprobation!

The Vision

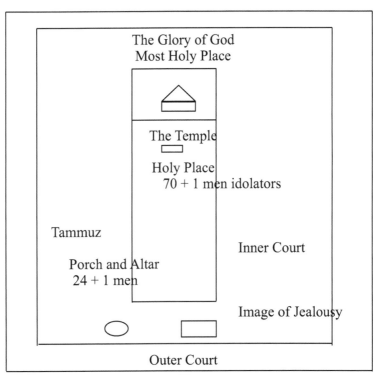

EZEKIEL CHAPTER NINE

1.   **THE MAN WITH THE WRITER'S INKHORN** – vs 1-4.

Vs 1.   The men in charge of the City of Jerusalem are called to draw near. There are men in charge of all cities. All had a destroying weapon in their hand. Amp OT. Says "executioners".

Vs 2.   SIX men came from the way of the higher GATE facing the North. Each had a slaughter weapon in their hand. There was a SEVENTH man (?) amongst them, it seems, clothed with linen. He had a writer's inkhorn upon his loins. All went in and stood by the brazen Altar, cf. Ex 27:1-8; Lev 16:4; Rev 15:6. Brazen altar – the place of sin being judged. Judge or be judged!

Vs 3.   The Glory of the God of Israel was gone up from the Cherub and was now standing at the threshold of the House, cf 1:28; 3:23; 10:4, 18.
God in the Glory called to the Man clothed in linen having the writer's inkhorn.

Vs 4.   The Man in linen is commanded to go through the City of Jerusalem and set a mark (mark a mark, mark a TAU – a CROSS – sign, of Hebrew alphabet, last letter) on the foreheads of all who sigh and cry for the abominations done in the City as well as in the House of God.
Cf. 1.   Ex 12:7. The sign of blood on the houses of the Israelites.
2.   The seal of God in the forehead or the seal of Satan in the forehead. The forehead = the seat of the mind, the thoughts, reasons, imaginations. Rev 7:3; 9:4; 13:16-17; 20:4.
3.   In the OT the High Priest had the golden mitre with "Holiness to the Lord" on the forehead. Ex 28-29 chapters.
It speaks of the principle of the CROSS applied to the MIND in the Last Days also to the true Church, the godly remnant in the midst of a crooked and perverse generation.
Refer to Scriptures on the "mind", cf Rom 12:1-2.
All to be marked either for God or Satan.
1.   The Mark of Cain – mark of the damned. Gen 4:15. Murderer, liar, Lamb rejector.
2.   Mark of the Godly – mark of the intercessor. Ezek.9.

41

3.   Mark of the Intercessor – Paul the apostle. Gal 6:17. Mark of the crucified.

4.   Mark of the Sealed ones – Rev 14:1-4; 7:1-4. Thus intercessory ministry before the Lord. Psalm 119:53, 136; Jeremiah 13:17; 2 Cor 12:21; 2 Pet 2:8.

2.   **JUDGMENT BEGINS AT GOD'S HOUSE** – vs 5-7. Cf 1 Pet 4:17

Vs 5.   The 6 other men are called to go after the Man and smite with the sword.   Note – God seals His own FIRST before the sword goes through, cf Rev 7:1-3; Ex 12:7.
There is no pity for the unsealed ones, cf Rev 9:1-5 also. Ezekiel 9:10.

Vs 6.   All to be slain . Old and young, men and women. Not to go ever near the ones who have the MARK of their forehead. The seal of God's protection. 2 Chronicles 36:17; Rev 9:4.
Begin at my sanctuary, cf 1 Pet 4:17; Jeremiah 25:29.
Judgment begins at God's House.
The 6 men began with the Ancients (the Sanhedrin, 70+1 men) who were idol-incense burners. The leaders of the nation.   God begins with the leadership in judgment, cf Mt 23-24. AD 70 also.

Vs 7.   The City and the Sanctuary filled and defiled with the slain. So AD 70 also.

3.   **THE PROPHET'S UNAVAILING INTERCESSION** – vs 8-11.

Vs 8.   The prophet falls in intercession before the Lord in the midst of the slaying in God's fury.

Vs 9.   God told him that the iniquity of the House of Israel and Judah was exceeding great. 2 Kgs 21:16; Ezekiel 8:17. Full of blood, wresting of judgment in which the innocents were slain. Perverseness. The wicked should be judged or God's justice is at stake.
They reject God's omnipresence and omniscience, cf 8:12; Psalm 10:11; Isa 29:15.

Vs 10. Not pity. Refer again 5:11; 7:4; 8:18; 11:21.

Vs 11. The Man in his linen garment reported that it was done as commanded.
Note also Jeremiah 15:1.   Jeremiah also is not to pray or intercede for the people, and even Moses and Samuel – great intercessors – would not be heard; so Ezekiel here.

EZEKIEL CHAPTER TEN

1. **COALS OF FIRE OVER THE CITY** – vs 1-7

Vs 1. Ezekiel sees again the likeness of a throne above the firmament over the head of the Cherubim.
The throne like a sapphire stone – footstool, cf. Ex 24:9-11.
Cf. 1:22, 26.   1.   John sees a throne. Rev 4-5.
                2.   Ezekiel sees a throne. Ezek 1, 10.
                3.   Isaiah sees a throne. Isa 6.
Though earthly thrones fall, the throne of God stands supreme and secure.

Vs 2. The Lord speaks to the Man clothed in linen, calling Him to go in between the wheels of the Cherubim and fill His hand with coals of fire, scattering them over the City of Jerusalem. Ezekiel sees Him do so.
Fire – symbol of Divine judgment and holiness in action against sin. "I am come to send a fire in the earth." - Lk 12:49; Heb 12:29; Rev 8:5; Ezekiel 1:13.

Vs 3. Cherubim stood on the right side of the House, slowing, reluctantly departing. The Shekinah Glory-Cloud filled the inner court. The Man in linen went in to get the coals of fire.

Vs 4. The Glory of the Lord went up from the Cherub and now stands over the threshold of the House. House filled with the Cloud, and the Court filled with the brightness of the Lord's Glory.
Cf. 1:28; 3:23; 1 Kgs 8:10-11; Ezek 10:18-19; 43:5.

Vs 5. Sound of the wings of the Cherubim heard in the Outer Court. A voice of majesty speaks when the Lord speaks. 1:24; Psalm 29:3, 4.

Vs 6. The Man in linen goes in and stands between the wheels of the Cherubim, cf. vs 2, 3.

Vs 7. One of the Cherub sends forth his hand and places the fiery coals into the hand of the Man clothed in linen. He receives it and goes out.

2.   **THE CHERUBIM AND THE DEPARTING GLORY** – vs 8-22.

Vs 8.   The form of hands under the wings of the Cherubim = service, cf. Vs 21; 1:6.

Vs 9.   The four wheels, as the colour of a beryl stone, cf 1:15 notes. Transport, movement.

Vs 10.   The four wheels alike, as a wheel in the middle of a wheel, cf 1:16-19.

HISTORY 1 Samuel 1-6	PROPHECY Jeremiah 7	VISIONARY Ezekiel 1-10
Shiloh – The Place	Jerusalem – The Place	Jerusalem – the Place
Samuel the Prophet	Jeremiah the Prophet	Ezekiel the Prophet
Eli Priesthood	Corrupt Priesthood	Corrupt Priesthood
Tabernacle of Moses	Temple of Jerusalem	Temple of Jerusalem
Ichabod – Glory departs	Ark of God disappears	Glory departs
Ark taken captive by Philistines	Ark not to be mentioned or visited	Ark not mentioned once

Vs 11.   Refer again to notes on 1:16. Amp OT Went in any one of the four directions in which their four individual faces were turned.

Vs 12.   Full of eyes. Body, backs, hands, wings, wheels – full of eyes round about.
Eyes = 1:18. Symbolic of sight, insight, perception, intelligence, all seeing into the purposes of God in the past, present and future. Seeing as God sees. The eyes of the Lord run to and fro through the whole earth ....

Vs 13.   The wheel called whirling wheels. Margin, Galgal. Margin.

Vs 14.   The four faces. Refer to notes on 1:6, 10.

Vs 15.   The Cherubim mounted up.   Same vision as Chapter 1. Confirmation to the Prophet when God speaks the same thing twice or thrice.
1. So Pharaoh's dream. Gen 41:32;   Num23:19;   Isa 46:10-11.
2. So Joseph's dreams. Gen 37.
3. So Peter's vision. Acts 10.
4. So Jeremiah's call. Jeremiah 1.
God speaks plenty of times – but once, yet twice. Job 33:14; Psalm 62:11; Num 12:6

44

Vs 16. Cherubim and wheels as one in all their movements, cf. 1:19.

Vs 17. Unity of Cherubim and wheels because of the Spirit of the Living Creature in them which was the Spirit of Life. Cf. 1:12, 20, 21.

Vs 18. The Glory departs from off the threshold and stands over the Cherubim, cf. Vs 4.
So the Glory leaves the Cherubimed Ark of the Covenant in the earthly Temple (cf. Jeremiah 3:16) and goes over the heavenly Cherubim. Hos 9:12.

Vs 19. The Cherubim mount up on their wings and stand at the Door of the EAST Gate of the Lord's House. The Shekinah Glory-Cloud was over them. Departing step by step, cf. 11:22.

Vs 20. Confirmation of the vision of Chapter 1, cf. Vs 15: 1:22.

Vs 21. Refer to notes on 1:6. Four faces, four wings and hands under their wings.

Vs 22. Faces and likeness and appearances as previously seen, cf. 1:10, 12. All went straight forward.
But note – The Glory is reluctantly leaving the Sanctuary step by step, unnoticed, and unseen by all except the Prophet in vision.

NOTE: Progressive development of the theme of the Departing Glory.

1. Ezekiel 1:4-28. The Glory of the Lord in vision in the heavenly Temple.
2. Ezekiel 8:4. Earthly Temple and abominations there, cf Solomon's Temple and Glory that came originally. 2 Chronicles 1-8. Ex 40 also.
3. Ezekiel 10:4. 9:3. The Glory begins to depart from the Temple.
4. Ezekiel 10:4. The Glory leaves the Cherubim on the threshold.
5. Ezekiel 10:18-19. The Glory leaves then to the East Gate.
6. Ezekiel 11:22-23. The Glory leaves then for the Mt Olives, thus leaving the TEMPLE and the CITY of God.

Gradually, reluctantly, majestically – none noticing the departing Glory. After which came the Babylonian Captivity.

Typical of "Ichabod" – "The Glory is departed" or "There is no Glory" or "Where is the Glory". 1 Sam 1-6 chapters. Ark of the Covenant into Captivity.

7. Ezekiel 43:1-2. The Glory returns to the NEW Temple by way of the EAST Gate. Thus it leaves the OLD material Temple and comes to the NEW and spiritual Temple, the Church.

Note how years later, the Messiah would come to the Temple and City and cleanse it at the beginning and ending of His ministry, which cleansing they would reject. Abominations were there. Then He departs as the Glory of God, and prophesies of its coming desolation under the NT Babylon – Rome. Mt 23:38 – 24:1-3. He was THE GLORY – John 1:14-18, and He departed also from the Mt of Olives, to which He will return again. Zech 14:1-10.

Worthy to compare the past under Samuel with Jeremiah and Ezekiel.

The Church is now God's Temple. The Glory of God is in the Church. Came on the Day of Pentecost, forsaking the material Temple and coming to the New and Spiritual Temple, the Church. 1 Cor 3:16; Col 1:27. Christ in you, the Hope of Glory. Body of Christ is the New Covenant Temple now. Must not defile it or else "the glory" (ie, the Holy Spirit) will leave it to desolation also. As sure as God forsook the material Temple when it was defiled with abominations, so sure will He do that to the person or the group who defiles His Temple!

EZEKIEL CHAPTER ELEVEN

1. **THE 25 MEN OF WICKED COUNSEL** – vs 1-3

   Vs 1. The Spirit transports the prophet in his vision and brought him to the EAST Gate of the Lord's House that looks Eastward.
   The significance of the EAST and the Cherubim, cf Gen 3:24.
   There he sees 25 men there. Jaazaniah, the son of Azur – a Prince. And Pelatiah, the son of Benaniah – a Prince also.
   Two men, cf 10:19; 8:16. The Courses of David, no doubt in the 24 plus 1 man.

   Vs 2. These 25 men now stand with their Princes who devised mischief, giving wicked counsel to the people in the City.

   Vs 3. They influenced the people contrary to God's prophetic word, concerning building.
   Margin. "It is not for us to build houses near."
   The City – the Caldron.
   The People – the Flesh, cf. Vs 7, 11; Jer.1:13; Ezekiel 24:3, 6.

2. **THE CALDRON AND THE FLESH** – vs 4-12.

   Vs 4. Prophecy AGAINST them. Word of God against them, not for them, for they are against the Lord.

   Vs 5. Spirit of the Lord comes on the prophet to speak. God knows all the thoughts which come into their mind. Psalm 139:1-6.
   Omniscience.

   Vs 6. The streets to be filled with multiplied slain, cf. 7:23.

   Vs 7. The city to be like a caldron.
   The slain like the flesh therein, cf. Vs 3; 24:6.
   The 25 People and their Princes to be brought out of the City.

   Vs 8. The sword feared will come upon them.

   Vs 9. These men to be given to the hand of strangers and judgments to fall on them.

   Vs 10. To also fall by the sword in the border of Israel. Know that God is the Lord, cf. 2 Kgs 25:19-21; Jeremiah 39:6; 52:10.

Vs 11.   The City of Jerusalem (where most would like to die) will not be their caldron, nor they the flesh.   They will die in the border of Israel, cf. Vs 3, 7.

Vs 12.   They will know that the Lord He is God when he judges them for not walking in His statutes, judgments, but acting like heathen. Lev 18:3.

3.   **THE DEATH OF A PRINCE** - vs 13 cf. Vs 1

Vs 13.   As Ezekiel prophesied, Pelatiah dropped dead.   The prophet fell before the Lord in intercessory prayer that God would keep a remnant and not destroy all the people, cf. 9:8.   Cf. Acts 5 also. Sapphira and Ananias.
Cf.   Jeremiah 29 also.   Hananiah dropped dead in the 7th month of that year. Word of the Lord is life unto life, or death unto death.

4.   **NEW COVENANT PROMISES** – vs 14-21

Vs 14.   The Word of the Lord.

Vs 15.   The prophet's own brethren and kindred, as well as the House of Israel as a whole have been told by the inhabitants of Jerusalem to get far from the Lord and His land.   Claim the land was given for a possession to them.

Vs 16.   Although the House of Israel is driven and scattered in all various countries, the Lord says "Yet will I be to them as a LITTLE SANCTUARY ...."
The Old Covenant and the Old Sanctuary in Tabernacle and Temple.
Bereft of the material and physical Sanctuary and externals, they may find all that was symbolised in the material thing in God Himself, the True Sanctuary,   cf 37:26;   John 1:14-18; Heb 8; John 2:19-21; Isa 8:14.
Prophetic of the Lord Jesus Christ, the New Covenant Sanctuary. In A PERSON, not in A PLACE.

Vs 17.   Promises of gathering and assembling the people out of the countries and bringing them to the land of Israel.
Cf. 20:41; 28:25; 34:13; 36:24.

Vs 18.   To cleanse the land of detestable and abominable things.

Ezra 9:11; Ezekiel 37:23 (Rom 11:25-29). Fulfilled in measure in the Restoration from Babylon at close of 70 years for Remnant.

Vs 19. New Covenant Promises.
1. I will give to them one heart. United heart. Not divided. Jeremiah 32:39; Isa 8:14. Ezekiel 36:25-27. Regeneration.
2. I will put a new spirit within you. Psalm 51:10. Ezekiel 36:36. Recreated and new spirit as in regeneration. Renewing of the spirit by being born of the Spirit. John 3:1-5; Tit 3:5.
3. I will take away the stony heart out of them. Old Covenant commandments on Tables of Stone. 2 Cor 3.
4. I will give them a heart of flesh. Tender, soft, responsive. New Covenant Laws on such.

Vs 20 5. That they may walk in My statutes.
6. Keep Mine ordinances and do them. Ordinances of House of the Lord.
7. They shall be my people.
8. And I will be their God. Lev 26:12.
   Cf. Jeremiah 31:31-34; Heb 8. All only possible by the power of the NEW Covenant and NEW Sanctuary in the Messiah Himself, by His Spirit.
   Not a place now but a PERSON! Sanctuary and Law in Him – Christ.

Vs 21. Judgment on those whose heart walks after detestable things and abominations.
Own way to be recompensed on their heads. cf. 7:4.

5. THE GLORY DEPARTS TO THE MT OF OLIVES – vs 22-23

Vs 22. The Cherubim and chariot wheels mount up, with the Glory of God above them.
Cf. 10:19; 1:28.

Vs 23. The Glory Shekinah leaves the City and stood over on the Mountain on the EAST side of the City of Jerusalem.
i.e. The Glory departs from the Sanctuary and ascends by way of the East from Mt Olivet. Does not return to the material Temple but to the NEW vision Temple in Ezekiel 43:1-3; Zech 14:4.

6.   THE PROPHET'S RETURN TO CHALDEA – vs 24-25

Vs 24. The Spirit brings Ezekiel in his vision verily back to the Captivity in Chaldea. The vision closes off, cf 8:3.

Vs 25. Ezekiel relates to those of the Captivity what he had seen in the vision concerning
1.   The City – coals of fire.
2.   The Temple – departing Glory.
3.   The Rulers and their abominations.
4.   The Seal of God on the Faithful Remnant.
5.   The Judgment on Rulers, Princes and People.
6.   The New Covenant Promises given.

EZEKIEL CHAPTER TWELVE

1. **THE SIGN OF EZEKIEL MOVING HIS STUFF** – vs 1-7

Vs 1. The Word of the Lord.

Vs 2. The rebellious house, cf. 2:3, 5, 6-8; 3:26.
     a. Eyes to see – see not. Spiritual blindness Results of spiritual rebellion.
     b. Ears to hear – hear not. Spiritual deafness.
     Isa 6:9; 42:20; Jer 5:21; Mt 13:13-14; Acts 28:25-28.
     Thus lose what you do not use.
     Root cause – rebellion. 1 Sam 5:23. As sin of witchcraft.
     None so deaf as those who don't want to hear or blind as those who do not want to see.
     Rebellion brings spiritual blindness and deafness to persons or nations.

Vs 3. The prophet to prepare his stuff (instruments) for removing.
Move by day in their sight, from one place to another place.
Perhaps they may consider even though they be rebellious.

Vs 4. Stuff brought forth in the day. At even to go forth as one going into Captivity.

Vs 5. Ezekiel digs through the wall and carries his stuff out thereby.

Vs 6. As he does, he is told to bear it on his shoulders (as a slave) with face covered (stumbling, not see clearly where he is going).
The prophet to be A SIGN to the House of Israel, cf. Vs 11.
Refer also Isa 8:18; Heb 2:3; Psalm 71:7; Zech 3:8; Isa 20:2-3; Ezekiel 4:3; 24:24. Signs to a hardened and rejecting people, those who reject the Word.

Vs 7. The prophet obeys the word of the Lord, removing his stuff as in preparation for going into Captivity.
Thus "creative" and "illustrative" prophecy here!

2. **THE SIGN INTERPRETED TO THE PEOPLE** – vs 8-16

Vs 8. The Word of the Lord in the morning.

Vs 9. The rebellious House of Israel asked the prophet what he was digging in the wall for, what was he doing.

cf. 2:5; 17:12; 24:19. Too blind to interpret the sign for themselves.

Vs 10. The Interpretation. The prophetic burden concerns the Prince in Jerusalem and all the House of Israel there. Cf. Burden – Mal. 1:1.

Vs 11. Ezekiel is their SIGN. AS ... SO.
As Ezekiel had removed his stuff as going into captivity, so would the House of Israel. Cf. Vs 6. 2 Kgs 24:4-7.

Vs 12. The Prince ..... cf. Jeremiah 39:4-7. Probably Zedekiah. God's omniscience, foreknowledge and prophecy.
Seeking to escape Jerusalem and from the city, getting out between the gates and the two walls as he tried to.
Typified in what Ezekiel did in Babylonia, Zedekiah would do in Jerusalem what the prophet was doing.

Vs 13. God will spread His net over him and take him in His snare. He will be taken to Babylon. He will see it not, but he shall die there.
Cf. Jeremiah and Ezekiel prophecies concerning Zedekiah. Zedekiah sees his sons slain and sees the King of Babylon face to face, then his eyes are put out and he is taken to Babylon and does not see it.
Job 19:6; Jer 52:9; Lam 1:13; Ezek 17:20; 2 Kgs 25:7; Jer 52:11; Ezek 17:16.

Vs 14. All the King's helpers will be scattered. His body guard. 2 Kgs 25:4; Ezekiel 5:2, 10, 12.
The sword after him.

Vs 15. The scattered and dispersed among the nations will recognise that it was the Lord's judgments on them. Cf. Vs 16, 20: Psalm 9:16; Ezekiel 6:7, 14; 11:10.

Vs 16. God will leave a REMNANT from the sword/famine/ pestilence. They will be a testimony that the captivity came because of their abominations in their own land, cf. 6:8-10.

3.   **THE SIGN OF EZEKIEL'S MEALS** – vs 17-20.

Vs 17. Word of the Lord.

Vs 18. The prophet to eat his bread and drink the water with quaking, trembling added to carefulness, cf. 4:16.

Vs 19. The interpretation of vs 18, cf. 4:16 prophecy. Significant of the famine and scarcity of food in the siege. They also would eat and drink as such in food rationing.   Zech 7:14. Desolation because of the violence of the inhabitants.

Vs 20. Cities and land to be desolated. Know that the Lord is God.

4.   **THE PROVERB AND THE VISION** – vs 21-25.

Vs 21. The Word of the Lord.

Vs 22. Proverbial saying among the people that the days are prolonged, (put off, postponed) and the vision of the prophet Ezekiel fails to come to pass.
2 Pet 3:4; Ezekiel 12:27; 11:3; Amos 6:3; read.

Vs 23. God will make the proverb to cease. It will be reversed.
The days are at hand – not prolonged.
The vision is effected – not failed.
Joel 2:1; Zeph 1:14.

Vs 24. The vain vision and flattering divinations of false prophets in Israel to cease.
Joel 2:1; Lam 2:13; Ezek 13:23.

Vs 25. God the Lord alone. What He speaks shall come to pass. Not to be prolonged, but to be performed in the days of the rebellious house.
Cf. Vs 28; Isa 55:11; Dan 9:12; Lk 21:33.

5.   **THE VISION CONFIRMED** – vs 26-28

Vs 26. The Word of the Lord. Amos 6:3.

Vs 27. The people of Israel say Ezekiel's vision is not for now; that it is far off, for the days and time to come, cf vs 22.

Vs 28. God says His Word shall be no longer delayed. It shall be done, cf. Vs 3, 23, 25 again. Isa 55:11.

EZEKIEL CHAPTER THIRTEEN

1.　**THE FALSE PROPHETS IN ISRAEL** – vs 1-9.

Vs 1.　The Word of the Lord.

Vs 2.　The true prophet, Ezekiel, is the prophecy against the false prophets in Israel.
Sign –

Vs 3.　1. Prophesy out of their own hearts, cf vs 17. Jeremiah 14:14; Jeremiah 23:16, 26.
　　　　2. Foolish prophets.
　　　　3. Follow their own spirit.
　　　　4. Have seen nothing – no vision. Things they have not seen.
　　　　　Hedge – wall.

Vs 4.　The prophets of Israel like FOXES in the desert, cf Song 2:15; Lk 13:31-32; Lam 5:18.
Deceitful, sly, cunning, smelly. Ready to devour the sheep and lambs of the flock of God. Isa 5:5.

Vs 5.　Prophets not gone up into the GAPS (breaches). True prophet called to "stand in the gap". Cf. Psalm 106:23, 30; Ezekiel 22:23, 30; Psalm 80:8-15; Isa 59:16.
Also to make up the hedge by standing in the gap as an intercessor in the day of the battle. Job 1:10.
Symbolic – of the enemy breaking in, causing a breach in the wall, and someone should be there to stand in the gap, making up the hedge of protection.

Vs 6.　False prophets see lying divinations. Use the Lord's Name in vain. Not sent of the Lord. Hope for others to confirm their word.
Cf. Vs 23; 12:24; 22:28; Deut 13:1-6; 18:15-22.

Vs 7.　Challenge of the Lord to them. God has not spoken, yet they spoke. Vain and lying visions of divination. Rev 22:18-19.

Vs 8.　Because of this God is against them.

Vs 9.　Judgment on the false prophets. God's hand on these liars. Not to be in the Assembly of the people, secret or council.

Not to be written in the writing of Israel. Ezra 2:59, 62:
Nehemiah 7:5.
Not to enter the land of Israel. 11:10,12. Names taken out of
Book of Life. Psalm 69:28.
Know that the Lord is the Lord. 20:38.

SUMMARY:
This section above sets forth the characteristics of the False Prophet.

1. They prophesy out of their own heart, not from the heart of God.
2. They are foolish.
3. They follow their own spirit. Walk after own spirit, not the Spirit of God.
4. They have seen nothing. Things not seen.
5. They are like sly foxes.
6. They fail to go up and fill the gaps as intercessors.
7. They fail to make up the hedge of protection.
8. They see vanity and lying divination, divine lies. Not the truth.
9. They say the Lord said when He spoke not to them. Deut 18:18-20.
10. They hope for others to confirm their false word.
11. They seduce the people into a false peace and security. Vs 10, 16.
12. They pollute God among the people. Vs 19.
13. They are greedy for gain. Vs 19.
14. They are false princes. Vs 22.

Thus they are self-deceived and deceive others for they do not have a love for the truth. 2 Thess 2:1-12. Lying spirits. 1 Kgs 22.

2. **THE WALL OF UNTEMPERED MORTAR** – vs 10-16.

Vs 10. False prophets prophesy "Peace" where there is none, cf. Vs 16. So the prophets up at Jerusalem against Jeremiah.
They build up a slight wall and others daub it with untempered mortar. Mortar that should consolidate and hold the wall up and together for protection.
Lacks that 'temper' – quality which binds as cement, strengthens the wall. 22:28.

Vs 11. The wall shall fall which they have built. An overflowing shower shall wash out the mortar causing the wall to fall.

Wind and rain and hailstones – worst things for a newly built wall. Cf 38:22.

Vs 12. When the wall falls, the people will challenge the prophets about the mortar they put in it.

Vs 13. The Interpretation. Vs 13-16.
God will send a stormy wind, hailstones and great overflowing shower to destroy that false wall of security here that they have built up.

Vs 14. The whole wall will be broken down. The foundation of the wall will be seen. Wall to destroy the false prophets. They will know that God is the Lord, cf. Vs 9, 21, 23; 14:8.

Vs 15. The wall and those that daubed it to come under the wrath of God.

Vs 16. The ones who daubed the wall with untempered mortar are the prophets of Israel prophesying of Jerusalem and the false visions of peace. Cf. Jeremiah 6:14; 28:9.
Symbolics:
1.   The Wall – false security.
2.   The untempered mortar – False prophecies.
3.   The Builders daubing it – False prophets.
4.   The Storm, showers, hail and wind – the wrath and judgments of God.

3.   **THE FALSE PROPHETESSES** – vs 17-23.

Vs 17. Ezekiel to prophesy against the women prophetesses also. Hunting souls.
Also prophesy out of their own hearts cf. Vs 2: 20:46; 21:2.

Vs 18. Woe to the women.
Sew pillows to arm holes (elbows). Make kerchief on head of statues to hunt souls, cf. 2 Pet 2:14. Undoubtedly the "crystal ball" kind of means of divining for information for the souls of people. Witchcraft. By false utterances deceived people that they would live and not die.

Vs 19. The Lord's Name polluted by their lying in His Name to the people.   His Name is truth, yet they lie in His Name. Prophesying death on the ones that live and life on the ones that should die. Reversal.
Their reward and wages for divination = barley and bread. Food in the siege and the famine. Prov 28:21; Mic 3:5.

Vs 20. God will judge their pillows and their equipment used to hunt souls. The gardens (margin), the groves of witchcraft.

Vs 21. God will tear their kerchiefs and deliver His people out of their hand. They will know God did this, cf vs 9.

Vs 22. Lies have saddened the heart of the righteous. Lies have strengthened the hands of the wicked. Life promised to the wicked, yet not turn him from his wicked way.
Cf. 3:17-21; Jer. 23:14. A true prophet will seek to do this.

Vs 23. False prophetesses not see any more vanity and divinations. God will deliver His own people. Cf. Vs 9.

Thus the whole chapter is judgment against the False Prophets and Prophetesses.

EZEKIEL CHAPTER FOURTEEN

1.   **THE IDOLATROUS ELDERS OF ISRAEL** – vs 1-5.

Vs 1.   Certain elders come and sit before Ezekiel waiting the word of the Lord. Enquiry of God via the Prophet, cf. 8:1; 20:1; 33:31.

Vs 2.   The Word of the Lord came.

Vs 3.   Two great evils of these Elders. 1 John 5:20.
1.   Idols set up in their hearts – Internal.
2.   Stumbling-block of iniquity before their face – External. Vs 2. Vs 4,7; 7:19.
Should the Living God be enquired at by such idolatrous Elders? 2 Kgs 3:13.

Vs 4.   Everyone who is guilty of these things, yet they come to seek the Prophet. God will answer them according to the multitude of their idols.

Vs 5.   The House of Israel to be dealt with according to their heart condition. Idols estranged them from the Lord. Violation of the Ten Commandments. Ex 20.

2.   **CALL TO GENUINE REPENTANCE** – vs 6-11

Vs 6.   Call to the House of Israel.
1.   Repent – A change of mind in relation to God and sin. The ROOT. Internal.
2.   Turn – from your idols and abominations. FRUIT. External. Evidence. Thus right about turn. Change of mind and change of direction. Root and fruit of genuine repentance.

Vs 7.   The people of the House of Israel like their Elders. Israel, strangers among them, separated from God, set up idols in the HEART, put stumbling-blocks of iniquity before them and their face.
God will answer them if they come to a prophet for direction and guidance.

Vs 8.   God will set His face against that man. Divine judgment. He will make the prophet:
1.   A sign –

2. A reproach –
3. Cut him off from among the people. Know that God is the Lord, cf. 6:7; Lev 17:10.
Lev 20:3, 5, 6; Jer 44:11; Ezek 15:7.

Vs 9. A deceived prophet is permitted to be deceived because of no love for the truth. 2 Thess 2:1-12. God shall stretch out His hand and destroy that prophet from Israel. 2 Kgs 22.
Cf. 1 Kgs 22:23; Job 12:16; Jer 4:10; 2 Thess 2:11.

Vs 10. All to be punished. The Elders, the Prophet and the People. Reward to such to the people who follow them.

Vs 11. The divine purpose. To cause Israel to cease going astray, polluting themselves with their transgressions.
Yet to experience New Covenant promises.
1. Be My people, cf. 11:20: 37:27.
2. I will be their God. 2 Pet 2:15.

3. **GOD'S FOUR SORE JUDGMENTS** – vs 12-21; Jn 5:22; Mal 3:5.

Vs 12. Word of the Lord. Prophetic formula. Three witnesses.

Vs 13. When the land sins grievously against God, He will stretch out His hand on it and break the staff of bread in sending FAMINE on it, cutting off man and beast.
Judgment No 1. Cf. Lev 26:26; Isa 3:1; Ezek 4:16; 5:16.

Vs 14. Even if these three men, Noah, Daniel and Job were in, they would be delivered only, by reason of their righteousness.
Cf. Vs 16, 18, 20 also.
Cf. Jeremiah 15:1; 7:16; 11:14; Prov 11:4. Jeremiah, Moses and Samuel = Three witnesses, as Intercessors.

Vs 15. Judgment No 2. NOISOME Beasts pass through the land.
Literal beasts = Lev 26:22; Ezekiel 5:17; 2 Kgs 17:25-26.
Symbolic of national beasts – Gentile nations. Political – see Assyria, Babylonia etc. Dan 7; Dan 8; Rev 12-13, 17.

Vs 16. Refer to vs 14, 18, 20 and notes. These THREE MEN – three witnesses – not even deliver their own sons and daughters, only themselves. No guarantee of households saved even.

Vs 17. Judgment No 3. A SWORD. Lev 26:25; Ezekiel 5:12; 21:3, 4; 29:8; 38:21. The Sword of war to go through the land cutting off man and beast.

cf. Jeremiah 25. The Cup and the Sword.

Vs 18. Refer to vs 14, 18, 20 and notes.

Vs 19. Judgment No 4. A PESTILENCE (Plague). Cf. 2 Sam 24:15;
Ezekiel 38:22; 7:8. God's fury on the land in blood cutting
off man and beast.

Vs 20. Cf. Vs 14, 16, 18, 20. These 3 men. Repeated 4 times in all.
God always has His 3 Witnesses, cf. Deut 17:6-7; Num
35:30; 1 Tim 5:19; 2 Cor 13:1; John 8:17; Deut 19:15; Mt
18:16; Heb 10:28. Thus:

1. Three men in the fiery furnace. Dan 3.
2. Three men on the Mt of Transfiguration. Mt 17:1-6.
3. Three men in this time as examples of righteous men.
Ezekiel 14.
4. Three men in all sent into each city of Judah. Lk 10:1-2.
Two plus the Son of God.

Three – number of the Godhead, three witness, complete
testimony. 1 John 5:5-8.

Note the men in their Dispensational setting.

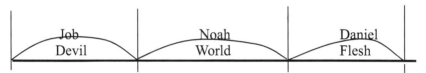

Each were overcomers in their generation. Each were 'sign'
men of the Last Day Church.
1. Noah – Gen 6-9 chapters. Overcomer of the world, by
faith. Lk 17, Mt 24.
2. Daniel – Dan 1-5. Overcomer of the flesh. Mt 24:9-14.
The 70 Weeks prophecy to him.
3. Job – Job 1-2, 40-42. Overcomer of the devil. Jas 5:11.

Each of the three men were sign men in their generation. All
are used in the New Testament as such concerning the second
coming of the Lord.
They were faith – righteous men. Only delivered by their own
righteousness.   So wicked   was the House of Israel in
Ezekiel's time, that God would not deliver any households,
but only those who were faith-righteous men, cf. 5:17; 33:27.

Vs 21. God's four sore judgments.   Number of earth, universal, worldwide.
    1. The Sword – cf. Second Seal. Red horse. Rev 6:4.
    2. The Famine – cf. Third Seal. Black horse. Rev 6:3.
    3. The Noisome Beasts – Fourth Seal. Pale Horse. Rev 6:8.
    4. The Pestilence – cf. Fourth Seal. The Pale Horse. Rev 6:8.
Vs 22. 5. The Remnant – cf. First Seal. The White Horse, Righteousness. Rev 6:1-2.

4.   **THE FAITHFUL REMNANT** – vs 22-23.

Vs 22. God, as always, leaves a REMNANT, both sons and daughters, who will come forth. That is, another generation. In seeing their way and their doings, the older generation shall be comforted concerning the judgment that god permitted on Jerusalem, cf 6:8; 20:43.

Vs 23. These sons and daughters – a godly remnant – shall comfort the older generation.   Recognise that Jerusalem was not judged with Divine cause, cf. 22:8, 9.

This chapter in its final section can be applied to the final generation in the Last Days also, in the Book of Revelation.

1. The four sore judgments – the 2nd, 3rd and 4th Seals.
2. Noah, Daniel and Job – The Overcomer Church, overcoming the world, the flesh and devil or the Church of the Last Days, the Bride of Christ.
3. The Remnant that God preserves – Rev 12:17. The remnant also here.

EZEKIEL CHAPTER FIFTEEN

1. **THE SYMBOL OF THE VINE TREE** – Vs 1-5, cf. Isa 5:1-7.

Vs 1.   The Word of the Lord.

Vs 2.   What is the Vine tree more than any tree, or branch thereof compared with the forest?

Vs 3.   The wood is useless for any special work. Cannot even be used for wooden pins (pegs) to hang vessels thereon. Only purpose for its existence is to bear FRUIT.

Vs 4.   Good only for the fire fuel, not for work. Fruit or Fire? Cf. John 15:6.

Vs 5.   If useless for work as a vine, much more so when reduced to ashes by the fire.

2. **THE INTERPRETATION** – vs 6-8.

Vs 6.   AS ... SO. As the tree given to the fire, so the inhabitants of Jerusalem to the fuel. Comparative principle.

Vs 7.   To be burned from fire to fire, devoured by the judgment of the Lord. Cf. Lev 17:10; Ezekiel 14:8; 7:4; Isa 24:18.

Vs 8.   The land to be desolated because of Israel's trespasses.

Summary:
1. The vine taken out of Egypt. Psalm 80.
2. The vine planted and protected. Isa 5:1-7.
3. The vine fruitless. Jeremiah 2:21; Hos 10:1.
4. The vine degenerated. Jeremiah 2:21.
5. The vine visited and rejected. Mt 21:33-46.
6. The vine burnt and wasted – useless when unfruitful. Ezekiel 15.
7. Christ and His Church now the true vine. John 15:1-15.

EZEKIEL CHAPTER SIXTEEN

This chapter, under the figure of a Woman, sets forth the history of the Nation of Israel from its infancy to marriage to the Lord, and then its violation of the marriage contract by spiritual harlotry. Cf. Ezekiel 23 also.

1. **THE NATION'S BIRTH** – vs 1-5.

Vs 1.   The Word of the Lord.

Vs 2.   God desires to cause Jerusalem to know her abominations. He does this under the figure of a Harlot. Cf. 20:4; 22:2.

Vs 3.   Birth and nativity of the land of Canaan. Gen 35:1-4. Land of Promise, cf. 21:30.
    1. Thy father – an Amorite
    2. Thy mother – a Hittite
    Figurative language here. Abraham and Sarah (Idolatrous before call.   Josh 24:14;   Ezekiel 20 also). Family association of idolatry. Isa 51:2. Symbolic names used there.

Vs 4.   3. Thy naval not cut. Figurative language also.
    a. Day of nativity and birth – Birth of a Nation.
    b. Naval not cut – no separation from mother.
    c. Not washed in water to supple thee – no cleansing by water of the Word.
    d. Not salted at all – cleansing by salt of impurities of birth.
    e. Not swaddled at all – for warmth, comfort etc.

Vs 5
    f. No eye pitied three – no midwife.
    g. None had compassion – unloved nation.
    h. Cast out into the open field – rejected as an infant. Infanticide.
    i. Loathed in the day of birth – unwanted, despised child, infant nation.

2. **THE NATION'S INFANCY TO WOMANHOOD** – vs 6-14.

Vs 6.   A. God passed by and saw the infant nation polluted in own blood. Cf. Lev 12. Margin. Trodden under foot.
    B. God gave the word of life, the good news "Live".

Vs 7.   C. God caused the infant nation to multiply, increase and wax great. Book of Exodus. Margin. Made thee a million. Ex 1:17.
    D. Came to ornaments.

            E.   Breasts fashioned – maturity coming forth

            F.   Hair grown, not naked & bare. Beauty & glory. Ex 1-18.

Vs 8.   G. God passed by thee at the time of love.

            H. Spread His skirt over thee, cf. Ruth 3:9. Symbol of coming Marriage. Covered nakedness.

            I.   God entered into Covenant with the nation. Swore to her. She became His.   The Marriage Vows and contract. Mosaic

               Or Law Covenant. Mt Sinai. Ex 19; Jer 2:2.

Vs 9.   J.   God washed Israel with water, cf. Red Sea Baptism of Nation. 1 Cor. 10:1-4.

               Ceremonial cleansing of the Law. Washing by Word. Heb 9:10; Tit 3:5; Ephesians 5:23-32.

Vs 10. K. Thoroughly washed way thy bloods. Source of pollution.

            L.   Anointed thee with oil. The Holy anointing oil. Olive tree Nation. Ex 30:22-31.

            M. Clothed thee with embroidered work, shod with badgers Skins, girded with fine linen and covered with silk. i.e. The Tabernacle and Priesthood garments. Ex 25-40 chapters.

Vs 11. N. Decked with ornaments, bracelets, chain. As young bride. Cf. Gen 24:22; Isa 61:10, Prov 1:9.

Vs 12. O. Jewel in nose, earrings on ear, crown on head. Decked as a Queen, a Royal Bride. Isa 3:21. Bride & wife of Jehovah.

Vs 13. P. Decked with gold and silver, fine linen, silk, embroidered work.

            Q. Food – fine flour, honey and oil. Best of food in promised Land. Deut 32:13-14.

            R. Exceeding beautiful, cf. Psalm 48:2. Beauty of the nation Compared with other nations.

            S. Prospered into A KINGDOM. Cf. Glory of the Kingdom under David and Solomon.

Vs 14. Renown and beauty that God had put on the nation known amongst other nations. Lam 2:15.

3.   **THE NATION'S HARLOTRY** – vs 15-34.

Vs 15. Israel trusted in her own beauty. – Self confidence. Beauty deceives. Lam 2:15. Yet all was God-given. She played the harlot, began to fornicate with surrounding nations. Cf. Deut 32:15; Jer 7:4; Mic 3:11; Isa 1:21; 57:8; Jer 2:20; Ezek 23:3, 8.

Vs 16. Israel took her beautiful garments and used them to deck the High

Places and played the harlot there.
Never been like it before, for no other nation was ever brought into marriage relationship with God like Israel was, cf. 2 Kgs 23:7; Ezekiel 7:20; Hos 2:8.

Vs 17. Israel took of the jewels God had given her, of silver and gold, and used them to make images of a male (Margin) and used them in sex-worship. Spiritual whoredoms.

Vs 18. Israel used the embroidered wedding garments to cover the images. Used God's holy anointing oil and God's incense before them also.
All this God had given Israel, cf. Vs 14, 17, 18, 19.
Hos 1-2 chapters also. MY comeliness. My gold, MY silver, MINE oil, MINE incense, MY meat, etc.

Vs 19. Israel used God's food-offering of Canaan land, made of fine flour, oil, honey, which God had given and used them as a Meal offering (Lev 2) to the images for a sweet savour., ie, savour of rest.
Thus all the ordinances of the Tabernacle, priesthood garments, anointing oil, incense, meal offerings, etc., were all used now for idolatrous purposes.
Such is human nature. It prostitutes that which is God-given and ordained and uses the same things to worship idols and commit spiritual fornication. So did the Scribes and Pharisees in Messiah's Times, cf. Isa 1:10-15; 66:1-4.

Vs 20. Israel took her own sons and daughters, who belonged to God (Firstborn – Ex 13:1-6) and offered them in sacrifice to these gods to be devoured.
Their whoredoms were no small matter.
Cf. 2 Kgs 16:3; Psa 106:37; Isa 57:5; Jer 7:31; Ezek 20:36.

Vs 21. Caused their children to pass through the fire. Idolatrous Molech worship. Child-sacrifice.

Vs 22. Israel did not REMEMBER the days of youth and her polluted condition when God took her up. Wild harlotry. Forgetting God.
Cf. Vs 43, 60. Vs 4, 5, 6; Jer 2:2; Hos 11:1.

Vs 23. A double WOE pronounced on Israel's wickedness.

Vs 24. Israel built an eminent house (Margin. Brothel House) and made High Places in every street, i.e. The Temple of Samaria and all other idols groves. Isa 57:5, 7; Jeremiah 2:20; 3:2.

Vs 25. Israel built High Places everywhere. Her beauty became abhorred and she opened her being to all who passed by in her multiplied whoredoms. Prov 9:14.

Vs 26. EGYPTIAN idolatry – Israel's fornications and whoredoms provoke God to anger, cf. 8:10, 14. Israel and Egyptian alliances.
Cf. 20:6-10; 23:3. Idolators in Egypt before her redemption also.
Ezekiel only prophet, and also Joshua, mentioned Israel's idolatry in Egypt slavery.
Note also Jer. 42-43-44. House of Judah & Egyptian follies.

Vs 27. God punishes Israel by famine and by captivity into the various cities of the Philistines which are ashamed of her evil ways, cf vs 57; 2 Chronicles 28:18.

Vs 28. ASSYRIAN – Israel's harlotry and whoredoms as an insatiable harlot. Cf Assyrian idolatry and alliance and captivity.

Vs 29. BABYLONIAN – Israel's spiritual fornication from Canaan to Babylon, yet not satisfied, cf. 23:14.
Cf. Josh 7. Achan's Babylonish gold wedge and garment to House of Israel and Judah and their Captivities. Illustrate this.
Cf. Isa 39; Jer 50-51; Isa 47-48.

Vs 30. Israel's WEAK HEART condition. Weak and imperious whorish women.

Vs 31. Israel's weakness revealed in the rebuilding lots of places of idolatry in eminent places in every street. Also she sold herself to whoredoms yet did not receive hire for it as a harlot generally does. Scorned hire! Cf. Vs 24, 39.

Vs 32. Israel as an adulterous wife, having strangers instead of her husband Jehovah, cf. Jeremiah 31:31-34.

Vs 33. Israel does the opposite to a regular harlot. Strangers give gifts to whore lovers for hire.
Israel gave gifts to strangers and hired or bribed them for whoredoms. Isa 30:6; Hos 8:9.

Vs 34. Israel absolutely contrary to harlot women – none follow her as she does. Israel gave rewards to strangers, yet they gave her no reward for whoredoms. Dumb harlot – not even business-like!

4. **THE NATION'S BROKEN MARRIAGE AND JUDGMENT** – vs 35-43.

Vs 35. Because of this, O HARLOT, hear the word of the Lord. Terrible indictment from God to His wife!

Vs 36. Israel's sins discovered:
1. Her filthiness, nakedness, discovered by whoredoms.
2. Idols of abomination.
3. Blood of sacrificed children.
The 3 major sins dealt with in this chapter, cf vs 20; Jeremiah 2:34.

Vs 37. God will use the lover (nations) that Israel has had love with and pleasure with, as well as the nations she hated, and cause them to expose her nakedness.
Thus humiliation by other nations. Jeremiah 12:33, 26; Lam 1:8; Hos 2:10; 8:10; Nah 3:5; Ezekiel 23:9, 10, 22, 29.

Vs 38. God will judge Israel as A WOMAN THAT BREAKS WEDLOCK and kill her children. God will give her blood judgment in fury and jealousy.
Cf. Vs 20, 36; Gen 9:6; Ex 21:12.

Vs 39. Israel to be given into the hands of her lovers. They will break down her places of idolatry. They shall strip her naked and bare her of her glory, cf. Vs 20, 36.
Note the SEVEN I shall's of vs 39-41.

Vs 40. Israel to have a company against her, and stone her and thrust her through with their swords.
Cf. 23:46; John 8:5, 7; Lev 20:10; Deut 22:22; Num 25:1-9. The Law commanded that a wife who played the harlot be stoned!

Vs 41. Israel's lovers will burn her houses with fire, execute judgments on her in the sight of many women (nations) and also cause her to cease playing the harlot for no hire.

Vs 42. God's fury and jealousy will be satisfied then, and He will cease to be angry once she is punished, cf. 5:13; Deut 13:16;

2 Kgs 25:9; Jeremiah 39:8; 52:13; Ezekiel 5:8; 23:10, 48; 23:27.

Vs 43. Israel failed to remember the days of her youth, but caused the Lord to fret because of her desire to attract other lovers, cf. 5:13. God will recompense her way on her head to cause her not to commit lewdness above all her abominations, cf vs 22; 9:10; 11:21; 22:31; Psalm 78:42.

The whole picture is that of an enraged and jealous husband, Jehovah, because of all His loved bestowed upon His Bride and Wife, Israel, yet she plays the harlot with other gods who use her, abuse her, and then will turn upon her and destroy her.

5.   THE NATION'S SPIRITUAL CONDITION WORSE THAN OTHER NATIONS – vs 44-59.

Vs 44. Those that use proverbs will use this proverb against Israel. "AS is the Mother, SO is the daughter ....."

Vs 45. MOTHER an Hittite – FATHER an Amorite, cf. Vs 3 notes.
Judah/Israel – the daughter loathed her Husband.
Israel's sisters loathed their Husbands.   Like Mother, like Daughters!

Vs 46. THE ELDER SISTER is SAMARIA – she and her daughters – at the left hand.
THE YOUNGER SISTER is SODOM – she and her daughters – at the right hand.
Perhaps symbolic name used here for Judah, cf. Isa 1:1, 10; Rev 11:8.

Vs 47. Israel did not walk after their ways and abominations, but became more corrupted than they were, cf. 5:6, 7; cf. 48, 51; 2 Kgs 21:9.

Vs 48. Sodom and her daughters were not guilty of what Israel/Judah and her daughters were guilty of, cf Mt 10:15; 11:24.

Vs 49. The sins of Sodom listed as:
1. Pride –
2. Fulness of bread – material prosperity.
3. Abundance of idleness - #2 leads to this.
4. Not strengthen the hand of the poor – selfishness.
Vs 50. 5. Haughtiness – as #1.
6. Committed abominations before God, cf. Gen 13:10-13;

18:20; 19:5.

God judged Sodom as He saw fit, taking it away with fire and brimstone. Gen 19:24; Jude 7. Example city to other cities.

Vs 51. The sin of Samaria. The House of Israel did not commit half the sins of Judah. The House of Judah multiplied her abominations by bringing such into the very Temple of God at Jerusalem.

Her sisters, Samaria and Sodom, will rise to condemn her, because they were judged by God for less, cf. Jeremiah 3:11; Mt 12:41.

Vs 52. House of Judah judged her sister nations, Israel and Sodom; yet she is more evil than they. They were more righteous than she. Therefore the House of Judah shall bear her shame for herself the more for judging her sisters.

Vs 53. The Captivity to be turned, i.e.Always symbolic of God bringing back to blessing, and restoration, cf. Psalm 126:1-2; Isa 1:9; Jeremiah 20:16.
1. The Captivity of Sodom and her daughters.
2. The Captivity of Samaria and her daughters.
3. The Captives of Judah in the midst of Sodom and Samaria.

Vs 54. To bear her own shame and confusion for all that she has done. It will be a comfort to Samaria and sodom that God will also judge Judah, cf. 14:22.

Vs 55. Sodom, Samaria and Jerusalem – all to return to former estate in due time.

Vs 56. House of Judah not mention Sodom in the day of her pride. Not take any warnings from her sins and judgment.

Vs 57. Her wickedness is discovered, while she is reproaching Syria (Aram), etc, and all those round about her. They despise and spoil her. 2 Kgs 16:5; 2 Chronicles 28:18; Isa 7:1; 14:28.

Vs 58. Nation borne her lewdness and abominations. Cf. 23:49.

Vs 59. God will deal with the nation according to what she has done. Israel despised the OATH in breaking the marriage covenant, ie. The vows and promise of Israel to the Lord at Mt Sinai, under the Mosaic Covenant.

Cf. Ex 24. "All that the Lord hath said, we will do."
Ezekiel 17:13; Deut 29:1, 10-15, 21; 29:1-29; 30:1-20. No
doubt more especially the Palestinian Covenant concerning
the LAND and the conditions for remaining in it. The only
hope for anyone now is the NEW COVENANT!

6. **THE COVENANTS OF GOD TO THE NATION** – vs 60-63; Rom
9:4-5.

Vs 60.   However, God will remember His Covenant made with Israel
in the days of her youth, i.e. The Abrahamic Covenant. Psalm
106:45.
God will establish an Everlasting Covenant, i.e. Points to the
Everlasting and New Covenant. Heb 13:20; Jeremiah
31:31-34; Heb 8; Mt 26:26-28; Jeremiah 32:40; 50:5.

Vs 61.   Judah to be ashamed of her ways. Also to receive her sister
nations, Samaria and Sodom, as daughters. However, not by
her Covenant (ie, The Law or Mosaic Covenant). Cf. 20:43;
36:31; Isa 54:1; 60:4; Gal 4:26; Jeremiah 31:31-34.

Vs 62.   God will establish (make firm, strengthen) His Covenant with
Judah and they shall know that He is Jehovah, i.e. cf. Vs 60.
Prophetic of the NEW Covenant, when all shall know the
Lord from the least to the greatest. Hos 2:19.

Vs 63.   Divine purpose is to cause Judah to remember her shame, be
confounded and never open her mouth again anymore because
of her own shame. Not to condemn other nations. God will be
pacified to her after her punishment is accomplished. Rom
3:19.

SUMMARY:
Note the whole chapter in each relationship to the Covenantal
Principle and Israel's history in particular.

	Figurative		Interpretative
1.	vs1-5. The infant child	-	Birth of the Nation.
2.	vs 6-14. Infancy to womanhood	-	Development of the nation
3.	vs 15-34. Nation's harlotry	-	The Nation's idolatry
4.	vs 35-43. Broken marriage	-	vs 26. Egyptian idolatry
5.	vs 44-59. Spiritual state	-	vs 28. Assyrian idolatry
6.	vs 44-59. Captivities	-	vs 29. Babylonian idolatry – Captivity.
7.	vs 60-63. The Covenants	-	New Covenant relationship.

Covenant of Youth Abrahamic Covenant			New Covenant vs 60, 62
Seed – Gen 15-50 Vs 60. Ezek 16.			Everlasting Covenant Heb 13:20
	Thy Covenant, vs 59, 61 Mosaic Covenant		Only Hope "In Christ"
Sodom Egypt	Wilderness Land/Food		
Birth/Captivity vs 6-14 Vs 1-5. Canaan Abram/Isaac/Jacob	Sinai Marriage Tabernacle Palestinian Covenant Ex 19-40; Dt 29-30.		Kingdom Kings Chronicles
			Samaria/Israel Jerusalem/Judah Sodom state Harlot/Wedlock Captivities

EZEKIEL CHAPTER SEVENTEEN

1. **THE RIDDLE AND PARABLE OF BIRDS AND TREES** – vs 1-10

Note – this chapter should be studied in connection with the following chapters. 2 Kings, Jeremiah and Ezekiel. Thus History/Prophecy/Parable.

HISTORY	HISTORY	PROPHECY	PARABLE
2 Kings 24	Jeremiah 39/52	Jeremiah	Ezekiel 17

Vs 1. The Word of the Lord.

Vs 2. Ezekiel told to put forth a RIDDLE (difficult or perplexing problem for solution; but there is a solution for every riddle in God), and A PARABLE (comparison of two things moving from known to the unknown, seen to unseen) to the House of Israel.
NOTE: House of Judah spoken of "House of Israel" much in Ezekiel's prophecy, yet he does make distinction in both Houses at times.

THE FIRST EAGLE

Vs 3-6. <u>The SYMBOLICS of the Riddle and Parable</u> – vs 11-14.

	The INTERPRETATION Of Symbols.
a. A Great Eagle King of birds Lev 11:13; Dt 28:49; Nation as	- Nebuchadnezzar, King of Babylon. Job 39:27-30; Jer 48:40; 49:16; Hos 8:1; Prov 30:17. Dan 4:33.
b. Nation from afar. Not. understand the tongue. Great wings, strength	- Flight, rapidity, speed
c. Long-winged	- Extension of kingdom, stretched out, north to south world kingdom.
d. Full of feathers, plummage, pomp, pride, ruffles feathers as male bird to show off.	- Pride of Babylon as world
e. Divers colours - embroidery	- Entwined army of soldiers of all nations. Like UN Army of best of soldiers of all nationalities he conquered.

f.	Came to Lebanon - Jer.22:6; Zech 10:1. House of Cedar.	-	Jerusalem, 2 Kgs 24:11-16. Royal House
g.	Took the highest cedar. Royal tree, House of David. Jer 22:7	-	King Jehoiachin (2 Kgs 24: 14-16) taken to Babylon
h.	Cropped off young Twigs. Offshoots (Ezek 19:11-14) Cut off – cropped	-	The Princes and King's seed.
i.	Carried to land of traffic Canaan=traffickers	-	To Babylon
j.	Set in City of Merchants.	-	Babylonia (Rev 18:11-15)
k.	Took also Seed of the. land	-	King's seed and also the poorest of the land of Judah
l.	Planted in fruitful field.	-	Palestine land under Babylon
m.	Planted by great waters		
n.	Set it as willow tree	-	Lowly kingdom subject to Him.
o.	It grew, became a low. spreading vine	-	Kingdom to be low stature, submitted, base. Jer 27:10-11
p.	Her branches turned. towards him	-	Made a Covenant and oath with King of Babylon. So did Zedekiah when made king.
q.	Her roots under him.	-	Subject and vassal kingdom
r.	It became a vine	-	Lowly kingdom
s.	Brought forth branches		
t.	Shot forth sprigs	-	Further offspring

THE SECOND EAGLE

Read also 2 Kgs 24:17-20; 25:1-30; Jeremiah 37:1-10.

Vs 7-8. a.	Another great eagle	-	Egypt and Pharaoh
b.	Great wings	-	Great kingdom also
c.	Many feathers	-	Many peoples
d.	Vine bend roots towards him	-	Zedekiah sent to Egypt for help and horses instead of submitting to a Babylon King
e.	Shot forth branches to him	-	To Pharaoh
f.	Desired watering by furrows of his plantation	-	Place of planting
g.	Already in good soil.	-	Already under good rule

by great waters, to   though subject to Babylon
bring forth branches
and fruit as goodly vines

Vs 9.   Shall it prosper? Roots to be pulled up, fruit cut off, leaves to
wither, not take many people to do it. Note vs 15; Jeremiah
1:10. Rooting out here.

Vs 10. To utterly wither as by an East wind in the very furrows
where it was planted to grow, cf. Vs 16.

3.   **THE INTERPRETATION OF THE FIRST RIDDLE AND
PARABLE** – vs 11-14, with vs 1-6

Vs 11. The Word of the Lord.

Vs 12. Rebellious House to know what these things mean.
     a.   King of Babylon, cf vs 3. Great Eagle.
     b.   Came to Jerusalem, ie. Lebanon. Vs 3.
     c.   Took the King, princes to Babylon, cf. Vs 3. Highest
        Branch of Royal House of David. To Babylon, the land
        of traffic.
Vs 13 d.   Took the King's Seed, cf. Vs 4. The young twigs.
     e.   Made Covenant with the King, Zedekiah, took oath, cf.
        2 Kgs 24:11-17.
     f.   Took of the mighty of the land, cf vs 3-4. Princes and
        industrious of land.
Vs 14 g.   The Kingdom to be base, not lift itself up, stand lowly by
        Keeping the Covenant with Nebuchadnezzar, cf. Vs 5-6.
        Lowly vine under the eagle, dependant upon him, as vassal
        Kingdom.

4.   **THE INTERPRETATION OF THE SECOND RIDDLE AND
PARABLE** – vs 7-10, with vs 15-21.

Vs 15. The King rebelled by sending his ambassadors (roots) to
Egypt to get help from there and horses. Deut 17:16; Isa
31:1, 3; 36:6, 9. To get people, cf. Vs 7, 8.
The vine bending her roots towards him, this other great
eagle.
Thus broke the Covenant between himself and
Nebuchadnezzar, yet taken oath in the Name of the LORD.
Cf. Vs 9-10; 2 Kgs 24:20; 2 Chronicles 36:13.

Vs 16. The King, Zedekiah, to die in Babylon because of the broken
Covenant.

Cf. Jer 32:5; 34:3; Ezek 12:13.

Vs 17   Pharaoh, King of the South, of Egypt, not be able to help Zedekiah in the attack on the Babylonians. Jeremiah 37:7; 52:4.

Vs 18.   Zedekiah despised the OATH and broke the COVENANT after he had given his word to submit in the Name of the Lord. Cf. 1 Chronicles 29:24; Lam 5:6.
Any Covenant confirmed with an OATH was to be binding, unbreakable   cf. Heb 7:20, 28;   9:16; Gal 3:15-17; Heb 6:15-20.
Undoubtedly Zedekiah had given this oath in the Name of the Lord to be a subject king, and he had violated this oath by sending to Egypt for help, plus breaking the Laws for Kings in Deut 17, for horses, and also bringing reproach on the Lord, the true God.
He would not escape!

Vs 19.   God declares that the King has broken HIS oath and HIS Covenant, thus will be recompensed by God Himself.
God is a Covenant-making and Covenant-keeping God, and expects the same from His people. He takes Covenants very serious even if made with a Gentile king in His Name.

Vs 20.   The King to be taken in God's net and snare (as a fish or prey is caught), trapped.
Then taken to Babylon to plead with him because of his trespass against GOD. The sin is against GOD, not only Nebuchadnezzar, cf. Psalm 51:1-4; Ezekiel 12:13; 20:36.

Vs 21.   The fugitives and his bands to fall by the sword and the rest to be scattered to the winds.
Fulfilment – now to know that God hath spoken. Ezek. 12:14.

5.   **THE THIRD RIDDLE AND PARABLE – UNINTERPRETED –** vs 22-24.

Note – this third riddle and parable is left uninterpreted, but the 'keys' of interpretation are to be found in the interpretation of the symbols in the previous two parables. This speaks of restoration of the tree here in this parable. Note – Job 18:16-21; 14:7-9. Hope of a tree, if cut down, that through the scent of waters it shall grow again. Note how trees are used as symbolic of kingdoms. Dan 4.

Vs 22. The Lord to take the highest branch of the high cedar and set it, i.e. Take of Zedekiah of the Royal House of David.

Symbolics			Interpretation
a.	The Highest Branch	-	King Zedekiah
b.	High Cedar	-	Royal House of David and Judah tribe
c.	The young twigs	-	Zedekiah's offspring
d.	A tender twig	-	A daughter (as all sons were slain)
e.	Plant it on high mount. and eminent	-	Transplant it to another Kingdom
Vs 23 f.	In Mt of Israel to plant. It	-	In Kingdom of Israel, House, outside Land
g.	Bring forth boughs, bear fruit	-	Offspring, royal seed
h.	Become goodly cedar.	-	House of David
i.	Fowls to dwell under branches	-	Various peoples protected thereunder
Vs 24 j.	All trees of field to Know	-	Other kingdoms in world to know
k.	High tree brought down. Green tree dried up	-	House of Zedekiah/Pharez/ Judah line
l.	Low tree exalted Dry tree made to Flourish	-	House of Israel (Zarah/Judah line)

The Lord has said it and done it!

DUAL INTERPRETATION

Some expositors suggest one or the other or both of the following interpretations. There seems to be that which is National and the other which is Messianic.

1. Natural and National Interpretation:
    The History of Judah's twin sons, Pharez and Zarah (Gen 38) sets the Judo line of kings. Pharez meaning "The Breach" was the line of Judah to David, and David through to King Zedekiah. His name was prophetic. With the slaying of the sons of Zedekiah, and the curse of Jeremiah on the seed or Jeconiah, there came "the breach" as prophesied in the Pharez name.
    The Pharez line had been the High or exalted tree, and the green or flourishing tree.
    Now it was to be brought down and dried up.

The Zarah (or, "The Seed", "Sprout") line should have received the Birthright or Sceptre but lost it at birth. Thus this line was the low (humiliated) tree, and the dry (the stifled) tree.
With the collapse of the Judo-Davidic-Zedekiah throne, the change over of Ezekiel 21:25-27 came.

Thus Zedekiah is left with, at least, a couple of DAUGHTERS (Refer to Notes) (Jeremiah 39-42 chapters). It is one of these "tender twigs" that is taken to another place and planted in the House of Israel and there prospers into a great cedar (Royal House). In other words, the daughter of the Judo-Pharez-David-Zedekiah line is joined to a son of the Judo-Zarah line and the Covenant of the Sceptre to Judah continues its natural line, as well as the Davidic Covenant being unbroken.

For a fuller exposition also refer to "Judah's Sceptre and Joseph's Birthright" by A.A. Allen and "The Royal Seed" and "Abrahamic Covenants and Davidic" by Kevin J. Conner.

2. The Spiritual and Messianic Interpretation:
   The Spiritual and Messianic interpretation, which most Bible expositors follow is seen in the following breakdown of symbols and interpretations:

Symbolics		Interpretation
a. The highest branch of cedar.	-	Zedekiah – David
b. The young twigs	-	His daughters
c. The tender one	-	The virgin Mary
d. The high mountain	-	The Kingdom of God
e. Bring forth fruit	-	The Church
f. Goodly cedar tree	-	The glory of the Church
g. Fowls under its branches	-	Gentiles coming into the shadow of the Church
h. All trees know Natural Israel dried up and Brought down	-	All world to see glory of the Church, which is spiritual Israel, exalted, flourishing

Mat 13. Parable of the Mustard Seed which becomes a great tree, birds under it. Isa 53:2, 11. The natural and national, once the high and green tree, now becomes the dry and brought down tree (cf. Lk 23:31), and the NT spiritual Israel now becomes the flourishing and green tree.

EZEKIEL CHAPTER EIGHTEEN

This chapter compares favourably with Ezekiel 3; Ezekiel 33. The whole chapter teaches personal RESPONSIBILITY and ACCOUNTABILITY before God of every individual. It shows the balancing scales how men try to balance out "the guilt" and "the blame" for their sins. God's scales are just, His weights and balances equal.

1. **THE PROVERB AND THE INTERPRETATION** – vs 1-4.

    Vs 1. The Word of the Lord.

    Vs 2. Proverb concerning the land of Israel.
    "The fathers have eaten sour grapes, and the children's teeth are set on edge."
    Jeremiah 31:29; Lam 5:7, i.e. The fathers have sinned and the children are suffering and paying for it. They ate the sour grapes and it offended the teeth of the children, i.e. This generation is suffering for the sins of the previous generations.

    Vs 3. Proverb not to be used any more in Israel.

    Vs 4. The proverb refuted. All souls are God's; father and son. The soul that sins it shall die. Rom 6:23. AS .... SO ....

    That generation answered and said that they were paying for the sins of the fathers, not for their own sins. Based upon a misinterpretation of Ex 20:4-6 and Deut 5:9-10. They said they were having the sins of the fathers visited upon them. They failed to interpret properly vs 6 of Exodus 20. The sins of the fathers are visited upon the children to the third and fourth generation of them that HATE Me, but there is mercy to all those who LOVE Me!! This is the fact. So it depends on the "hating" and "loving" of God that determines whether a generation is judged or not. If generation after generation HATE God, then the sins are visited in judgment on them. But if they LOVE God, then that generation can receive the mercy of God and commence the generations of them that LOVE God, i.e. Godly generations.

2. **CHARACTERISTICS OF THE JUST FATHER – The FIRST Generation** – vs 5-9.

    Vs 5. Characteristics of the JUST or justified man. He does that which is:

	1.	Lawful and right (margin. Judgment and justice).
Vs 6.	2.	Not eaten on mountains. 22:9. Idolatrous feasts. Ex 20.
	3.	Not lift up eyes to idols of House of Israel. Idolatry. The 2nd commandment.
	4.	Not defiled his neighbour's wife. Adultery. Lev 18:20; 20:10.
	5.	Not come near menstruous woman. Uncleanness. Lev 18: 19; 20:18.
Vs 7.	6.	Not oppressed any but restored the pledge to the debtor. Ex 22:21; Lev 19:15; 25:14.
	7.	Not spoil by violence. Oppression. Ex 22:26; Dt 24:12
	8.	Gave bread to the hungry. Deut 15:7; Isa 58:7; Mt 25:35. Hospitable.
	9.	Covers the naked with a garment. Mt 25:35.
Vs 8.	10.	Not given forth to usury. Ex 22:25; Lev 25:36; Dt.23:19 Neh 5:7; Psa 15:5.
	11.	Not taking increase.
	12.	Withdraws his hand from iniquity.
	13.	Executes true judgment between man and man. Peace maker, reconciler, justice. Zech 8:16; Deut 1:16.
Vs 9.	14.	Walk in God's statutes.
	15.	Keep God's judgments.
	16.	All to do truly – according to truth.

This man is JUST. Characteristics of the just.

This man shall LIVE. Promise for the just, cf.   20:11; Amos 5:4.

Thus keeping of Commandments of God, moral and civil Commandments, or the laws of God are seen here.

3.   **CHARACTERISTICS OF THE WICKED SON – The SECOND Generation** – Vs 10-13.

Vs10.   The characteristics of the wicked son, born of his father, are described here.

They are the opposite to the fathers.

1.	A robber, or breaker up of an house. Stealing.
2.	A shedder of blood. Killer, murderer. Ex 21:12; Num 35:31; Gen 9:6.
3.	Does evil to his brother of the list above.

Vs 11.	4.	Does not do the godly duties listed above.
	5.	Eats on the mountains. Idolatrous feasts.
	6.	Defiles his neighbour's wife. Adultery.
Vs 12.	7.	Oppresses the poor and the needy.
	8.	Takes spoils by violence.
	9.	Does not restore the pledge.
	10.	Does not restore the pledge. Lifts up his eyes to idols. Idolatry.

11. Commits abominations. 8:6, 17.

Vs 13. 12. Given to usury.

13. Takes increase.

This man shall NOT LIVE. These things are an abomination
To God and man. He shall surely DIE. His blood is on his
Own head, cf. 3:18; Lev 20:9, 11-13, 16, 27: Acts 18:6.

4. **CHARACTERISTICS OF THE GOOD GRAND-SON – The
THIRD Generation** – vs 14-18

Note: This brings us to the THIRD generation now. (Refer to Tract of
Generations of the Godly and Ungodly Family and "Household
Salvation".

Thus:

Father – First generation. Vs 1-9. A just father.

Son – Second generation. Vs 10-13. An evil son.

Grandson – Third generation. Vs 14-18. A good and just son.

Vs 14. Son begotten of the second generation. If he sees all the
wickedness of his father and considers it, learns by it, what
not to do, then he shall live. Thus he becomes like his godly
grand-father, not his ungodly father.

Vs 15-17.

These verses list 12 of the positive qualities of his righteous
grandfather. Refer to notes in list vs 1-9.

If he walks in God's judgments and statutes, he shall not die
for the iniquity of his ungodly father. He shall surely LIVE!

NOTE: All this had to be spelled out because of the
misinterpretation of punishment on sin thus to the
third and fourth generation. See notes on vs 4. The
answer to Ex 20:4-6 and Deut 4:24 is that
JUDGMENT is visited on the third and fourth
generation of those that HATE the Lord, but MERCY
is shown to them that LOVE the Lord! So each
generation is dealt with accordingly by God. Each
generation can invoke or change the judgment of God
by genuine repentance. This is the burden of the rest
of the chapter.

Vs 18. The father who cruelly oppressed, spoiled by violence, and
did evil to his brother amongst the people bears his own
iniquity and dies in it, cf. 3:18.

83

5. **GOD'S MERCY UNTO THE REPENTANT WICKED** – vs 19-23.

Vs 19. Israel challenges God by charging that the son is suffering for the iniquity of the Father. In these words they felt they were suffering judgment in their generation because of the sins of their fathers, or the previous generation(s).

God says that the son who does that which is right shall LIVE. Ex 20:5; Deut 5:9; 2 Kgs 23:26; 24:3, 4.

Vs 20. The soul that sins shall die. Neither the son nor the father bears the other's iniquity. Each individual is accountable for themselves before the Lord.

The righteous is accountable for his righteousness.

The wicked is accountable for his own wickedness. Personal responsibility and personal accountability, cf. Vs 4.

Deut 24:16; 2 Kgs 14:6; 2 Chronicles 25:4; Jer 31:29-30; Isa 3:10-11; Rom 2:9.

Vs 21. Promise to the wicked of any generation. If he TURNS from his sins and keeps God's laws, judgments and statutes, he shall LIVE and not die. Cf. Vs 27; 33:12, 19.

Vs 22. Further promise to the repentant wicked. All his transgressions will never be mentioned to him. God will only remember his righteousness. 33:16.

His sins will be cast into the sea of God's forgetfulness. NEW COVENANT promises. Jeremiah 31:31-34.

Vs 23. God has no desire or pleasure in the wicked dying. God desires all to come to repentance and turn from their wicked ways and live. cf. Vs 32; 33:11; 1 Tim 2:4; 2 Pet 3:9. Not will that any should perish.

6. **GOD'S JUDGMENT ON THE FALLEN RIGHTEOUS** – vs 24.

Vs 24. All that God says of the wicked is also true in the opposite relative to the righteous. If a righteous man turns from his righteousness and commits iniquity, and does the abominations of the wicked man, he shall die. None of his righteousness shall be remembered. Only his sins will be remembered and in them he dies. 3:20; 33:12, 13, 18; 2 Pet 2:20.

7. **THE EQUALITY OF GOD'S WAYS AND DEALINGS** – vs 25-29 30a.

Vs 25. Israel complains against the ways of God. Charge God with foolishness, charge against the justice and equality of God's dealings.

Cf. Vs 19. "Yet YE say ... Why do we bear the father's iniquity?"

Cf. Vs 25. "Yet YE say ... God's ways are not equal." Vs 29. However, the very opposite is true. God's ways are equal. Man's ways are not equal, not perfectly balanced. Man became imbalanced in the Fall of Adam.

Vs 26-28.

These verses set forth the equality of God's ways in His dealings with the righteous and the wicked. God's balances are just and equal.

God gave Israel laws for balances and just weights and measures. He Himself demonstrates such in His dealings with His creatures.

God's moral attributes reveal that He will never do anything with His creatures which is inconsistent with His character.

Note Scriptures on "balances" and "just weights". Lev 19:36; Prov 16:11; Job 37:16; Prov 11:1; 20:23; Hos 12:7. He hates a false balance and unjust weights.

Righteous man	-	Wicked man considers (vs 14)
Turns from righteousness	-	Turns from his wickedness and Transgression
Commits iniquity	-	Does the lawful and right
Dies in them	-	Save his soul alive
Vs 24, 26	-	Vs 21-22, 27-28
Dies for his iniquity	-	Surely live and not die.

Vs 29. God's ways are indeed equal. Israel's ways are not equal, vs 25. God's ways versus man's. Ways. Isa 55:8. God weighs the motives and actions of all in His balances. ob 31:6; Isa 26:7; Dan 5:27. Weighed in the balances and found wanting ....

Vs 30. God will judge every one in the House of Israel according to their ways. 7:3; 33:20. We judge God's ways and God will surely judge our ways.

8.   CALL TO REPENTANCE – vs 30b, 31-32.

Vs 30b. God calls to REPENTANCE and TURNING away from all

transgressions. 1 John 3:4. Sin is transgression of the Law.
Rom 6:23. The wages of sin is death.

1. Repent – change of mind towards God and sin. Root of repentance. Internal.
2. Turn others – the fruit of repentance. Thus inwards and outward, the evidences. Mt 3:2, 17; Rev 2:1-5; Heb 6:1-2. Positive and negative.
   So iniquity shall not be your ruin! Iniquity (lawlessness) is the violation of God's law individually or nationally in any or every generation.

Vs 31. 3. Cast away all transgressions and the cause of them. Fruits meets for repentance. Ephesians 4:22-23.
4. Make a new heart. Jeremiah 31:31-34; 32:39.
5. And a new spirit – 11:19; 36:26. Attitude of spirit.
   These things involve the NEW Covenant work also.
   Why will ye die? No need to. Death is the result of sin.
   Rom 6:23; Ezek 18:20.

Vs 32. God has pleasure in them that turn to Him. He has no pleasure in any one's death, or dying in sin. Vs 23. Call to turn themselves as well as others.

6. Live. 16:6; 18:22, 27; Lam 3:33; Ezek 33:11; 2 Pet.3:9.

NOTE: Four recurring words here.
1. Sin, iniquity or transgressions.
2. Die, dies, death.
3. Live, liveth.
4. Lawful, right, righteousness, just.
   Vs 4, 9, 13, 17, 18, 19, 20, 21, 22, 23, 24, 26, 27, 28, 31, 32. The same truth holds true for the NT Church believer as for the OT Church – Israel.

ILLUSTRATIONS:
Refer to line of Godly and Ungodly Kings, i.e. Hezekiah, Manasseh, Amon, Josiah, Jehoahaz, Jeconiah, Jehoiakim and Zedekiah. Note the

Godly fathers and ungodly sons and judgments accordingly. Refer to Jeremiah's ministry to the last 5 kings, several generations here.

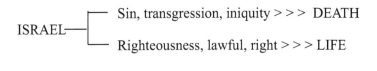

ISRAEL — ┌─ Sin, transgression, iniquity > > > DEATH
          └─ Righteousness, lawful, right > > > LIFE

EZEKIEL CHAPTER NINETEEN

1. **THE PARABLE OF THE LION'S WHELPS** – vs 1-9.

The key to this chapter is found in the "seed-prophecy" over a son named Judah in Gen 49:8-10. There is the symbol of (a) The Lion and (b) the Vine, and both are used in symbolic prophecy here. The Parable of the Lion's whelps concerns "the pride of Lions" of Judah's last several kings.

1. Concerning Jehoahaz or Shallum – vs 1-4.
    Vs 1. The lamentation for the PRINCES of Israel. 26:17; 27:2.
    Vs 2. What is thy mother? A Lioness, ie, the lion of the tribe of Judah. Kingly, and royalty. Picture the mother lion, laying down with her pride (whelps)
    Nourishing them amongst the young lions (lion = symbol of Egypt, Assyria, Babylon also). Here symbolic of the Princes Of the throne or royal house of David.
    Vs 3. One of the whelps brought up became a young lion learned to catch the prey and devoured men. Vs 6.
    i.e. King Jehoahaz (or Shallum) born of his mother, Hamutal. 2 Kgs 23:31-32.
    Vs 4. The nations heard of him, took him in their pit (to catch lions) and took him and bound him in chains in Egypt. 2 Kgs 23:33; 2 Chronicles 36:1-4; Jer 22:10-12.
    i.e. The nations, Egypt (King of South) and Babylon (King of North) against Judah. Pharoah-Neco took Jehoahaz and bound him and took him to Egypt, where he died, according to the word of the Lord by Jeremiah.

    Note: Jeremiah and Ezekiel flow together in the prophetic word; One in clear prophecy in Jerusalem and the other in parabolic Prophecy.

2. Concerning Jehoiachin – vs 5-9.
    Vs 5. When the lioness saw that her hope was lost, she took another of her whelps (or princes) and made him a young lion, or King over Judah.
    Note: Judah, Egypt and Babylon all symbolised by Lions. Perhaps the young lion here is Jehoiakim or Jehoiachin. Maybe both alluded to here.   2 Kgs 23:34-37; 24:1-7. Remembering that Jehoiakim reigned 11 years while Jehoiachin reigned only three months.
    Vs 6. Jehoiachin walked up and down amongst the other princes, Learning to catch and devour men, cf vs 3. Or Jehoiakim?

Vs 7. Palaces and cities and land desolated under his roaring.
Perhaps significant of the oppression of his own people to
Maintain his kingdom. Jeremiah 22:13-19, 20-30.

Vs 8. The nations (Babylonia and surrounding nations) set on him
From the provinces and spread the lions net over him and
Caught him in their pit. 2 Kgs 24:2; 24:8-16.

Vs 9. Jehoiachin (Jeconiah, or Coniah) was put in ward and taken
to Babylon and his voice was heard no more in the
mountains of Israel. 6:2.
Thus fulfilling the word of the Lord through Jeremiah.
2 Kgs 24:15; 2 Chronicles 36:9-10; Jer 22:20-30.

Thus under the symbol of ravaging and roaring lions, Jehoahaz'
captivity and death in Egypt and Jehoiachin's captivity and death in
Babylon are depicted.
Both of these parables and interpretation could be columnised.

2. **THE PARABLE OF THE VINE AND THE SCEPTRE** – vs 10-14

The second lamentation takes up another symbol of Israel – the
symbol of the Vine. It depicts the desolate condition and scene in
Judah of the last of her kings being dethroned and no apparent heir to
the throne of David after the death of Zedekiah, and the slaying of his
sons – Zedekiah being the last of the kings of Judah ever to reign in
Palestine over the House of Judah.

Vs 10. 1. The Mother vine – Psalm 80; Isa 5:1-7. Judah, His pleasant
plant. Vine in thy blood. Royalty, royal red blood. Cf 17:
6-10.

2. Planted by the waters, i.e., Mediterranean Sea, Jordan,
Galilee etc.

3. Fruitful and full of branches by reason of many waters
Deut. 8:7-9. Prosperity of Israel in the land. The 12 tribes,
as branches of the vine.

Vs 11. 4. Strong rods for sceptres to bear rule – i.e. the Princes of
Judah - of David's throne line.

5. Stature exalted among the thick branches – i.e. Judah
exalted
Amongst all the tribes of Israel, as the royal line. 31:3;
Dan 4:11; Psa 80:8-11.

Vs 12. 6. Plucked up in fury – i.e. Ps. 80:12. By the judgment of God
Using Babylon (Egypt also) to judge her.

7. Cast down to the ground – i.e. Dethroned.

8. East wind dried up her fruit – i.e. 17:10; Hos 13:15. East
wind, symbolic of Babylon from East coming by way of
the North also.

88

9. Her strong rods broken and withered – i.e. Princes to rule Broken and dethroned.
10. The fire consumed them – i.e. judgment and death. Psalm 80:16.

Vs 13. 11. Planted in the wilderness, in dry and thirsty land – i.e. Desolation of Judah's condition under Babylon.

Vs 14. 12. Fire gone out of a rod of her branches – i.e. cf. Jud. 9:15. Bow or burn spirit. The rod – no doubt Zedekiah, the last Judo-Davidic king. 2 Kgs 24:17-20.
13. Devoured her fruit – i.e. destroyed the last chance of the royal throne surviving his wickedness.
14. So that the vine has no strong rod to be a sceptre to rule – i.e. Destruction of Zedekiah's royal sons by the King of Babylon. No royal seed (apparently) left to rule and take the

Sceptre of Judah, cf. Gen 49:10. The sceptre not to depart From Judah until Shiloh comes.

2 Kgs 25:1-7; 2 Chronicles 36:11-21; Jer 52:1-11.

This is a lamentation and shall be for one. The problem of God's unbreakable covenant seems to be at stake. What of the Sceptre? What of David's throne? Psalm 89. What of the unbreakable Covenant concerning David? Psalm 89:38-52.

Thus under the two Parables, of the lion and the vine, the last several Kings of Judah are dealt with. Both are lamentations of Ezekiel. Remember Jeremiah's lamentation over godly king Josiah.

EZEKIEL CHAPTER TWENTY

The key words and thoughts in this chapter have to do with the third and fourth commandments, even as chapter 18 have to do with the third and fourth generations.
Ezekiel 18 with Ex 20:1-6 - The third and fourth generations. Commandment against idolatry.
Ezekiel 20 with Ex 20:7, 8-11 - The third and fourth generation. Commandments concerning the taking of the Lord's Name in vain and the violation of the Sabbath.
The key word 'rebel' is used in this chapter. Thus 22 times in the Book of Ezekiel.
Note the word 'sabbath' used 6 times in this chapter. Note also "My Name's sake". All are connected in the people of God.

1. **THE ELDERS COME TO ENQUIRE OF EZEKIEL** – vs 1-4.

   Vs 1.   The Elders of Israel come before Ezekiel to inquire of the Lord on the 7th year, the 5th month and the 10th day.
            Cf. 8:1. Sat before him waiting for the prophecy to flow.

   Vs 2.   The Word of the Lord came.

   Vs 3.   The Lord tells Ezekiel that He will not be enquired of by these Elders. What was in their heart, and what was their motivation? Curiosity or desire to obey? Cf 14:3 note.

   Vs 4.   The Lord told Ezekiel that he should remind them of their abominations. Should Ezekiel plead for them with these motivations?
            "If I regard iniquity in my heart, the Lord will not hear me." Psalm 66:18. Useless to enquire of God through the prophet if sin is not dealt with. 22:2; 16:2.

2. **ISRAEL'S PAST IDOLATRY IN EGYPT** – Exodus Book – vs 5-9.

   Vs 5.   1. Israel Chosen in Egypt by the Lord.
               The Lord reminds the Elders through the prophet of the day When He chose Israel as a nation, and lifted up His hand (swore) in covenant deliverance, making Himself known to them as the LORD in Egypt. Abrahamic Covenant.
               Ex 6:7-8; Deut 7:6; Ex 3:8; 4:31; Deut 4:34; Ex 20:2.

            2. Deliverance from Egypt.
               His desire was to bring them forth from the land of Egypt to

A land of milk and honey. Canaan land called "the GLORY Of all lands" – cf. Vs 15. Ex 3:8, 17; Deut 8:7-9; Jer. 32:22; Psa 48:2; Dan 8:9; Zech 7:14.

Vs 7.   3. Idolatry in Egypt
God called them to cast away their abominations and idols Of the Egyptians they had. 18:31; 2 Chron. 15:8; Lev 18:3; Deut 29:16; Josh 24:14.
Both Joshua and Ezekiel speak of Israel's idolatry in Egypt.

Vs 8.   However, Israel did not cast away their abominable idols of Egypt but rebelled and would not hearken to the Lord, even though He was delivering them out of the House of Bondage.
Note: Amos 5:25-26; Isa 43:23. Allusions to these idols in the Wilderness. The Lord even intended to pour out His fury on them in Egypt for this rebellion. 7:8.

Vs 9.   The Lord, however, preserved for HIS NAME'S SAKE, or else His Name would have become polluted among the heathen in whose sight it had been magnified by the plagues and the Exodus of Israel from Egypt.
God's Name was at stake – Note. Ex 3:13-16. Revelation of His Name.
Ex 5:23. Demonstration of the power of His Name. Ex 6:1-8; 9:16.
Ex 25. The Tabernacle was a dwelling place for His Name. A Place.
Num 6:24-27. Then His Name was placed upon the children of Israel by High Priestly blessing. 2 Chronicles 7:14.   My people which are called by My Name.

Note: His Name's sake. Ezek. 20:9, 14, 22, 39, 44; 36:21-22; Num 14:13.
The foundational purpose of the Exodus was that His Name would be known through out all the earth.

3.   **ISRAEL'S IDOLATRY IN THE WILDERNESS** – Numbers Book – vs 10-26.

Vs 10.   The First Generation – vs 10-17.
Vs 10. God, in spite of Israel's idolatry and rebellion in Egypt, Brought them out into the Wilderness. Ex 13:18.
Vs 11. The Lord gave His statutes and judgments to them. Obedience meant life. Mt Sinai, the giving of the Moral,

Civil and Ceremonial Laws.   Ex 20-24. Mosaic
Covenant. Deut 4:8; Nehemiah 9:13;   Psalm 147:19;
Lev 18:5; Gal 3:12.

Vs 12. The Lord also gave them the SABBATH to be A
SIGN of the Mosaic Covenant between them and
Himself. A sign that the Lord had set them apart for
Himself.

Note: Sabbaths in vs 12, 13, 16, 20, 21, 24. Sign of a
separated people.   Failure to keep the land Sabbaths
was the reason for the Captivity. 2 Chronicles 36:21.

Note the various "Sabbaths" Israel was commanded
to keep as a sign.

1. The Weekly Sabbath –
    Sign and seal of the Mosaic Covenant. Ex 20:8;
    Deut 5:12; Nehemiah 9:14; Ex 31:12-18.
    Note also "The Name" and "The Sabbath"
    connected in this chapter of Ezekiel.   They
    involved the 3rd and 4th Commandments of the
    Decalogue. Ex 20:7-11.

2. The Festival Sabbaths – Lev 23; Num 28.
    The Feast Days were also counted as extra
    Sabbaths in Israel and were extra Sabbaths in the
    weeks they fell in, beside the weekly Sabbath.

3. The Sabbath Years – Lev 25:1-7
    Every seventh year was also a Sabbath year for
    the people and the land and was a time of
    celebration. As noted, failure to keep such was
    the reason for the 70 years Captivity in Babylon,
    so the land could enjoy its Sabbaths.

4. The Jubilee Years – Lev 25:8-22
    Every 50th year was also a Sabbath year, called
    the Year of Jubilee. This was besides the Sabbath
    Years.

Thus the nation was sealed by God in the Covenant by the SABBATH
SIGN, the Sabbath days and years.   It was the significant and
distinctive sign of the sanctification of the nation unto the Lord.

Vs 13. Israel REBELLED against God in the Wilderness.
Israel REBELLED against God in Egypt also, vs 8.
Further rebellion, walked not in God's statutes and judgments.
They polluted God's Sabbaths, cf. Num 14:22, 29; Psalm
78:40; 95:8-10; Prov 1:25; Ex 16:27; Psalm 106:23. Both
morally and spiritually defiling God's rest, as also
ceremonially. God again threatened to pour out His fury on
them as in vs 8.

Vs 14. Again, God restrained His fury for HIS NAME'S SAKE, so it would not be polluted amongst the heathen who had heard of God's deliverance of Israel from Egypt, cf. Vs 9, 22.
They POLLUTED God's Sabbaths. God would not allow His Name, however, to be POLLUTED!

Vs 15. The Lord did punish this generation by not bringing them into the Promised Land. They knew God's "breach of promise" (Num 14:34, Marginal also – "Altering of My purpose").
Num 13-14 chapters, Psalm 95:11; 106:26.
They missed "the glory of all lands" - vs 6.

Vs 16. Israel despised God's judgments and statutes, polluting His Sabbaths and continued in heart-idolatry, cf. Vs 13, 24.
Num 15:39; Psalm 78:37; Amos 5:25-26; Acts 7:39-43.
Golden Calf idolatry. Ex 32-33-34.

Vs 17. However, the Lord did save the second generation from total extinction, allowing them to wander in the Wilderness for 40 years until the old generation passed on. Psalm 78:38.

The Second Generation – vs 18-26

Vs 18. The Lord exhorted the second generation not to walk in the idolatry of their fathers.

Vs 19. Called upon them to walk in His statutes and judgments. Deut 5:32; Deut 6-7-8-9-10-11-12 chapters.

Vs 20. Called on them to hallow His sign-Sabbaths. Jeremiah 17:22.

Vs 21. What was their response? The same as those in Egypt and the Wilderness. REBELLION!
Note vs 8, 13, 21 with 1 Sam 16:22-23.
Rebellion is as the sin of witchcraft and stubbornness as iniquity and idolatry. Num 25:1; Deut 9:23.
Again this generation failed to walk in God's statutes and judgments and keep His Sabbaths. The Lord again threatened to pour out His fury on them as in vs 8, 13 with 21.

Vs 22. But the Lord once more withdrew His hand of judgment for HIS NAME'S SAKE, to uphold His testimony before the heathen, cf vs 17, 9, 14.

Vs 23. Even though the Lord spared them in the Wilderness, He did swear (lift up His hand) that He would scatter and disperse them among the heathen countries.
Lev 26:33; Deut 28:64; Psalm 106:27; Jeremiah 15:4. This was because of His Covenant to the Fathers, Abraham, Isaac and Jacob.

Vs 24. Thus, because Israel failed to keep God's word and law and Sabbaths, though He would NOT DESTROY them, He would SCATTER THEM for their idolatry vs 13, 16; 6:9; Acts 7:42.

Vs 25. The Lord gave them certain statutes and judgments that were not good and that would bring about their death in these self-imposed judgments, i.e. Ps. 81:12; Rom 1:24; 2 Thess 2:11.
He gave them up to their own lusts which brought on themselves their own destruction!

Vs 26. Desolation also came near them for offering their sons as gifts to idols, causing them to pass through the fire. 2 Kgs 17:17; 21:6; 2 Chron. 28:3; 33:6; Jer. 32:35; Ezekiel 16:20; 6:7.

4.   **ISRAEL'S IDOLATRY IN CANAAN** – Judges Book – vs 27-32.

Vs 27. In spite of God's preserving grace and mercy and exhortations to that second generation, they BLASPHEMED God and trespassed against Him.
They were blasphemous. The way they did this was the LIFE they lived, thus the Name of God was blasphemed among the Gentiles by the ways the Israelites lived.
Rom 2:24; Num 6:24-27; 1 Tim 6:1; Tit 2:5, 8.

Vs 28. For when God brought Israel into the Promised Land, that He had sworn to them, they committed further idolatry.
High Hills and Thick Trees = sacrifices and offerings, drink offerings to idols.
Isa 57:5; Ezek 6:13; 16:19.

Vs 29. The Name of the High Place was BAMAH, meaning "High Place".

Vs 30. Thus the present generation was also guilty of spiritual whoredoms and abominations as the previous generations.

Vs 31. They polluted God by offering their sons in the fire to idols. Therefore should God be inquired of them by them? The answer is No! Cf. Vs 1-4, 26.

Vs 32. In the mind of Israel, they wanted to be as the heathen and serve gods of wood and stone and not the true and living God, cf   11:5. Thus Israel's history has been one of continual idolatry, and yet amidst God's amazing grace!

5. **PROMISES OF RESTORATION TO THE LAND** – Restoration Books, Haggai, Zechariah, Malachi, and Esther, Ezra and Nehemiah – vs 33-44.

In this section we have the promises of Restoration of Israel.   It should be remembered that they are in Babylonian Captivity for 70 years and Jeremiah also has spoken of their restoration to the land of Judah at the close.
Ezekiel's prophecy had its immediate fulfilment after the Babylonian Captivity in the restoration to the land and the revival under Ezra and Nehemiah.
No doubt there is a fuller and richer spiritual fulfilment reaching over into New Covenant times also.

Vs 33. The Lord says that He has, in spite of them, ruled over them with a mighty and stretched out arm and poured out His fury on them in the Captivities.   Jeremiah 21:5.

Vs 34. He promises again to bring them out of the countries they have been scattered in God's fury.

Vs 35. They will be brought into the Wilderness (cf. Hosea 2) and God will plead with them face to face.   Jeremiah 2:9, 35; Ezeiel 17:20.
I.e. Like God brought them out of Egypt into the Wilderness, so symbolically here also.

Vs 36. It will be similar to that pleasing of God in the Wilderness when God brought forth Israel out of Egypt (South).   Num 14:21-23, 28.

Vs 37. The Lord will cause all to "pass under the rod" and bring them into the bond (Margin, delivering) of the Covenant.
Cf. Lev 27:32; Jeremiah 33:13.   Like a shepherd has his sheep pass under the rod for numbering and discipline, so the Lord as the Shepherd of Israel will do likewise. The Rod and the Staff for His people. Psalm 23.

Vs 38. There will be a time of PURGING out of the Rebels and Transgressors, cf. Vs 8, 13, 21.

God will bring them forth out of the countries wherein they are, but they will not enter into the land of Israel, cf. 34:17; Mt 25:32; Jeremiah 44:14.

Vs 39. God tells the House of Israel to go and serve their idols, but tells them not to pollute HIS NAME in association with such corrupt practices.
Judges 10:14; Psa 81:12; Amos 4:4; Isa 1:13; Ezek 23:38.

Vs 40. In God's holy mountain, all those that God brings into the land, after purging out the rebels, will serve Him.
God will accept them and their offerings and first-fruits and oblations and holy things, cf. 17:23; Isa 2:2-3; Isa 56:7; 60:7; Zech 8:20; Mal 3:4; Rom 12:1.

Vs 41. God will accept them with their sweet savour offerings in this restoration to the law.
God will be sanctified by such living.

Vs 42. Israel shall know the Lord when He restores them to the land that He swore to their Fathers. Cf. Vs 38, 44; 36:23; 11:17; 34:13; 36:24.

Vs 43. Evidences of true cleansing will be seen.
1. Remembrance of their evil ways and doings.
2. Detesting their defilements by idols.
3. Loathing of themselves for these evils.
Vs 44. 4. Knowing the Lord in His Name.
5. That God did it for His Name's sake and did not deal with them according to their corrupt ways and doings.

6. **PARABLE OF THE FOREST** – vs 45-49.

Vs 45. The Word of the Lord.

Vs 46. Ezekiel to set his face towards the SOUTH and prophecy the Word of the Lord against the south field, i.e. Jerusalem and its holy places. 21:2.

Vs 47. The word of prophecy that the Lord would kindle a fire in the south field which would devour all the trees. A fire that would not be quenched from south to north. 21:4; with Jeremiah 21:14.
Note: 1. The GREEN tree. Luke 23:31.
2. The DRY tree, i.e. The righteous = green tree and the wicked = the dry tree. 21:3, 4.

Vs 48.   All flesh to see it and recognise that God kindled this unquenchable fire.

Vs 49.   Ezekiel feels that the Princes of the people will say that he is talking in Parables which cannot be understood.   Cf. Mt 13:9-17, 34-35. The Lord only resorted to Parables when the people refused to listen to His clear words.   Only the ones who had an ear to hear would perceive the interpretation of the parable. The rest would be blinded. So when God spoke in parables through the prophets, it was because they had rejected the clear word of the Lord.

Thus God had spoken to the people clearly by Jeremiah, now it is through parabolic prophecy in Ezekiel!

EZEKIEL CHAPTER TWENTY-ONE

1. **THE INTERPRETED CLEAR WORD OF THE FOREST** – vs 1-7.

    This section is so like the previous that it seems clearly to be the interpretation of the parabolic language, cf. 20:46 with 21:2, "Drop the word".

    Vs 1.   The Word of the Lord.

    Vs 2.   Make comparison with 20:46. Ezekiel to DROP the prophetic word against Jerusalem and its holy places in the land of Israel. Amos 7:16.

    Vs 3.   The word of the Lord against the LAND. The sword to be taken out of the sheath and to cut off both righteous and wicked. Cf Job 9:22.

    Vs 4.   The sword to cut off all from the south to the north.

    Vs 5.   All flesh to recognise that God has drawn out His sword. Isa 45:23; 55:11. Note also Jeremiah 25 with "The Cup" and "The SWORD". Compare 20:45-49 with 21:1-5.

	Ezekiel 25:45-49		Ezekiel 21:1-5
1.	The Word of the Lord	-	The Word of the Lord
2.	Son of Man	-	Son of Man
3.	Set face to the south	-	Set thy face to Jerusalem
4.	Drop words towards south, against the forest	-	Drop words towards holy places and the land of Israel
5.	Say to the forest	-	Say to the land of Israel
6.	Kindle a fire in thee	-	Draw my sword from its sheath
7.	Devour green and dry tree	-	Cut off righteous and wicked
8.	Flaming fire not quenched	-	Sword not return any more to sheath
9.	South to the north	-	South to the north
10.	All flesh know God kindled it	-	All flesh know Lord drew the sword.

    Vs 6.   Ezekiel to sigh with bitterness before their eyes. Spiritual travail. Isa 22:4.

Vs 7. Physical sighing interpreted to them – because of the travail of tidings. Melting hearts, feeble hands, fainting spirit, weak knees because of the terrible tidings to come. 7:17.

2. **THE SWORD** – vs 8-17

Vs 8. The Word of the Lord.

Vs 9. The sword to come. Prophetic word. Sword sharpened and furbished. Key word "sword" here in verses. Vs 3, 4, 5, 15, 28. Deut 32:41.

Vs 10. The sword sharpened and furbished to make a slaughter and glitter in so doing. Not a time for mirth. The sword becomes God's chastening rod (Margin) for His son, Israel (Ex 4:22-23).

Vs 11. The sword sharpened and furbished to be used and it is given by the Lord into the hands of the slayer, i.e. The King of Babylon. Vs 19 cf. Jeremiah 25 again.

Vs 12. Ezekiel called to demonstrate the sorrows of the people by reason of the sword. Crying, howling, smiting on his thigh. The people and princes of Israel shall do likewise in that time. Jeremiah 31:19.

Vs 13. It is God's trial and chastening rod on the nation, cf. Vs 10. Marginal. Job 9:23; 2 Cor 8:2.

Vs 14. Ezekiel commanded to prophesy and smite his hands together. Symbolic action of the clash of the sword on the grand and great men and the slain. Num 24:10; 1 Kgs 20:30.

Vs 15. The point of the sword is set at all gates. The 12 gates of the City the only way of escape. Hearts will faint. Great will be the ruin because of the bright sharpened sword. Vs 10, 28.

Vs 16. Facing the sword of the gates, the people will have to flee one way or another, wherever escape may seem possible. 14:17.

Vs 17. The Lord will do what He told Ezekiel to do and smite His hand together (vs 14) and then rest His fury. 22:13.

3. **THE INTERPRETATION OF THE SWORD** – vs 18-24.

Vs 18. The Word of the Lord.

Vs 19. The prophet to appoint TWO WAYS for the Lord's sword, in the hands of the slayer, King of Babylon, who is to come. Both ways out of the same land. The prophet to choose a place at the head of the way to the city.

Vs 20. The sword to come:
1. To Rabbath, of Ammonites – vs 28-32; Jeremiah 49:2; Amos 1:14.
2. To Judah and Jerusalem.

Vs 21. What Ezekiel did was symbolic of what the King of Babylon would do. King of Babylon stood before his teraphim, his images and liver to divine which way he should approach.

Vs 22. The divination went to the right hand for Jerusalem, for battering and slaughter in the sieges. Jeremiah 51:14; Ezekiel 4:2.

Vs 23. Refer to 17:13. Amp. OT. It will seem like a lying divination to them who have sworn to Nebuchadnezzar. Will he now fight against their homeland? But he will remind them of their guilt and iniquity in violating those oaths that they may be caught.
2 Chronicles 36:10; 13; Ezek 17:15, 18.

Vs 24. As Israel caused their iniquities and transgressions and sins to be remembered, so God remembers them for judgment. He will punish them by allowing them to be taken by Babylon's hand.

4. **PROPHECY AGAINST PRINCE ZEDEKIAH** – vs 25-27.

Vs 25.	1.	The profane wicked Prince of Israel	-	Prince Zedekiah – Jer. 52:2.
	2.	Whose day is come, iniquity to end	-	Wicked Prince, day of his judgment, to death, vs 29
Vs 26.	3.	Remove the diadem	-	The Priestly mitre.
	4.	Take off the crown	-	The Kingly crown.
	5.	This shall not be the same	-	Things no longer to continue as they have.

(ie Aaronic, Levi Priesthood & Kingly rule not to continue here. Thus Levi and Judah here under Babylonian Judgments.)

	6.	Exalt him that is low	-	i.e. Zarah line. Cf Lk 1:52
	7.	Abase him that is high.	-	i.e. Pharez line. Gen 38.
Vs 27.	8.	I will overturn, over	-	Perverted, perverted, perver-

Turn, overturn it	- ted will I make it (Margin).
Thus three overturns.	
9. And it shall no more. be (overturned).	- Remain same
10. Until He come	- Until Jesus comes.
11. Whose right (birth right) it is	- Gen 49:10
12. And I will give it to him.	- Luke 1:32

Undoubtedly natural and national fulfilment in the throne of David being transferred and overturned from the Judo-Pharez-Davidic line to the Judo-Zarah-line.

The ultimate fulfilment is in the Lord Jesus Christ Himself, the overturn from the natural to the spiritual. It is He, as Shiloh – who is to come – and it is His birthright, and God will give to Him the PRIESTLY DIADEM and the KINGLY CROWN, because He is the King-Priest after the order of Melchizedek. Lk 1:30-33; Isa 9:6-9; Heb 7; Psalm 110; Gen 49:10.

5. **THE SWORD AGAINST THE AMMONITES** – vs 28-32
Vs 28. Prophecy against the Ammonites (cf. 25:2, 3) and their reproach. The sword is drawn and furbished for the slaughter.

Vs 29. Cf. 12:24; Job 18:20; Psalm 37:13. Refer to Amp. OT. False divinations, divine lies, slain to be there, day of reckoning upon Amon.

Vs 30. The sword not to return to its sheath, cf. Vs 5. It will judge the Ammonites in the place of its nativity. Jeremiah 47:6, 7; Gen 15:14; Ezekiel 16:3.

Vs 31. Indignation, and fire of God's wrath to be upon them and they, as Israel, will be delivered into the hands of brutish men who will destroy them, cf. 7:8; 22:20.

Vs 32. The Ammonites to be fuel for the fire, and their blood to be poured out. Not to be remembered. The Lord has spoken it, cf. Isa 55:10-11.

Summary:
The chapter reveals the sword of the Lord unsheathed and being given into the hands of the King of Babylon. He will be used to judge Jerusalem and Judah and Rabbath and the Ammonites, cf Jeremiah 25:15-33. Fulfilment of "The Cup" and "The Sword" amongst all nations.

EZEKIEL CHAPTER TWENTY-TWO

1. **JERUSALEM – THE BLOODY CITY** – vs 1-12

Vs 1.   The Word of the Lord.

Vs 2.   Ezekiel is not to judge (plead for, Margin) the bloody city but show her her abominations. 20:2; Nah 3:1.

Vs 3.   A city that sheds blood and is idolatrous. Murder and idolatry here.

Vs 4.   Blood shed brings guilt. Idolatry brings defilement. Both bring times of judgment on the city guilty of such. So God used the heathen to do so to Jerusalem. 2 Kgs 21:16; Deut 28:37; Dan 9:16.

Vs 5.   Nations near and far will mock Jerusalem because of her pollutions and vexations.

Vs 6.   The Princes guilty of blood shed, cf Isa 1:23.
        Note the key word here is "blood".

Vs 7.   Note the catalogue of following sins:
1. Setting light by father and mother, cf. Deut 27:16; Ex 20:12; 21:17; Lev 19:3; Deut 21:18. Not honouring them as the 5th Commandment. Moral Law broken.
2. Oppression of the stranger by deceit. Civil Law violated. Ex 22:21.
3. Vexed the fatherless and the widow.

Vs 8. 4. Despising God's holy things.
5. Profaning God's Sabbaths. Lev 19:3.

Vs 9. 6. Slander and false witness to see people killed. Men of Slander, cf. Ex 20:16; 23:1; Deut 5:20.
7. Eating upon the mountains, cf. 18:6, 11. Idolatrous feasts.
8. Committing lewdness.

Vs 10. 9. Discovering father's nakedness. Lev 18:7, 8. Sin of Ham. Gen 9.
10. Defiling women in their uncleanness. Lev 18:19.

Vs 11. 11. Adultery with another's wife. Lev 18:20.
12. Fornication with daughter-in-law. Lev 18:15. Incest. Sin of Lot. Gen 19.
13. Defilement with one's sister, his father's daughter. Lev 18:9
     Note - #8-13 all to do with Morals.

Vs 12.   14. Taking bribes to shed innocent blood. Ex 23:8; Deut 16:19.
         15. Usury and increase. Extortion. Ex 22:25.
         16. Forgetting God's laws. Jeremiah 3:21. Root of the whole matter.

Thus Moral and Civil commandments of God broken here. 1 John 3:4. Penalty to be executed on broken law, and the law works wrath. Rom 4:15.
Note also the use of the word "blood" in vs 2, 3, 4, 6, 9, 12 and clauses associated with such.
Num 35:30-34.   BLOOD defiles the land and the land cannot be cleansed but by the blood of him that shed it.   Innocent blood to be avenged. God is THE AVENGER of Blood. Thus He uses Babylon to avenge the blood of the innocents.
Because of the laws of blood in the land, God would allow their blood to be shed in the land because they shed innocent blood. The curse of innocent blood comes on them in judgment.
The blood CRIES OUT TO GOD FOR VENGEANCE. Gen 9:6; Mt 27:25; Heb 12:22-24; Gen 4.

2.   **SCATTERING AND DISPERSION OF ISRAEL (JUDAH)** – vs 13-16.

Vs 13.   God smites His hand at the dishonest gain and the blood that has been shed there. Symbolised by Ezekiel in 21:17 also.

Vs 14.   Will their heart or hands be able to endure the dealings of God when He does what He has spoken? 21:7; 17:24.

Vs 15.   Israel and Judah to be SCATTERED and DISPERSED among the heathen in order to cleanse away their idolatry and filthiness, cf. Deut 4:27; Ezekiel 23:27; Lev 26:33; Nehemiah 1:8.
         Note: God used the captivity of Judah in Babylon to cleanse them of idol worship. The Jews have never been worshippers of idols since then.

Vs 16.   Their inheritance would be profaned by the heathen in their sight, so they would know the Lord was Lord. Psalm 9:16.

3.   **THE FIERY FURNACE OF JERUSALEM** – vs 17-22

Vs 17. The Word of the Lord.

Vs 18. The House of Israel becomes as dross in God's sight. Brass/ tin/iron/lead and as the dross of silver – fit for removal. Psalm 119:119; Isa 1:22; Jeremiah 6:28.

Vs 19. All to be gathered into Jerusalem.

Vs 20. As silver, brass, iron and lead and tin are gathered into a furnace to set the fire for purging on them, so would the various classes of people be gathered to be melted, cf. Dan 2. Metals in the Image represented Kingdoms of this world, in depreciating value and weight.
So the 5 metals listed here symbol the depreciating weight and value of these classifications in Israel.

Vs 21. To be gathered, blown upon by God's breath and melted in the fire of God's wrath.

Vs 22. As silver is melted, so they would be by God's fury and wrath. The dross comes to the surface in the fires of purification, cf. 20:8, 33.

4. **INDIGNATION OF PROPHETS, PRIESTS, PRINCES AND PEOPLE** – vs 23-31.

Vs 23. The Word of the Lord.

Vs 24. The land not cleansed but defiled by their sins. The land not rained on in "the day of indignation" – vs 31.
Note – The 4 groupings or classes referred to and their particular sins. Mainly the Leadership of the nation. Like leadership, like people.

Vs 25. 1. The Prophets
A conspiracy amongst the prophets like roaring lions
Ravening the prey. Hos 6:9; 1 Pet 5:8. They have:
a. Devoured souls – Mt 23:14.
b. Taken treasure and precious things – Mic 3:11.
c. Made many widows in the midst.
Vs 28   d. Daubed with untempered mortar – 13:10.
e. Seen vanity and divining lies to the people in the Name of the Lord when He has not spoken to them – 13:6, 7.

Vs 26. 2. The Priests
They have:
a. Violated the laws of God. Offered violence. Margin Ma 12:8.

      b.   Profaned God's holy things. 1 Sam 2:29.

      c.   Put no difference between the holy and the profane. Lev 10:10.

      d.   Not showed difference between the clean and unclean.

      e.   God's Sabbaths been hid from their eyes.

      f.   God is profaned (spoken lightly of) among them.

Vs 27. 3. <u>The Princes</u>

Like ravening wolves in the midst of the prey. Ezek.22:6; Mt 7:15; Acts 20:29. They try to:

      a.   Shed blood.

      b.   Destroy souls.

      c.   Get dishonest gain.

Vs 29. 4. <u>The People</u>

The congregation of the Lord, like their leaders have:

      a.   Used deceit and oppression.

      b.   Exercised robbery.

      c.   Vexed the poor and the needy.

      d.   Oppressed the stranger wrongfully. Ex 23:9; Lev 19:33.

Vs 30. God sought for a man amongst these classes to make up the breach in the hedge or stand in the gap to make intercession for the people and the land but He found none, cf. Jeremiah 5:1; Ezekiel 13:5; Psalm 106:23; Isa 59:16.

Vs 31. Because of no intercessors to stand in the gap, God poured out His wrath and indignation on them and recompensed their own way on their heads, cf. Vs 22; 9:10.

    <u>Thus</u>:

      1.   The Prophets – inspirational, spiritual ministry, representing God to man.

      2.   The Priests – ecclesiastical, devotional and ceremonial and mediatorial ministry, representing man to God.

      3.   The Princes – legal, civil, governmental ministry, representing God's government to man. All were corrupted and corrupted the people also.

      4.   The People – followed their leadership. Reveals the spiritual, moral and political and national decay of God's people.

EZEKIEL CHAPTER TWENTY-THREE

1.   **THE PARABLE OF THE TWO WOMEN** – vs 1-21.

Vs 1.   The Word of the Lord.

Vs 2.   The two women, daughters of one mother, cf. Jeremiah 3:7-8. Symbolic of TWO Houses of the ONE nation.

Vs 3.   Both women committed whoredoms and immorality play in Egypt, cf. Lev 17:7; Josh 24:17; Ezekiel 16:22.
Note: Ezekiel 23 follows the same basic principles as in Ezekiel 16.

Vs 4.   The names of the two women were:
1.   Aholah – Elder, or Samaria, House of Israel – Capital city. Meaning "His Tent, or Tabernacle".
2.   Aholibah – Sister, or Jerusalem. House of Judah – Capitol city. Meaning "My Tabernacle is in her." 1 Kgs 8:29.
Both were the Lord's by marriage covenant. 16:8, 20.
Both had sons and daughters. Children of the House of Israel and House of Judah as in the various tribes.

Vs 5.   Aholoh (Samaria) played the harlot though joined to the Lord. Doted upon her lovers, which were the Assyrians. Hos 8:9.

Vs 6.   The Assyrians clothed with blue; their captains, rulers on horses. God ornaments on Assyrian garments. Rank, power, authority – symbol of wealth, transport also.

Vs 7.   Israel committed spiritual whoredoms with the Assyrians and doted on them and their idols. Jas 4:4; As down in Egypt – vs 3. 2 Kgs 17:3; 16:10.

Vs 8.   Israel did not leave her whoredoms in Egypt either, cf. Vs 3.

Vs 9.   God delivered Israel into ASSYRIAN captivity, into the hands of her lovers. 2 Kgs 17. BC 721.

Vs 10.   Assyrians stripped Israel, slaying her sons and daughters and executing judgment on her.

Vs 11.   Aholibah (Jerusalem) saw this, yet she became worse in her whoredoms than Aholah,   cf. Jeremiah 3:8-11.

Vs 12. Judah dotes on the Assyrians also, their captains, rulers and horsemen, cf. Vs 6, 23.
Note the word "doted" in vs 7, 9, 12, 16, 20. 2 Kgs 16:7.
Israel as pastoral nation attacked by the great Metropolis of Nineveh and other cities of great nations. Jerusalem had the Temple as her binding power.

Vs 13. Thus both Judah and Samaria defiled, both going the same way and playing the harlot.

Vs 14. Judah increased her whoredoms, following the images of the BABYLONIANS. Archeologists show the beauty of such and the colours and art work.
God's law was to destroy their pictures and images. Pornography and perversion.
Num 32:52; Isa 23:16.

Vs 15. The Babylonian images girded and attired Chaldea was the land of their nativity, for God had called Abraham their father out of the land or Ur of the Chaldees.
Acts 7:1-5; Gen 11:31; 12:1, 4, 5.

Vs 16. Judah doted on the Babylonians and their images and sent messengers to Babylon. 2 Kgs 24:1.

Vs 17. The children of Babel came and committed whoredoms with Judah and defiled her. Vs 22, 28.

Vs 18. God's mind was ALIENATED from Judah as her mind had been alienated from Him. Jeremiah 6:8.

Vs 19. Judah repeated her whoredoms like as she had played the harlot in Egypt, cf. Vs 3. Josh 24:14; Lev 17:7.

Vs 20. Judah doted. Vs 12 notes.
Flesh as donkeys, issue as horses, cf. Psalm 32:8-9.

Vs 21. Judah's idolatrous whoredoms with the Babylonians were just a reminder to them of their lewdness in Egypt.

2. **THE INTERPRETATIVE WORD TO AHOLAH (JUDAH) – vs 22-35**

Vs 22. God will raise up Judah's lovers against her from every side, vs 28; 16:37.

Vs 23. The Babylonians and Assyrians (of the North) and their armies and horsemen against her, cf. Vs 12. Jeremiah 50:21.

Vs 24. The whole army and cavalry to come against Jerusalem and judge the city.

Vs 25. God's jealousy and fury to be against Judah. Babylon to take away her sons and daughters and devour by fire.

Vs 26. Judah to be stripped of everything. 16:39.

Vs 27. God will cause the lewdness and whoredoms brought from Egypt to cease. As noted, idolatry was cleansed from Judah after or by reason of the Babylonian captivity. Vs.3, 19; 16:41; 22:15.

Vs 28. God will deliver Judah into the hands of the Babylonians who she loved and now hates and is alienated from her in mind. Vs 17; 16:37.

Vs 29. To be dealt with hatefully and shamefully. Vs 26. 16:39. Most humiliating for any woman to be stripped naked. Cf. Lev 18. Laws concerning nakedness. Thus symbolic of being stripped of all resources, disarmed, exposed to danger, open to national rape.

Vs 30. The CAUSE. God is doing this because of Judah's heathenish whoredoms and idolatrous pollutions.

Vs 31. Judah walked in the same way as Israel, therefore her cup of judgment is the same. Jeremiah 25:15.

Vs 32. Judah to drink of Israel's cup deep and large. To be laughed and scorned at because of it. 22:4.

Vs 33. It is the cup of astonishment, drunkenness, sorrow and desolation. The same cup that sister Samaria drunk. Note – the CUP, vs 31, 32, 33 with Jeremiah 25:15-33. All nations to drink the cup of judgment, because their cup of iniquity was full. Gen 15:16; Mt 23:32; 1 Thess 2:16.

Vs 34. Judah will drink this cup even to sucking the dregs and do despite to herself. The dregs are the bitterest part. Psalm 75:8; Isa 51:17.

Vs 35.   Judah to bear the punishment of her whoredoms because she forgot her true Husband, Jehovah.   Jeremiah 2:32;   3:21; 13:25; Ezekiel 22:12; 1 Kgs 14:9; Nehemiah 9:26.

3.   **THE PROPHETIC WORD TO AHOLIBAH AND AHOLAH** – vs 36-44.

Vs 36.   Ezekiel to declare to both Houses their abominations.   Isa 58:1. As a true prophet of God.

Vs 37.   Note the list of abominations here, cf. Vs 45; 16:38, 20, 21, 36, 45; 20:26, 31.
1.   Committed adultery.
2.   Blood in their hands.
3.   Spiritual harlotry and adultery.
4.   Sons caused to pass through the fire.

Vs 38.   5.   Defiled God's sanctuary.
6.   Profaned God's sabbath. 22:8.

Vs 39.   7.   Offering their children, they then profaned God's House. 2 Kgs 21:4.

Vs 40.   8.   Sent for foreigners to come to her, decked herself as Attractive woman. Isa 57:9; Ruth 3:3; 2 Kgs 9:30; Jer 4:30.

Vs 41.   9.   Prepared a bed and table with incense and oil perfumes for Adultery.
Esther 1:6; Isa 57:7; Amos 2:8; 6:4; Prov 7:17; Ezek 16:18, 19: Hos 2:8.

Vs 42.   The multitude of drunkards come with bracelets on their hands and crowns on their heads. Men of the common sort, who go to those who play the harlot.

Vs 43.   God watched to see if whoredoms would be committed.

Vs 44.   10.   Spiritual adultery took place with the two women who Belonged to Jehovah. Thus both Samaria and Jerusalem Played as lewd and harlot women.

4.   **THE HARLOTS TO BE JUDGED** – vs 45-49.

Vs 45.   Righteous men shall judge these women as the Law said concerning adultery and shedding of blood. Vs 37. 16:38.

Vs 46.   God will bring a company of them to spoil and remove them by way of captivity.

Vs 47. This company will stone these harlots with stones and destroy them and their offspring with swords and burn their harlot houses. The LAW commanded that an adulterous wife be stoned. 16:40; 2 Chronicles 36:17, 19; Ezekiel 24:21; Lev 20:10; 18:20, Deut 22:22.

Vs 48. God will use this to cleanse the lewdness out of the land and as a lesson for other people to learn. 22:15; Deut 13:11; 2 Pet 2:6.

Vs 49. Sin and lewdness brings its punishment upon the heads of those who persist in it. Idolatry and adultery are spiritual whoredoms. Jas 4:4; Ezekiel 20:38, 42, 44; 25:5.

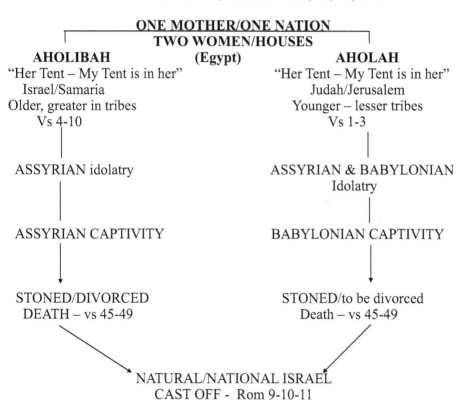

ONE MOTHER/ONE NATION
TWO WOMEN/HOUSES

AHOLIBAH	(Egypt)	AHOLAH
"Her Tent – My Tent is in her"		"Her Tent – My Tent is in her"
Israel/Samaria		Judah/Jerusalem
Older, greater in tribes		Younger – lesser tribes
Vs 4-10		Vs 1-3
ASSYRIAN idolatry		ASSYRIAN & BABYLONIAN Idolatry
ASSYRIAN CAPTIVITY		BABYLONIAN CAPTIVITY
STONED/DIVORCED DEATH – vs 45-49		STONED/to be divorced Death – vs 45-49

NATURAL/NATIONAL ISRAEL
CAST OFF - Rom 9-10-11

EZEKIEL CHAPTER TWENTY-FOUR

1. **THE PARABLE OF THE SEETHING POT** – vs 1-5.

Vs 1.   The Word of the Lord, in the 9th year, and 10th day of the 10th month.

Vs 2.   This was the very same day that Nebuchadnezzar set himself against Jerusalem.
Cf. 2 Kgs 25:1; Jer 39:1; 52:4 and Ezek 24:1.
Place in three columns. Note how remarkable this is. While Jeremiah is prophesying up in Jerusalem and the King of Babylon is besieging the city, God is speaking to Ezekiel in Babylon the exact same day.

Vs 3.   Parable of the pot with the water poured into it. To be spoken to the rebellious House of Judah. 17:12; Jeremiah 1:13; Ezekiel 11:3.

Vs 4.   The pieces, thigh, shoulder, and choice bones to be put into the pot.

Vs 5.   The bones to be burnt beneath and the bones in the pot to seethe and boil well.

2. **THE PARABLE OF THE POT INTERPRETED** – vs 6-14.

Vs 6.   The bloody city of Jerusalem is the pot full of scum. It has gone to pieces.
2 Sam 8:2; Joel 13:3; Obadiah 11; Nah 3:10.

Vs 7.   The blood is in its midst, set on the rock, poured out on the ground and covered with dust. Lev 17:13; Deut 12:16. So blood of animals to be poured out and covered with dust.

Vs 8.   God has set the blood of Jerusalem on the rock, not to be covered. Time of vengeance. Mt 7:2.

Vs 9.   Jerusalem, a bloody city. Vs 6. Hab 2:12. Pile for the fire to be great.

Vs 10. Wood to be heaped on the fire and the flesh and bones to cook, being spiced, i.e. The people. Wood heaped up = armies of Babylon piled up.

Vs 11. Jerusalem a pot to be set on the coals of fire, and all the filthiness and scum to be consumed. 22:15.

Vs 12. The lies and scum of Jerusalem to be in the fire. Note the word "scum" in vs 6, 6, 11, 12, 12. Fire brings the scum to the surface.

Vs 13. God endeavoured to purge this filthiness but it was not purged and will not be until God's fury rests on it. 8:18.

Vs 14. God has spoken it and it will come to pass.
1. I will do it.
2. I will not go back.
3. I will not spare.
4. I will not repent, or change My mind.
The ways and doings of Jerusalem to be judged. 5:11; 1 Sam 15:29.

3.   **EZEKIEL'S WIFE DIES** – vs 15-18.

Vs 15. The Word of the Lord.

Vs 16. God tells Ezekiel that He will take away his wife with a stroke ("the desire of thine eyes"), yet he is not to mourn or weep for her with tears.

Vs 17. He is not to cry or make mourning for his dead, nor is he to dis-attire himself of his clothes, cover his lips or eat the bread of mourning. Vs 22.
Cf. Jer 16:5; Lev 10:6; 21:10; 2 Sam 15:30; Mic 3:7; Lev 13:45.

Vs 18. He spoke the word of the Lord to the people in the MORNING and in the EVENING his wife died. Ezekiel totally obeyed the Lord's instructions concerning his wife.
This was hard for him. Human grief, sorrow and emotions suppressed in obedience to the word of the Lord.
Symbolic of that which God Himself went through over His wife, Israel.

4.   **EZEKIEL'S WIFE'S DEATH INTERPRETED** – vs 19-27.

Vs 19. The people ask the prophet to interpret these things to them, cf. 12:9; 37:18.

Vs 20. The prophet's answer of the word of the Lord.

Surely the people would realise the sorrow that the prophet went through, and what God went through over them?

Vs 21. God will do to His Sanctuary, which is the excellency of strength, and "the desire of their eyes" which they pity, that which was done to Ezekiel's wife. Their sons and daughters will die by the sword. Jeremiah 7:14; Ezekiel 7:20; 23:47.

Vs 22. The people will do as Ezekiel did. They will not cover their lips nor eat the bread of mourning. Vs 17; Jeremiah 16:6, 7.

Vs 23. They will not dis-attire or put on sackcloth and ashes on their heads as in mourning. They will pine away in their iniquities and mourn towards one another, not over the Sanctuary. Job 27:15; Psa 78:64; Lev 26:39.

Vs 24. Ezekiel is THE SIGN. Vs 27; Isa 20:3. They will do what he has done and when it happens they will recognise that God did it. 4:3; 12:6, 11; Jeremiah 17:15; John 13:19; 14:29; Ezekiel 6:7; 25:5.

Vs 25-26.
In that day that all these events happened to the Sanctuary and the people, those that escape will come to the prophet and tell him exactly what he said is what happened. 33:21.

Vs 27. In that day the prophet will no longer be dumb but his mouth will be opened to speak for God has made him their sign of God's word. 3:26.

Thus:

Ezekiel's Wife		The Temple & People
1. Delight of thine eyes, his wife	-	Delight of their eyes, the Temple
2. Taken away in a stroke.	-	Taken away suddenly
3. Not to mourn, weep nor cover lips	-	People will not mourn or weep
4. Not to eat bread of mourning	-	Not eat bread, as terrible famine/seige

EZEKIEL CHAPTER TWENTY-FIVE

IN THIS SECTION, Chapters 25, 26, 27, 28, 29, 30, 31, 32 and 35 we deal more especially with the surrounding Gentile nations. It is the "Gentile Section" of Ezekiel, even as in the other Major and Minor Prophets there is a Gentile section. There are SEVEN nations dealt with specifically.

1. **PROPHECY CONCERNING THE AMMONITES** – vs 1-7
    Vs 1.   The Word of the Lord.

    Vs 2.   Prophecy against the Ammonites. 35:2; Jeremiah 49:1; Ezekiel 21:28; Zeph 2:9. Younger daughter of Lot's incest and the son born, named Ammon. Gen 19:30-38.

    Vs 3.   The Ammonites, the flesh-seed, mocked in derision:
    1. The Sanctuary profaned
    2. The Land desolated
    3. The People of Judah taken captive, 26:2; Prov 17:5.

    Vs 4.   Because of this God will deliver them to the children of the East and they will possess the possessions of Ammon, eating and drinking their fruit and milk. Law of Divine retribution. As you do to others, SO shall it be done to you.

    Vs 5.   Rabbah, their city, shall be a stable place for camels and Ammon a place for flocks. 21:20; 24:24; Isa 17:2.

    Vs 6.   Because of clapping hands/stamping feet/rejoicing in heart of despite over the fall and judgment of Israel. Ezekiel 36:5; Job 27:23; Lam 2:15; Zeph 2:15.

    Vs 7.   God will stretch out His hand and judge Ammon of the heathen and cut them off and make them perish out of the countries. The lesson to be learned from this prophecy is that which concerns the Law of Divine retribution. God will do to them what was done to Israel, because of their wicked attitude to God's judgment on His own people. Note: Psalm 18:25-27; Lev 26:23-28; Prov 3:34; 1 Kgs 8:32; Obadiah 15.

2. **PROPHECY CONCERNING THE MOABITES** – vs 8-11
    Vs 8.   The word concerning Moab and Mt Seir, their capital city and mount. Read also Isa15-16; Jer. 48:1; Amos 2:1; Ezek. 35:2,5.

    Vs 9.   God will open the shoulder of Moab and his frontier cities, three named here.

Vs 10. The children of the East (vs 4) will come on them as they do on the Ammonites (21:32). Both Moab and Ammon were the sons of Lot by his incest with his daughters (Gen 19:30-38). The flesh-seed!

Vs 11. God's judgments to be executed on Moab and they shall recognise that God is the Lord over the nations.

3. **PROPHECY CONCERNING THE EDOMITES** – vs 12-14
Vs 12. Edom also took advantage of the captivity of Judah and revenged himself of Judah. 2Chron.28:17; Ps.137:7; Jer.49:7-8; Amos 1:11; Obad.10. Edom comes of Esau, the birthright-despiser and seller. Gen 25 and 27. That conflict always between Jacob and Esau since birth, and on into national history. Note the prophecies concerning Esau, the firstborn after the flesh. Refer to notes on Obadiah for fuller exposition of this judgment on Esau/Edom or the flesh-seed. That which was in Esau against Jacob manifested itself in the succeeding generations of Edom. Law of Divine retribution.

Vs 13. God will also stretch out His hand on Edom, cutting off man and beast, making all desolate in their cities.

Vs 14. God's vengeance will be laid on Edom and he will use the house of Israel to fulfil His anger. Isa 11:14.

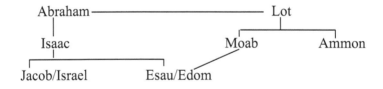

4. **PROPHECY CONCERNING THE PHILISTINES** – vs 15-17
Vs 15. Word against the Philistines, ancient enemies of Israel from the time of Samson onwards. Revenge and despiteful heart of hatred in the nation here. The old, perpetual hatred. Jer.25:20; Amos 1-6; 2Chron.28:18. Hate is murder. Hatred is not necessarily the absence of violence, but can reject a person.

Vs 16. God will stretch out His hand on them also and cut off and destroy them. Zeph 2:4; 1 Sam 30:14; Jeremiah 47:4.

Vs 17. God's vengeance will be upon them as on others who are against Israel. Note the word "vengeance" in vs 14, 14, 15, 17, 17, cf. 5:15; Psalm 9:16; Isa 63:1-4. Vengeance is in the heart of God at certain times. Heb 10:30; Deut 32:36.

EZEKIEL CHAPTER TWENTY-SIX

It should be noted here that Chapters 26, 27, 28 concern Tyrus, a great seaport and mercantile city, Phoenician city, and also island place too. The island city was about ¾ mile off the mainland surrounded by about a 150 foot wall. No army could get across the walk-way to the island city. Refer to the History of its eventual Fall. Hiram, King of Tyre, was a great friend of King David and King Solomon in the early times of Israel's glory.

1. **PROPHECY CONCERNING TYRUS** – vs 1-6.

   Vs 1. The Word of the Lord in the 11th year, 1st day of the month.

   Vs 2. Tyrus boasting herself over the Fall of Jerusalem, that everything would now turn to her. 25:3; Isa 23; Jeremiah 25:22; Amos 1:9; Zech 9:2.

   Vs 3. God is against her and will cause many nations to come up against her, as the sea causes waves to overcome and come up on the shore. Note the symbol of the sea and waves as nations. Rev 17:15; Isa 17:12-13; 57:20-21.

   Vs 4. Walls and towers to be broken down, and dust (dirt) to be scraped off and the place to be bare as the top of the rocks. Note vs 14. Literally fulfilled in her destruction and subsequent years.

   Vs 5. The city to be for a place to spread nets in the midst of the sea and to be a spoil to the nations. 27:32.

   Vs 6. Daughters of Tyrus in the field to be shown by the sword and they will know that God did it. 25:5.

   Note: History has shown how literally this was fulfilled, as the old city was destroyed and parts of it are still seen in the midst of the sea, and men still spread their nets there. The city has never been rebuilt as vs 14 says and the dirt was taken away and left the old city as bare as a rock.

2. **THE KING OF BABYLON TO DESTROY TYRUS** – vs 7-14

   Vs 7. God's instrument of judgment on Tyrus will be the King of Babylon. Nebuchadnezzar, a king of kings, from the north will come with his whole army and cavalry. Ezra 7:12; Dan 2:37.

119

Vs 8.   He will slay their sons and daughters. He will make a fort, pour out engine shot and use the buckler against Tyrus.

Vs 10. So great will be his cavalry and armies and chariots that the city walls would shake at such. He shall enter in the GATES like men enter into a breach in the wall of a city when broken up. The Gates were an important part of the city.

Vs 11. People will be slain with the sword and the strong garrison smashed to the ground.

Vs 12. Their riches and merchandise will be spoiled and their luxury houses and business houses to be smashed and left in the midst of water.

Vs 13. Their songs to cease and harps not to be heard. Isa 14:11; 24:8; Jeremiah 7:34; 25:10; Isa 23:16; Ezekiel 28:13; Rev 18:22.

Vs 14. Tyrus to be bare as the top of a rock, a place for nets, and never to be built again. God has spoken it. Vs 4, 5.
Note – Other cities have been rebuilt, but not Tyrus.

3.   **THE LAMENTATION OF THE ISLES OVER THE FALL OF TYRUS** – vs 15-21.

Vs 15. The isles will shake when they hear of the Fall of Tyrus. Vs 18. Jeremiah 49:21: Ezekiel 27:18.

Vs 16. The Princes of the sea (merchants) will lay off their royal robes and vacate their thrones and put on mourning robes as they sit in the dust, trembling and astonished.   27:32; Rev 18:9; Isa 23:4.

Vs 18. The isles will tremble at the Fall of Tyrus. Vs 15.

Vs 19. God will make Tyrus a desolate city, uninhabited , and cause the waters of the sea to cover it.

Vs 20. Tyrus to be brought down to desolation, the lower parts of the earth, down to the pit. 32:18,23. God's glory seen in the land of the living.

Vs 21. Tyrus to be no more, though sought for, not to be found. As buried in the sea, not excavated.

EZEKIEL CHAPTER TWENTY-SEVEN

NOTE: Much of the language of the things of Commerce are taken up and applied to the End-time Babylon in Revelation 18. Here in Ezekiel is listed the great merchants who brought there the wares to Tyrus for business. The Fall of the great city Tyrus, becomes prophetical of the Fall of Babylon in the Last Day, as well as the other great cities of Commerce and Trade. The business world will be judged in due time. Jude 7. Examples.

1. **THE MERCHANTS OF THE ISLES, THE LANDS AND THEIR WARES** – vs 1-25.

   Vs 1.   The Word of the Lord.

   Vs 2.   Take up a Lamentation for Tyrus. 26:17.

   Vs 3.   Tyrus situated at the entry of the sea as a great seaport and was renowned merchant city for many isles and lands. The pride of beauty. 28:2, 12; Isa 23:3.

   Vs 4.   The borders of the sea right on the sea. City builders perfected its beauty. Vs 3, 4, 11.
   Note: Following in vs 5-25 we have the list of the islands and products brought to Tyrus for trade. Note the exact and detailed list given by the Lord through the prophet. Much of this is repeated in Revelation 18.

   Vs 5.   1.   The Shipping Industry of Tyrus – vs 5-9
   1.   Ships built of fir trees of Senir. Deut 3:9. Ezekiel 27:5. Masts made of the cedars of Lebanon.
   Vs 6.   2.   Oars made of the oaks of Bashan. Benches made of ivory out of the isles of Chittim. Jer 2:10.
   Vs 7.   3.   Fine embroidered linen from Egypt for the ship's sails. Purple, blue and scarlet from the isles of Elishah.
   Vs 8.   4.   Mariners of Zidon and Arvad. The wise men of Tyrus were their pilots.
   Vs 9.   5.   Ancients and wise men of Gebel (1 Kgs 5:18; Ps.83:7) Were the ship's repairers or "stoppers of chinks" (Margin). Stabilisers. Thus we have a detailed description of their ship-Building industry.

   2.   The Army of Tyrus – vs 10-11
   Vs 10.   1.   Men of Persia, Lud and Phut is the standing army of Tyrus, with their shields and helmets.

Vs 11.   2.   The standing army on the walls of the city and at the Watchtowers were men of Arvid and Gammadims with their shields. These shields (probably brass) shining in the sun would certainly add beauty to the appearance of the city. Vs 3, 4.

Great cities like this always had their Military forces ready on the walls and at the watchtowers day and night for any attack, cf. Babylon. Rev 18.

3.   The Merchants of Tyrus – vs 12-25.
1. Tarshish – vs 12. Silver, iron, tin and lead. Gen 10:4; 2 Chronicles 20:36.
2. Javan, Tubal and Meshech – vs 13. Slaves, vessels of brass. Gen 10:2; Rev 18:13.
3. Togamarh – vs 14. Horses and horsemen and mules. 38:6.
4. Dedan and cities – vs 15. Horns of ivory and ebony. Gen 10:7.
5. Syria – vs 16. Emeralds, purple and embroidered work, fine linen, coral and agate (Margin, chrysoprase).
6. Judah and Israel – vs 17. Wheat, honey, oil and balm (Margin, raisin). Judges 11:33; Jeremiah 8:22.
7. Damascus – vs 18. Wine and wine wool.
8. Dan and Javan – vs 19. Bright iron, cassia and calamus.
9. Dedan – vs 20, 15. Precious clothes for chariots. Gen 25:3.
10. Arabia and princes of Kedar – vs 21. Lambs, rams and goats. Gen 25:13; Isa 60:7.
11. Sheba and Raamah – vs 22. Chief spices, precious stones and gold. Gen 10:7; 1 Kgs 10:1-2; Psalm 72:10; Isa 60:6.
12. Horon, Canneh and Eden, Sheba, Asshur and Chilmad – vs 23-24. All sorts of things, blue clothes, embroidered work, chests of rich apparel made of cedar wood bound with cords. Gen 11:31; 2 Kgs 19:12; Gen 25:3.
13. Ships of Tarshish did sing of Tyrus because of the good business and trade of the merchants. Vs 4; Psalm 48:7; Isa 2:16.

2.   THE LAMENTATION OF THE MERCHANTS AT THE FALL OF TYRUS - vs 26-36.

Vs 26. The East wind breaks the city by the waters, like tidal waves smashing it. Psalm 48:7.

Vs 27. The whole trade, shipping trade, and army are to fall into the sea in the day of ruin for Tyrus. Prov 11:4.

Vs 28. The suburbs (Margin, waves) will shake at the cry of the pilots as they see the destruction. 26:15.

Vs 29-30. The merchants of the sea shall leave their ships and come to the land, cry bitterly, wallow in ashes, casting dust on their heads, as they realise their business world has collapsed. Rev 18:17-19; Job 2:12; Esther 4:1, 3; Jeremiah 6:26.

Vs 31. Baldness, sackcloth, weeping and bitterness of heart will be on them. Jeremiah 16:6.

Vs 32. They shall lament over Tyrus being destroyed in the midst of the sea. 26:17; Rev 18:18-19.

Vs 33. Lamentation over the wares, and riches and merchandise that use to come and go from Tyrus to many peoples and kingdoms of the earth, and their kings. Rev 18:19.

Vs 34. God will use the seas to break up the city and its merchandise and traders shall fall. Vs 27; 26:3.

Vs 35. The inhabitants of the isles and their kings shall be astonished and afraid at the news of its Fall. 26:15.

Vs 36. The merchants will hiss at her having lost the business and profits. Tyrus to be a terror and to be seen no more. 26:21; Jeremiah 18:16.

NOTE: There seems to be a double instrument of judgment used against the city of Tyrus.
1. The King of Babylon and the nations under him to destroy the city, and then
2. The waters of the sea destroying the city also; the latter being symbolic of the former.

In B.C. 332 Alexander the Great finally conquered the city, killing 8,000 in all and taking 30,000 slaves, while the sea played its part also.

EZEKIEL CHAPTER TWENTY-EIGHT

The progression of judgment against Tyrus in these chapters is seen to be as follows:

1. The FALL of the CITY under Nebuchadnezzar. Ch. 26.
2. The COLLAPSE of the BUSINESS world, the Merchants of Tyrus. Ch 27.
3. The JUDGMENT of God on the PRINCE and KING of Tyrus. Ch 28:1-19.

1. **PROPHECY CONCERNING THE PRINCE OF TYRUS** – vs 1-10, cf. Rev 18.

   Vs 1.   The Word of the Lord.

   Vs 2.   Word to Prince of Tyrus concerning his pride of heart and self-deification.
   Note the word "heart" in vs 1, 1, 5, 6, 6, 17. God sees the heart condition. Mark 7:21-23; Jeremiah 17:9-10. The sin of Satan seen here. Pride, setting oneself up as God. So did most of the kings of earth, The Pharaohs, the Kings of Babylonia, Roman Emperors, all set themselves up as deity to be worshipped, forgetting that they were but men. 27:3, 4; Isa 31:3.
   Note: Pride, joy over Judah's downfall, violated covenant with Jerusalem, Joel 3:4-8; Amos 1:9-10, and wealth.

   Vs 3.   The Prince of Tyrus was wiser than Daniel, no secrets hid from him. Zech 9:2. Ezekiel thus confirms the existence of the Prophet Daniel, who also was in Babylon at this period of time. Devil's wisdom was corrupted, though originally from God. Dan 1:17. The Prince of Tyrus was the Prince under the Devil's control. Jas 3:15-18.

   Vs 4.   With wisdom and understanding the Prince of Tyrus had gotten great riches and wealth and has built the city of Tyrus up to such fame and worldwide recognition amongst the nations and merchants.

   Vs 5.   Riches and wisdom increased business traffic and the end result was PRIDE. Psalm 62:10; Zech 9:3.

   Vs 6.   Pride led to DEIFICATION and claims to Divinity. Vs 1.

125

Vs 7. Because of pride God will bring strangers against the Prince and the terrible of the nations (i.e. Nebuchadnezzar at this time) and the sword will destroy his wisdom and brightness. 30:11; 31:12; 32:12.

Vs 8. The Prince will be brought down to the pit in death to die the deaths of those who drown in the seas.

Vs 9. No longer be able to deify self as God, but realise but a man in the hands of a God who judges.

Vs 10. Die the deaths of the uncircumcised. Note "deaths" in the plural here – physical, and spiritual and eternal or deaths, spirit, soul and body.

2.   **PROPHECY CONCERNING THE KING OF TYRUS** – vs 11-19.
Vs 11. The Word of the Lord.

Vs 12. Lamentation now over the King of Tyrus, as there was over the Prince. (Note – Many expositors believe that this is also a prophecy concerning Satan, who is THE PRINCE and KING of the Kingdom of Darkness, and his Fall. Thus the "Law of Double Reference"). We note his description is outlined form.

1. Sealed up the sum. The summation of all beings.
2. Full of wisdom. Note "wisdom" here in vs 3, 4, 5, 7, 12, 17 with Jas 3:13-18.
3. Perfect in beauty.
4. Been in Eden, the Garden of God (possible allusion to the Heavenly Paradise).
5. Coverings of precious stones (like the stones on the Breastplate of the High Priest, Ex 28). Vs 13.
    (1) The sardius (Margin. Ruby)
    (2) The topaz.
    (3) The diamond.
    (4) The beryl (chrysolite).
    (5) The onyx.
    (6) The jasper.
    (7) The sapphire.
    (8) The emerald (chrysoprase).
    (9) The carbuncle.
        All them in gold settings, it seems.
6. The workmanship of tabrets and pipes prepared in him the Day he was created. Created being. Ministry of music here.

7. The Anointed Cherub – Set by God. Vs 14.
8. The Covering Cherub, cf. Ex 25:1-22. The Cherubim on the Ark of God, and the Anointed Cherub and the Ark-Throne. Thus high ministry, and God-given anointing.
9. Upon the Holy Mount of God, i.e. The Kingdom. Ezekiel 20:40.
10. Walked up and down in the midst of the stones of fire. Holiness of God.
11. Perfect in day he was created. Inapplicable to men only. Vs 15.
12. Iniquity found in him, cf. 2 Thess 2:3-10. Ezekiel 28:18. Mystery of Iniquity.
13. Multitude of merchandise (trafficking) filled with violence. Vs 16.
14. He has sinned, cf. 1 John 3:4.
15. To be CAST out of the Mt of God. Note the major steps in the "casting out" of Satan.
     (1) Cast out of heaven, the Paradise of God. Isa 14: 12-14; Ezek 28:16.
     (2) Cast out of heaven to earth. Rev 12; Ezekiel 28:17.
     (3) Cast out of earth to the bottomless pit. Rev 20:1-10.
     (4) Cast out of the bottomless pit to the Lake of Fire. Rev 20:11-15.
        Progressive steps over the 7000 years of Week of Redemption.
16. The profane Cherub.
17. To be destroyed out of the midst of the stones of fire.
18. Heart lifted by reason of beauty – yet it was God-given. Vs 17, 2.
19. Wisdom corrupted by reason of brightness. Yet all this beauty and wisdom was God-given. Not originated with him.
20. To be cast to the ground, cf. Rev 12.
21. To lay before Kings, cf. Rev 17. The 10 Kings of the Anti-christal Empire.
22. Sanctuaries (of Heavenly holy places) defiled by his iniquitous traffic. Vs 18.
23. Fire to be brought forth from him to devour and bring him to ashes on the earth in the sight of all.
24. All to be astonished at this judgment. Vs 19.
25. Not to be a terror any more.

Evidently the "Law of Double Reference" is seen here. Behind the Prince and King of Tyrus is King Satan. He was the Anointed covering Cherub of the throne of God in the heavenly Eden.

He was given the ministry of music, the leadership of the worship of the hosts of heaven. There came that time when the Mystery of Iniquity began and he was lifted up in pride. Beholding himself, his anointing, his ministry, his wisdom and beauty, he was lifted up in pride. After he fell, he began a traffic of slandering campaigns in the Holy Places of heaven, influencing other angels in his Fall. He was cast out of the immediate presence of God. The Scripture reveals the progressive steps in the casting out of Satan unto his ultimate casting into the Lake of Fire, cf. Isa 14; 12:12-14. God never divested him of his wisdom, beauty and ministry, but all became totally corrupted and with these he deceives the nations of the earth. The judgment on the Prince of Tyrus, and the King, shadows forth prophetically that judgment on Satan the Prince and King in God's time.

3. **PROPHECY AGAINST ZIDON** – vs 20-23
Tyre and Sidon were closely situated on the sea coasts.

Vs 20. The Word of the Lord.

Vs 21. Prophecy against Zidon.

Vs 22. God is against Zidon, and will be glorified and satisfied in the judgment executed on it.

Vs 23. Pestilence, blood and judgments by the sword on it.

4. **ISRAEL TO BE RESTORED TO THE LAND** – vs 24-26
Vs 24. No longer to be as a brier and thorn to the House of Israel. Num 33:55; Josh 23:13.

Vs 25. God will gather the House of Israel from the people scattered amongst them and then to cause them to dwell in the land again.

Vs 26. To dwell safely, build houses, plant vineyards in confidence. After God has executed judgments on all those nations that despised Israel.
Isa 65:21; Amos 9:14; Jer 31:5.
Probably this is referring to the restoration from Babylon and some from the House of Judah and some from House of Israel from Assyria.

EZEKIEL CHAPTER TWENTY-NINE

1. **PROPHECY AGAINST PHARAOH, KING OF EGYPT** – vs 1-7
    Vs 1.   The Word of the Lord, in the 10th year, 10th month, 12th day.

    Vs 2.   Ezekiel to prophesy against Egypt and Pharaoh the king, cf. 28:21; Isa 19-20; Jeremiah 25:19; 46:2, 25.

    Vs 3.   God is against Egypt and its king. Egypt as a Great Dragon in the midst of the rivers, boasting of its great river, the Nile. Psalm 74:13-14; Isa 27:1; 51:9; Ezekiel 32:2. The Devil is THE Dragon, the dragon behind the beastly kingdoms and dragon kingdoms of this world. E28:2; Isa 37:10; Rev 12:9.

    Vs 4.   God will put a hook into his jaws and all the fish in the river shall stick to his scales. Symbolic of Pharaoh and his people.

    Vs 5.   To be thrown as dragon and fish (i.e. King and people) into the wilderness to be meat for the beasts (other kingdoms) of the field and fowls of the heaven to feed on. Jeremiah 8:2; 16:4; 25:33; Jeremiah 7:33; 34:20.

    Vs 6.   Symbolic of fishermen taking up dragon of the sea and fish by the hook and leaving them to die on the land and be food for beasts. Egyptians to know God is the Lord because of what they have done to the House of Israel. 2 Kgs 18:21; Isa 36:6.

    Vs 7.   When Israel took hold of Egypt as a staff to lean upon for help, the staff broke under them. Jer.37:5, 7, 11; Ezek.17:17.

2. **EGYPT TO BE DESOLATED FOR 40 YEARS** – vs 8-12
    Vs 8.   A SWORD to be on man and beast, cf. Vs 4. Fish hook. 14:17; 32:11-13.

    Vs 9.   Egypt to be desolate because of what God will do to the river she boasts she owns.

    Vs 10. God is against Egypt and her rivers, which are to be wasted from the Tower of Syene to the border of Ethiopia. 30:12, 6; Ex 14:2; Jeremiah 44:1.

    Vs 11. Man or beast not to pass because of the desolation which is to last for 40 years. The number 40 = probation, testing period, end in victory or judgment. 32:13.
            Cf. The 40 years in the Wilderness for Israel. Num 13-14.

Vs 12. Land and cities of Egypt to be desolate for 40 years, and Egyptians to be scattered and dispersed through the countries. 30:7, 26.

3. **EGYPT TO BE RESTORED AFTER 40 YEARS** – vs 13-16.
Vs 13. At the end of 40 years the Egyptians to be gathered against from their scattering. Isa 19:23; Jeremiah 46:26.

Vs 14. Captivity to be turned and the people return to their own land, but to be a BASE Kingdom. Low kingdoms, never a world kingdom as in earliest history. 17:6, 14.

Vs 15. Egypt to be the basest of kingdoms and not to exalt itself above the nations anymore. To be diminished and not rule the nations again.
Note: Egypt was the first World Kingdom that ruled over Israel in their infancy as a nation, until the Exodus.

Vs 16. Egypt no longer to be the confidence of the House of Israel as had been in times of war. Know it is the Lord. Isa 30:2, 3; 36:4, 6. Note how Israel was always turning back to Egypt in their heart or deeds instead of to the Lord. Hence God would break the reed they leaned upon.

4. **EGYPT TO FALL UNDER NEBUCHADNEZZAR, THE KING OF BABYLON** – vs 17-20.
Vs 17. The Word of the Lord, in the 27th year, 1st month and 1st day.

Vs 18. God reminds Ezekiel what Nebuchadnezzar had done to Tyrus though he got no wages for it or for his army. Jeremiah 27:6; Ezekiel 26:7, 8.

Vs 19. God will give the land of Egypt into his hand and he will take a spoil and the prey will be the wages of his army, from here. Jeremiah 25:9.

5. **ISRAEL TO BE BLESSED** – vs 21.
The House of Israel to BUD forth and they will know that God is the Lord. Psalm 132:17; Ezek 24:27.

Vs 21. Cf. Aaron's rod that budded. Num 17.
Cf. Psa 132:17. David's rod to bud.
Israel to bud also. Significant of the Divine seal of appointed service and blessing and life out of death.

EZEKIEL CHAPTER THIRTY

1.   **JUDGMENT ON EGYPT AND ALL WHO UPHOLD HER** – vs 1-19.

Vs 1.   The Word of the Lord.

Vs 2.   Howling and woe over the coming day. Isa 13:6.

Vs 3.   The DAY OF THE LORD is near, a cloudy day on the heathen. 7:7, 12; Joel 2:1; Zeph 1:7.

Vs 4.   The sword to be on Egypt, Ethiopia to be in pain. Foundations to be broken down. 29:19; Jeremiah 50:15.

Vs 5.   Ethiopia, Libya, Lydia, Chub and the mingled people in league with Egypt to fall by the sword. Ezekiel 27:10; Jeremiah 25:20, 24.

Vs 6.   All who uphold Egypt to fall. Pride of Egypts power to come down by reason of the sword. 29:10.

Vs 7.   Land and desolation on the cities. 29:12.

Vs 8.   To know God did it when He sets a fire in Egypt and destroys her helpers.

Vs 9.   God also to send messengers in ships to frighten the careless Ethiopians, as in the day of Egypt. Isa 18:1, 2.

Vs 10. God will use Babylon to judge Egypt. 29:19.

Vs 11. Nebuchadnezzar to bring his people and fill the land of Egypt with those slain by the sword.

Vs 12. God will dry up Egypt's river, sell the land into the hand of wicked strangers and desolate the land. God has spoken it. Isa 19:4, 5, 6.

Vs 13. Idols of images to be destroyed out of Noph. Prince of Egypt to be no more. Fear in the land. Isa 19:1; Jeremiah 43:12; 46:25; Zech 10:11; Isa 19:16.

Vs 14. Cities of Egypt burnt = Pathos, Zoan, No; 29:14; Psalm 78:12, 43; Nah 3:9, 8-10.

Vs 15. Fury of God on Sin and No also. Jeremiah 46:25.

Vs 16. Fire on cities of Egypt. Cf. Vs 8.

Vs 17. Other cities of Egypt destroyed (Refer Margin).

Vs 18. Also the day on these cities will be dark, and the yokes to be broken. Egypt's strength to cease and her daughters to go into captivity. Jeremiah 2:16.

Vs 19. God executes judgments in Egypt by the sword of Babylon.

2.   **WORD AGAINST PHARAOH** – vs 20-26.

Vs 20. The Word of the Lord in the 11th year, the 1st month and 7th day.

Vs 21. Arm of Pharaoh to be broken by the Lord. Not to be bound by splint or healed   so as not to be able to hold a sword. Jeremiah 46:11; 48:25.

Vs 22. God is against Egypt's Pharaoh, and God will break his arms and cause the sword to fall out of his hand, cf. Vs 26; Psalm 37:17.

Vs 23. Egyptians to be scattered and dispersed amongst the nations, cf. Vs 26; 29:12.

Vs 24. God will strengthen the arms of the King of Babylon and put His sword into his hand. God will break Pharaoh's arms and he will groan before Babylon as a deadly wounded man. Sword fight!

Vs 25. Arms of Nebuchadnezzar strengthened – to use God's sword. Arms of Pharaoh broken – to drop the sword. Psalm 9:16.

Vs 26. Egyptians scattered and dispersed against and amongst the nations, cf. Vs 23; 29:12.

EZEKIEL CHAPTER THIRTY-ONE

1. **THE WORD TO PHARAOH** – vs 1-2.
    Vs 1.   The Word of the Lord in the 11th year, the 3rd month and the 1st day. Cf 30:20. That is, two months later.

    Vs 2.   Word to the King of Egypt and his multitude/Who can they be likened to for greatness? Cf. Vs 18.

2. **EGYPT'S GREATNESS LIKE UNTO ASSYRIA'S** – vs 3-9.
    Vs 3.   Assyrian Kingdom likened to a great Tree, cf. Dan 4:10. How often Kingdoms were likened to great trees, cf. Mt 13:31-32; Ezekiel 17; Judges 9: Ezekiel 15; Isa 10:18.

        1. A Cedar in Lebanon, i.e. Royalty, in the Mt or Kingdom.
        2. Fair branches.
        3. Shadowing shroud.
        4. High stature.
        5. Top among the thick branches.
    Vs 4.   6. Set in rivers and great waters to make it great. Source of Supply. Jeremiah 51:36.
        7. Little conduits to all trees of the field, i.e. The supply to kingdoms etc.
    Vs 5.   8. Height exalted above his fellow trees.
        9. Boughs multiplied. Peoples, extent of kingdom.
        10. Branches long by reason of the source of waters and shot forth everywhere, ie. The spread of the Empire. Dan 4:11.
    Vs 6.   11. Fowls made nests in its branches.
        12. Beasts dwelt under the shadow of the tree. So did nations, small and great put their trust in the greatness of the Assyrian Kingdom. 17:23; Dan 4:12.
    Vs 7.   13. Fair in greatness and length of branches.
        14. Root by great waters, i.e. Rivers and seas.
    Vs 8.   15. No other tree could compare with the beauty of the Assyrian Tree. No tree in the garden of God could hide its greatness. Gen 2:8; 13:10; Ezek 28:13.
    Vs 9.   16. All the trees of the field envied the greatness of this Kingdom.

3. **JUDGMENT ON THE TREE OF EGYPT** - vs 10-18.

    Vs 10. Pharaoh, King of Egypt, lifted himself up in pride as a tree with height and boughs as Assyria. Dan 5:20.

Vs 11. God has delivered Pharaoh into the hands of Babylon's king and he will deal with him. Egypt to be judged for its wickedness.

Vs 12. Strangers of the terrible of the nations (Babylon) to cut Egypt as a tree, branches, boughs, etc, and all the birds and beasts (peoples) to leave him. 28:7; 32:5, 8.
Note: As did the people to Nebuchadnezzar in his time of pride. Dan 4. The tree cut down and later restored.

Vs 13. Fowls and beasts of the field remain on his ruins. Isa 18:6; Ezekiel 32:4.

Vs 14. Purpose in the fact that none of the trees (i.e. smaller kingdoms) exalt themselves for height, or shoot out their power over others. Delivered to death in the earth with those going down to the pit. 32:18; Psalm 82:7.

Vs 15. Mourning for Egypt by Lebanon and all the trees of the field.

Vs 16. All nations to shake at the fall to hell and the pit of Pharaoh. All the trees of Lebanon relieved at it also. 32:31; Isa 6:15; 14:8, 15.

Vs 17. Also all other trees to go to hell when slain by the sword, those that trusted under his shadow.

Vs 18. Egypt likened to Assyria in greatness and its Fall. Vs 18 answers the question of vs 2. 32:19; 28:10; 32:19, 21, 24.

As a great tree is brought down, so will Egypt be, with other trees to the nether parts of the earth. This is Pharaoh and his multitude. Die the deaths of the uncircumcised, i.e. those out of covenant relationship with God.

Thus Pharaoh and his kingdom likened to a great tree and cut down by God, the tree cutter, who uses Babylon to do this as well as the other trees.

Symbolic of Nebuchadnezzar conquering Egypt and all surrounding nations, cf. Dan 4. Babylon as a tree. Mt 13:31-32. The Kingdom of God like a mustard tree.

EZEKIEL CHAPTER THIRTY-TWO

1. **LAMENTATION FOR PHAROAH** – vs 1-10.

    Vs 1.   The Word of the Lord in the 12th year, 12th month, and 1st day.

    Vs 2.   Lamentation for Pharaoh. Likened to:
    1. A young lion of the nations, and
    2. A dragon (Margin), whale in the seas, coming from and fouling the waters.
        Vs 16; 27:2; 19:3, 6; 38:13; 29:2; 34:18.

    Vs 3.   God will spread His net over him and his company of people. 12:13; 17:20; Hos 7:12.

    Vs 4.   Pharaoh and hosts to be cast out on the field, as meat to fowls and beasts. 29:2; 31:13.

    Vs 5.   Their flesh to be laid out in the mountains and also the valleys. 31:12.

    Vs 6.   Land to be watered with their blood, even to the mountains, and the rivers.

    Vs 7.   Heaven, the sun, moon and stars to be darkened in that day when Pharaoh is extinguished. Isa 13:10; Joel 12:31; 3:15; Amos 8:9; Mt 24:29; Rev 6:12-13.

    Vs 8.   All the bright lights of heaven to be darkened and the land.

    Vs 9.   Hearts of many to be vexed when God brings destruction by His word and sword on Egypt and scatters them into the countries.

    Vs 10. Many people and kings to be horribly afraid when they see God's sword and all will tremble for their lives. 26:16.

2. **BABYLON TO BE USED TO JUDGE EGYPT** – vs 11-16

    Vs 11. The sword of the King of Babylon to come on Pharaoh. 30:4; Jeremiah 46:26.

    Vs 12. The swords of Babylon, the terrible of the nations, to spoil the pomp of Egypt and its multitude. 28:7; 29:19.

Vs 13. God will destroy the beasts (Kingdoms) from beside the waters. No more trouble by man or beasts. 29:11.

Vs 14. God will make the rivers deep and run like oil.

Vs 15. The land of Egypt to be desolate, destitute, and smitten and know that it is the Lord. Ex 7:5; 14:4, 18; Ps.9:16; Ezek. 6:7.

Vs 16. This is the lamentation that the nations will lament over Egypt's judgment. 26:17 with vs 2; 2Sam1:17; 2Chron. 35:25.

3. **WAILING FOR EGYPT AND THEIR DAUGHTER NATIONS WITH HER** – vs 17-32

Vs 17. The Word of the Lord, in the 12th year, 12th month and 15th day, cf. Vs 1.

Vs 18. Wailing for Egypt and the daughter nations cast down to the pit with her. 26:20; 31:14.

Vs 19. Though beautiful, she goes down with uncircumcised (those not in covenant relationship with God), vs 21, 24; 31:2, 18.

Vs 20. Given over to the sword.

Vs 21. All slain by the sword and into the midst of hell. Vs 19, 25, 27; Isa 1:31; 14:9-10.

Vs 22. ASSHUR and her company are there, in their graves, slain by the sword. Isa 14:15.

Vs 24, 25. ELAM and her multitude are there, graves and the pit, slain by the sword. Though a terror to the land of the living, yet all die the deaths of the uncircumcised and go to the pit. Jeremiah 49:34.

Vs 26. MESHECH, and TUBAL and their multitude there also. Slain by the sword and sent to the pit. Though they counsel and cause terror in the land of the living, yet slain. Gen 10:2; Ezek 27:13.

Vs 27. Uncircumcised nation gone down to hell in their iniquity. Isa 14:18.

Vs 28. Repeat.

Vs 29. EDOM and her kings and princes, slain by the sword, and lie in the pit with the uncircumcised too (In the wicked section of Sheol). 25:12. Princes of the North.

Vs 30. ZIDONIANS gone with the slain by the sword also. 38:6, 15; 39:2; 28:21.

Vs 31. Pharaoh will feel consoled when he sees all the other daughter nations judged by the sword as well as her army. 31:16.

Vs 32. God has caused His terror by the sword in the lands of the uncircumcised nations. That is, Egypt and all the nations allied with her.

Note: UNCIRCUMCISED used so much here, referring to the non-Covenant nations.
THE SWORD – speaks of Babylon, the sword God used to judge these nations.
THE PIT and HELL – speaking of the grave and Sheol, the place for the bodies and souls of the slain.

EZEKIEL CHAPTER THIRTY-THREE

1.   **THE CALL OF THE WATCHMAN** – vs 1-6
Compare this chapter with Ezekiel Chapters 3 and 18 also.

Vs 1.   The Word of the Lord to Ezekiel.

Vs 2.   Son of Man = type of Christ. When God brings A SWORD on the land (cf. 3:11; 14:17) and the people take a man and make a man of their coasts to be their set watchman (cf. 2 Sam 18:24-25; 2 Kgs 9:17; Hos 9:8);

Vs 3.   The watchman is to:
1. Blow the trumpet, and
2. Warn the people, when he sees the sword coming.

    NOTE: "the sword" in 32:11, 20, 21, 22, 23, 24, 25 etc with Jeremiah 25:27, 31-33; Rev 6:3-4. The rider on the RED horse and the second seal.

Vs 4.   Whoever hears the trumpet and refuses to take the warning, then if the sword slay them, his blood is on his own head. 18:13.

Vs 5.   He heard and took no heed of the warning. The one that hears and takes warning delivers his own soul.

Vs 6.   If the watchman sees the sword come, and does not blow the warning trumpet and the people are slain in their sins, then the blood is required at the hands of the watchman, cf. Vs 8.

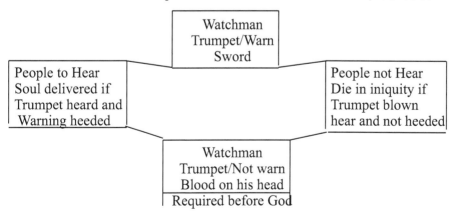

139

2. **EZEKIEL SET BY THE LORD AS A WATCHMAN** – vs 7-16

Vs 7.   Ezekiel, as Son of Man, SET as a watchman to the House of Israel, to hear the word from God's mouth and warn them.

Vs 8.   To warn the wicked not to die in his iniquity. If Ezekiel fails to warn then God will require it at his hand.

Vs 9.   However, if the wicked refuse to hear the warning of God through the prophet, and he dies in his iniquity, the prophet has delivered his soul. Thus - God/The Prophet/The House of Israel.

Vs 10.   If the House of Israel are really pining over their sins and transgressions and really desire to live, they can ask the prophet. 24:23; Isa 49:14.

Vs 11.   God's answer to them is that He has no pleasure in the death of the wicked. He desires that the wicked turn from his way and live. Why will Israel die, when God desires them to live? 18:31; 2 Sam 14:14; 2 Pet 3:9.

Vs 12.   Also warning to the righteous and the wicked here. The righteous are not to depend on their righteousness and then live in sin. Reverse for the wicked. If the wicked turn from his wickedness, God will not require it of him in his righteousness. 3:20; 18:24, 26; 2 Chronicles 7:14.

Vs 13.   If the righteous trusts his own righteousness and the promise of life, and then commits iniquity, his righteousness shall not be remembered if he dies in his sin. 3:20; 18:24.

Vs 14.   If the wicked is under the death penalty and he turns from his sin and do the lawful and right and he restore the pledge, that which he has robbed, and walk in the statutes of life, and not his iniquities, then shall receive life.

Vs 15.   Cf. 3:18, 19; 18:27; 18:7; Ex 22:1, 4; Lev 6:2, 4, 5; Lev 18:5; Ezek 20:11, 13, 21.

Vs 16.   The sins of the wicked shall not be remembered or mentioned – he shall have life.

3. **THE EQUALITY OF GOD'S DEALINGS** – vs 17-20 with 18:25-30a notes.

Vs 17. The children of Israel said God's ways are not equal (cf. Vs 7-16). God tells them His ways are equal, cf. Vs 20; 18:25, 29, 26.

Vs 18-19. Note the equality of God's ways.

Righteous turn from	Wicked turn from
His righteousness	his wickedness
Commits iniquity	Lives righteously
Dies in sin	Lives for God
Righteousness not to	Wickedness not to
Be remembered	be remembered

Vs 20. God's ways are equal. God will judge the House of Israel for their ways, which are just the opposite to God's. Vs 17; 18:25; Isa 55:6-8.

4. THE LAND DESOLATED ACCORDING TO THE PALESTINIAN COVENANT – vs 21-29.

NOTE: This passage has to do with the possession of the Land. Israel boasted that the land was theirs by inheritance according to the Abrahamic Covenant and should not be thus desolated by God. What they failed to realise was the relationship of the Abrahamic and Palestinian Covenants. The Abrahamic Covenant was the GIFT of the land by grace and faith, and the Palestinian Covenant gave the CONDITIONS for holding the land and that was by OBEDIENCE to the laws of the land, God's land.

Thus:

Abrahamic/Land/Gift		
Inheritance		
Grace/Faith/Obedience		
Unconditional		
Into the Land	Palestinian	
Gen 12-25	Conditional	
	In the Land	
	Obedience	
		Out of the Land
	Lev 26/	Assyria/Babylon
	Deut 27-32	Israel/Judah

Refer to Deut 29-30, 27-28 chapters for the conditions of holding the land. Note especially Lev 26 chapter.

Vs 21.   In the 12th year of the captivity, the 10th month and 5th day, one escaped from the smitten city of Jerusalem and came to Ezekiel, cf. 1:2, 3; 24:26-27; 2 Kgs 25:4.

Vs 22.   That very evening, before this one escapee arrived, God had opened the mouth of the prophet from the dumbness that had been brought upon him while the siege was on. So in the morning when the escapee arrived Ezekiel was prophesying again. 24:27.

Vs 23.   The Word of the Lord.

Vs 24.   The remnant who remained in the wastes of the land of Israel complained about the fact that Abraham was only one person, yet God gave him the land for an inheritance. Here they were many and the land was much more their inheritance. Boasted in their father Abraham.
Refer to notes on this remnant under Jeremiah 40-45 also. Here they are pleading the fact that the land being given to Abraham under the Covenant should not be taken from them. 34:2; 36:4; Josh 11:23; 21:43-45; Gen 12:1-3; 15:18; Josh 1:4.
However, GOD WAS THE LAND-LORD, the land-owner, and Israel were but the tenants. Lev 25:23.
The conditions for the tenants were laid out in the contract or Covenant in Deut 27-32.   If and when they failed to keep the conditions, they would be expelled. Refer to notes on Joshua (KJC. OT History). Isa 51:2; Acts 7:5; Mic 3:11; Mt 3:9; John 8:39.

Vs 25.   God challenges them on their sins and whether they are entitled to the possession of the land.
1.   Eating blood which was forbidden. Gen 9:4. Noahic Covenant and Mosaic also. Lev. 3:17;   7:26;   17:10; 19:26.
2.   Lifting up their eyes to idols. 18:6. Idolatry. Violate 1st and 2nd Commandments.
3.   Shedding blood. Murder. 22:6, 9. The 6th Commandment.

Vs 26.   4.   Stand on the sword and work abominations.
5.   Defile the neighbour's wife. Adultery. 18:6; 22:16. The 7th and 10th Commandments violated.
Note: The violations of the commandments of the Lord here. Ex 20:1-17. How could they remain in the land? They boasted of Abraham as their father, but he was not guilty of these things which defiled the land. He kept Covenant and obeyed

the Lord. They have violated the conditions of remaining in the Covenant land, so they were expelled – not entitled to remain.

Vs 27. God says that those remaining in the desolated land, in the open field, the forts and the caves will die by the sword, beasts and pestilence. Vs 24; 39:4; Judges 6:2; 1 Sam 13:6; Ezekiel 14:21. Refer also to Jeremiah's prophecies to this same remnant!!

Vs 28. The land to be desolated with great desolations. 7:24; 24:21; 6:2, 3, 6; Jeremiah 44:2, 6, 22. Note again Lev 26:31-35 especially.

Vs 29. Israel to recognise that God brought desolations about because of their iniquities. Hence it is important to understand the relationship of the Abrahamic Covenant to the Mosaic and Palestinian, in relation to the LAND of PALESTINE! Prov 26:2.

Thus: Ezek 1-10. The Temple / Ezek 11-24, The City / Ezek 23, The Land.

5. **THE HYPOCRISY OF THE PEOPLE TO THE PROPHET EZEKIEL** – vs 30-33.

Vs 30. God shows how the people were talking about him behind the walls of their houses, and saying to come and hear what the old prophet has got to say. Isa 29:13.

Vs 31. In mockery and hypocritical attitude they come and sit before the prophet, listen to his words and do not obey them. They show great love with their MOUTH but their HEART is covetous. 8:1; Ps.78:36-37. Margin – Loves – JESTS. Mt 13:22; Is.6:6-9. Mouth and heart far removed from each other.

Vs 32. The prophet is like a lovely song and the prophet's voice very pleasant as an instrument player (Note – Ezekiel was a priest, could also have been a singer-musician). They hear and disobey. Spiritual deafness, not having "ears to hear".

Vs 33. When it comes to pass, as it surely will, they will know that a prophet has been amongst them. 2:5; 1 Sam 3:20.

EZEKIEL CHAPTER THIRTY-FOUR

Note: The great Shepherd Chapters of the Bible, Jeremiah 23; Ezekiel 34; John 10; Acts 20; 1 Pet 5; Psalm 23.

1. **PROPHECY AGAINST THE SHEPHERDS OF ISRAEL** – vs 1-6.

Vs 1. The Word of the Lord.

Vs 2. Prophesy against the Shepherds of Israel, cf. Jeremiah 23 also.

Vs 3. The Shepherd represents the rulers of Israel – Kings, Prophets, priests, Scribes and Elders of the nation, all who had positions of leadership and rulership over the nation and were responsible to the people. Jeremiah 23:1; Zech 11:17; Isa 56:11; Zech 11:16; Lk 15:4.
Desolating prophecies against the shepherds that brought the sheep of Israel to the condition they were as a nation.
The word to the Shepherds:
1. Woe to the shepherds.
2. The shepherds should feed the flock. Lk 15:4; 1 Pet 5:3.
3. Eat the fat sheep.
4. Clothe themselves with the wool.
5. Kill the fed sheep.
6. Not feed the flocks.

Vs 4. 7. Not feed or strengthen the <u>diseased</u> sheep.
8. Not heal the <u>sick</u> sheep.
9. Not bind up the <u>broken</u> sheep.
10. Not bring again the <u>driven away</u> sheep.
11. Not seek the <u>lost</u> sheep.
12. Ruled with force and cruelty. 1 Pet 5:3.

Vs 5. 13. Sheep <u>scattered</u> because of no shepherd.
14. Sheep <u>devoured</u> by beasts of the field. 1 Kgs 22:17; Mt 9:36; Isa 56:9.

Vs 6. 15. Sheep <u>wandered</u> on mountains and hills.
16. God's flock scattered and none search for them.
Note the 5-fold condition of the sheep in vs 4, and vs 5, 6.

2. **FURTHER WORD TO THE SHEPHERDS** – vs 7-10.

Vs 7. The Word of the Lord to the shepherds.

Vs 8. God swears by Himself concerning His flock that have been a prey to the beasts because of the failure of the shepherds. Vs 5, 6, 2, 10.

Vs 9.   The Word of the Lord to the shepherds. Vs 1, 7.

Vs 10. God is AGAINST the shepherds.
1.   God will require His flock at their hands.
2.   God will cause them to cease feeding His flock.
3.   God will see that the shepherds do not feed themselves any more.
4.   God will deliver His flock from them. Vs 2, 8.

3.   **THE LORD IS THE TRUE SHEPHERD** – vs 11-16;   Isa 40:11; John 10.

Vs 11. The Lord will be the true shepherd to His flock.
1.   The Lord will search and seek out His sheep.
Vs 12. 2.   He will seek His scattered sheep.
3. Deliver them out of all places where scattered in the cloudy day. 30:3.
Vs 13. 4.   To be brought out from the people.
5.   To be gathered from the countries.
6.   To be brought back to their own land.
7.   To be fed on the mountains of Israel, by rivers and inhabited
Places. Isa 65:9, 10; Jer 33:12.
Vs 14. 8.   To be fed now in good pasture, a fat pasture.
9.   To have folds on high mountains, lie in good fold. Ps 23:2; Jer 33:12.
Vs 15. 10. God will feed His flock and make them lie down.
Vs 16. 11. The Lord will seek the lost.
12. The Lord will bring again the driven away.
13. The Lord will bind up the broken.
14. The Lord will strengthen the sick.
15. The Lord will destroy the fat and strong and feed them with judgment.
He will do all vs 4 says in the opposite, all that the shepherds
Failed to do and discern in the needs of the sheep.
Isa 40:11; Mic 4:6; Mt 18:11; Lk 5:32; Isa 10:16; Amos 4:1; Jer 10:24.

4.   **PROPHECY AGAINST THE FLOCK** – vs 17-19.

Vs 17. The Word to the flock now. Having pronounced judgments on the shepherds, now it is on the cattle, the rams and goats.

Thus "the flock" here consist of sheep and goats, cf. Mt 25:31-46. Both CLEAN animals, sheep and goats, yet symbolic of the unrighteous and righteous in Israel.

Vs 18. The rough cattle ate the good pasture and drank the deep waters and then fouled it up with their feet for others.

Vs 19. God's flock had to eat and drink that which had been trodden down and fouled up with their feet.
So is the custom amongst sheep and goats. They drink if the waters softly, then the strong ones pollute the waters with their feet, and the weaker sheep have to drink the muddied waters! Characteristic of God's people so often!

5.   **JUDGMENT ON THE CATTLE** – vs 20-22

Vs 20. God will judge the fat and the lean cattle. Vs 17.

Vs 21. These he goats thrust with their shoulder and horns the diseased and scattered sheep.

Vs 22. God will save His flock and judge between cattle and cattle.
Thus Shepherds and Sheep will come under judgment before God.
What happened in the O.T. Church is also prophetic of the N.T. Church, and ministries and people come for judgment.

6.   **THE MESSIANIC PROPHECIES** – vs 23-31.

Vs 23. Note the I WILL'S of the Lord in vs 7-31, vs 23-31.
1. I will set up One Shepherd over them.
2. He will feed them.
3. Even My servant David (Son of David). He will feed and shepherd them. Isa 40:11; John 10:11;   Pet 2:25; Jeremiah 30:9; Hos 3:5.
Vs 24. 4. I will be the Lord their God (i.e. The Father).
5. David My Servant will be Prince among them. God has spoken it (i.e. The Son). Ezekiel 37:22. Note – David, a Shepherd-King over the sheep and God's people. The Example Shepherd over God's people caring for the flock. 1 Sam 16:11-13; 2 Sam 24:17; Psa 78:70-72.
Vs 25. 6. I will make them a Covenant of Peace. Heb 13:20.
7. I will cause evil beasts to cease out of the land and the sheep to dwell safely in the wilderness and sheep in the woods. Lev 26:6; Isa 11:6-9; Hos 2:18; Ezek 37:26.

Vs 26. 8. I will make them and their places a blessing, refreshing
Revival showers of rain.
9. I will cause the showers of blessing to fall. Isa 56:7;
Gen 12:2; Isa 19:24; Zech 8:14; Lev 26:4; Psa 68:9.
Vs 27. 10. Trees and earth will yield fruit and increase and sheep will
Dwell safely.
11. God will break their bondage yokes and deliver them out
Of their captor's hands. Lev 26:4; Psalm 85:12; Isa 4:2.
Vs 28. 12. Not to be a prey to heathen beasts but dwell safe in the
Land, without fear. Jeremiah 30:10.
Vs 29. 13. I will raise them as a plant of renown.
14. Not to be consumed out of the land with hunger.
15. Not to bear the shame of the heathen ruling over them.
36:3,6.
Vs 30. 16. They shall come to know God as their God and they His
People. Vs 24.
Vs 31. 17. God's flock of His pasture are men. Ps.100:3; John 10:11.

This ultimately points to the Lord God and the Messiah who will be
the Prince and One Shepherd over the people of God. They will be,
by reason of the New Covenant made by the Good, Great and Chief
Shepherd of Calvary. Also points to true shepherds that Messiah raises
up to His Church in New Covenant times.

Thus lessons for ministry today. God will judge both shepherds and
sheep in the time of His advent. Mt 25:31-46.

EZEKIEL CHAPTER THIRTY-FIVE

1. **THE JUDGEMENT AGAINST MT SEIR** – vs 1-15.

Note – The burden of this prophetic words is against Mt Seir, or against the Esau/Edomites. Mt Seir was given as an inheritance to Esau, Jacob's brother nation. The Scripture reveals them to be always at enmity against Jacob/Israel, ever since the Birthright Blessings incidents. Gen 25:26-27.
Refer to Obadiah, Minor Prophets – KJC. Diagram = Isaac, then Jacob/Israel, Mt Sinai, and Esau/Edom, Mt Seir.

Vs 1. The Word of the Lord.

Vs 2. The Word of the Lord against Mt Seir. Face against it. Deut 2:5; Amos 1:11; Ezekiel 6:14.

Vs 3. God is against Mt Seir and His hand will be stretched out to make it desolate.

Vs 4. Cities to be wasted and desolated.

Vs 5. Mt Seir (Edomites) had a perpetual hatred and murderous spirit against Israel (Jacob) and in all their times of calamity used the sword against them. Psalm 137:7; Dan 9:24.

Vs 6. The Lord will cause blood to pursue Israel, it will be blood for blood. Shed blood in Israel and so Edom's blood will be shed, according to the Laws of innocent blood. Psalm 109:17; Num 35:33.

Vs 7. Mt Seir to be desolated and all to be cut off who go in or out. Judges 5:6.

Vs 8. Hills, mountains, valleys and rivers to be filled with the slain by the sword.

Vs 9. Mt Seir to be perpetual desolations and cities not to exist again. 36:11; Jeremiah 49:17.

Vs 10. Edom claimed Israel and Judah to be their inheritance, and wanted to possess it, but they did not realise that the land really was the Lord's land. Psalm 83:4, 12; 48:1-3.

Vs 11. God will do to Esau was Esau did to Israel. Note "thine anger" and "thy envy" and "thy blasphemies" and "thy hatred."
Mt 7:2; Jas 2:13; Ezekiel 35:12. Law of Divine retribution.
God's judgment will be known among them.

Vs 12. Edom to know that God has heard all their blasphemies against the mountains of Israel, claiming that they are theirs now that the Lord has destroyed them.
Psa 9:16.

Vs 13. The words of their mouth have been against the Lord and He has heard them. 1 Sam 2:3.

Vs 14. God will make Edom desolate when the rest of the earth is rejoicing. Isa 65:13.

Vs 15. Note the Law of Divine retribution. AS .... SO.
AS Edom rejoiced at Israel's desolation, so will God desolate Edom, Mt Seir and Idumea.   36:5.
Refer to notes on Obadiah.

Note: This prophecy of Ezekiel given about B.C. 587, and possibly Obadiah's also, B.C. 586-3 (although some suggest as late as B.C. 606). However, about the time of Babylon's rule.
The key word is "desolate" used about 8 times in vs 3, 4, 7, 9, 12, 14, 15.
Compare Ezekiel 35 with Obadiah 1-21 chapters.

EZEKIEL CHAPTER THIRTY-SIX

1. **PROPHECY TO THE MOUNTAINS OF ISRAEL** – vs 1-7

    Vs 1.   The Word of the Lord to the mountains of Israel. 6:2, 3.

    Vs 2.   The enemies of Israel mocked them saying that the ancient high places were their possessions. 35:10; 25:3; Deut 32:13; 28:37.

    Vs 3.   The enemies made these mountains desolate, claiming them as his possession and now took up slander and infamy against Israel's desolations. Deut 28:37.

    Vs 4.   Because of all that the enemies said the Lord did to these mountains, God will reverse it. God speaks to the mountains, hills, rivers, valleys, and waste places and cities that are in derision. 34:28; Psalm 79:4.

    Vs 5.   God spoke in the fire of His wrath to the heathen and Idumea, who rejoiced with despiteful minds against HIS LAND. Lev 25:23; Deut 4:24; Ezekiel 38:19; 35:10-12.

    Vs 6.   God told Ezekiel to prophesy to these mountains, hills and valleys and rivers that they had borne the shame of the heathen in His jealousy and fury. Vs 15; Psalm 123:3, 4; Ezekiel 34:29.

    Vs 7.   God will reverse His hand of judgment and the heathen round about shall bear the same shame that the land of Israel suffered.
    If God's people and God's land suffer judgment for sin, how much more shall heathen peoples and lands suffer judgment. 20:5.

2. **PROPHECY OF BLESSING ON THE MOUNTAINS OF ISRAEL** – vs 8-15.

    Vs 8.   Mountains of Israel to shoot forth branches, yield fruit for Israel.

    Vs 9.   God is for HIS LAND and will turn it and it shall be tilled and sown.

Vs 10. Men will be multiplied, cities inhabited and the waste places rebuilt. Vs 33; Isa 58:12; 61:4; Amos 9:14.

Vs 11. Men and beast to multiply, be fruitful. All to be settled in their old estates and God will do better for them than at their beginnings. Jeremiah 31:27; Ezekiel 35:9; 37:6, 13.

Vs 12. Israel to repossess their inheritance and the land no longer to be bereaved of people. Obadiah 17: Jeremiah 15:17.

Vs 13-14. Because the enemy mocked the land for devouring its nations (Israel and Judah), God says it shall be revived.

Vs 15. The land no more to hear the heathen and reproach of other nations upon it. 34:29.
Note again – This involves the Covenant LAND. It is God's land and although He must disinherit the tenants for their iniquities and desolate the land, yet He says it is still HIS LAND and He watches over it in judgment or in blessing. Ezekiel 33:21-29 notes.
Refer to Abrahamic and Palestinian Covenants. Lev 26; Deut 11; Deut 27-32 chapters.

3. **THE REASON GOD JUDGED THE LAND OF ISRAEL** – vs 16-20.

Vs 16. The Word of the Lord.

Vs 17. When Israel dwelt in the land, they defiled it by their own ways and doings and became as an unclean woman. Lev 18:25-28; Jeremiah 2:7; Lev 15:19-20.

Vs 18. Because of this God poured out His fury on them for their murders and idolatry in the polluted land. 16:36, 38; 23:37.

Vs 19. God also scattered them and dispersed them among the heathen countries. God judged them according to their idolatrous ways. 7:3; 18:30; 39:24.

Vs 20. Even in those lands, they polluted the Name of the Lord and the heathen reproached the Name of the Lord because of the way Israel lived. Isa 52:5; Rom 2:5; 2 Tim 2:19.

4.   **GOD'S CONCERN FOR HIS HOLY NAME** – vs 21-24.

Vs 21.   God is concerned for His Name which the House of Israel
           profaned among the heathen where they went.
           To profane God's Name is an attack on His holy character.
           Note the 3rd Commandment Ex 20:1-10; 2 Tim 2:19; Rom
           2:5, 24; Ezekiel 20:9, 14.

Vs 22.   God will act, not for their sakes, but for HIS NAME'S sake
           which was profaned. 20:41; 28:22.

Vs 23.   God will sanctify His Name in His people which was really
           profaned among the people and heathen lands. 20:41.

Vs 24.   God will gather them out from the heathen and bring them
           again to their own land. 34:13; 37:21.

5.   **MESSIANIC PROMISES AND PROPHECIES** – vs 25-38

Note the promises here which overflow into the Restoration from
Babylon (remnant from Assyria) into Messiah's Times and the
New Covenant era.

Vs 25.   1. To be sprinkled with clean water. The Laver, cf. Ephesians
              5:2527; Tit 3:5. Washing of water by the word. Ceremonial
              washings point to moral purification.
           2. To be cleansed from all filthiness. Heb 10:22; Jer. 33:8;
              2 Cor 7:1.
           3. To be cleaned from all idols. Isa 52:15; 1 John 5:8.
Vs 26.   4. To be given a new heart.
           5. To be given a new spirit within them, cf. John 3:1-5.
              Regenerated spirit.
           6. To have the stony heart taken out of them.
           7. To be given a heart of flesh. Tender, sensitive and
              responsive Jer32:39; Ezek11:19; 2 Cor3. Tables of Stone,
              the Old Covenant; Tables of Flesh, the New Covenant.
Vs 27.   8. To have God's Spirit put within them. 2 Cor3; Acts 2:1-4;
              John 16:9-12; Rom 8:25-29.
           9. To walk and keep God's statutes & judgments to do them.
              Heb 8; Jer 31:31-34; Ezek 11:19; 37:14.
Vs 28.   10. To dwell in the Covenant land given to the three fathers.
              Jer 30:22; Ezek 28:25; 37:25; Ezek 11:21; 37:27.
          11. To be His people and He be their God. New Covenant.
              Heb 10:16.
Vs 29.   12. To be saved from all uncleanness. Mt 1:21; Rom 11:26.
          13. To be blessed with corn and not famine. Psalm 105:16;

Ezek 34:29.

Vs 30. 14. To have fruitfulness, increase and multiply in the land and Not be the reproach of the heathen. 34:27.

Vs 31. 15. To remember their evil ways and to loathe themselves for Their iniquities and abominations. 16:61-63; Lev 26:39; Ezek 6:9; 20:43.

Vs 32. 16. To be done fo His Name's sake. Vs 22.

           17. To be ashamed and confounded for their evil ways. Deut 9:5.

Vs 33. 18. To dwell in own land and cities after THE DAY of cleansing. Vs 10. Lev 16, i.e. The Day of Atonement to cleanse the Land and people.

Vs 34. 19. To till the desolate land.

Vs 35. 20. To make the waste & desolate land as the Garden of Eden Inhabited. Isa 57:3; Ezek 28:13; Joel 2:3.

Vs 36. 21. To be a witness to the heathen that the Lord both BUILDS And PLANTS the ruined and desolate places. 17:24; 22:14; 37:14; Jer 1:10.

Vs 37. 22. To be enquired of by the House of Israel to do all this for Them. Responsibility to seek the Lord to fulfil His promises Not to be fatalistic about it. Vs 10; 14:3; 20:3, 31.

Vs 38. 23. To be increased like flocks, flocks of men.

           24. To keep the Solemn Feasts. Lev 23. To know that the Lord is God.

Undoubtedly much of this was fulfilled in the restoration from Babylon and on unto Messiah times. The burden of it definitely involves the NEW COVENANT in contrast to the OLD Covenant. The stony heart from the Old Covenant, the Mosaic and then the new heart, the new spirit under the New Covenant. From Moses to Jesus as Mediators of Covenants.

EZEKIEL CHAPTER THIRTY-SEVEN

1.   **THE VISION OF THE VALLEY OF DRY BONES** – vs 1-10.

Vs 1.   The HAND of the Lord on Ezekiel. 1:3. Carried out "in the Spirit" of the Lord. 3:14; 8:3; Lk 4:1; Ezekiel 11:24. Set down in the midst of the valley full of bones.

Vs 2.   Ezekiel caused to behold the state of the bones, very many and very dry.

Vs 3.   The Lord asks Ezekiel "Can these bones LIVE?" The answer "Thou knowest" was a wise answer from the prophet. It would involve the miracle of resurrection to make them live. Faith in the God of the resurrection. Deut 32:39; John 5:21; Rom 4:17; 2 Cor 1:9.

Vs 4.   Ezekiel commanded to prophesy upon the bones, and cause them to hear the Word of the Lord.

Vs 5.   Note the "I will's" of the Lord's word to the bones.
1.   I will cause breath to enter into you and ye shall live. Vs 9; Psalm 104:30.
2.   I will lay sinews upon you.

Vs 6.   3.   I will bring up flesh upon you.
4.   I will cover you with skin.
5.   I will put breath in you and ye shall live.
6.   You will know that He is the Lord. 6:7; 35:12; Joel 2:27; 3:17.

Vs 7.   Ezekiel prophesied as was commanded, nothing more, nothing less, nothing else. Only such would produce results. As he prophesied there was:
1.   A noise
2.   A shaking
3.   Bones coming together
4.   Bone to his bone.

Vs 8.   Response to the prophetic word. Sinews and flesh and skin came on the bones, but there was no breath in them.

Vs 9.   The Lord told Ezekiel to prophesy to the wind (the breath), calling it to come from the four winds and breathe upon the slain bodies. Vs 5; Psalm 104:30; Jas 2:26.

Note:
1. Prophecy of The WORD – vs 1-8a.
2. Prophecy of The WIND – vs 8b-10.

Thus the WORD and the SPIRIT. Note what the Word did and what the Spirit did. BOTH are needed. Spiritually in the Church, as nationally here in Israel. Refer to GBT of "The Word and The Spirit" (KJC). Gen 1:1-5; Rev 7:1-4; Dan 7:1-2. The four winds speak of that which is worldwide.
Though bones, skin, sinews, and flesh all together, yet death still prevailed. The LIFE breath was needed.

Vs 10. Ezekiel prophesied to the wind as commanded and breath came into them.
1. Breath came into them, i.e. the spirit.
2. They lived.
3. They stood on their feet.
4. They were an exceeding great army. Rev 11:11; Psalm 141:7; Isa 49:14; Ex 7:4.
Israel often spoken of as God's Army, the army of the Lord.

2.   THE VISION INTERPRETED – vs 11-14.

Vs 11. The bones are the WHOLE HOUSE of Israel, i.e. The 12 tribes, Israel and Judah.
Cf. Vs 1-3.
Bones dried, hope lost, cut off from our parts. Psalm 141:7; Isa 49:14.
1. Our bones – the tribe structure of Israel.
2. Our hope – The Messianic hope.
3. Our parts – the relationship of the tribes to each other.

Vs 12. God will open their graves and raise them up by resurrection into their land. Vs 25; 36:24; Isa 26:19; Hos 13:14. National resurrection.

Vs 13. Resurrection out of their graveyards in the nations.

Vs 14. God will put His Spirit (cf. Vs 9, the breath) into them and will bring them into their own land and they shall know the Lord has done it. 36:27.

Thus the whole vision is symbolic of the spiritual condition of death on the Nation, and their scattered condition in Assyrian and Babylonian Captivity. The situation looks helpless and hopeless. But God has given His prophetic word and the Spirit and by these the nation would experience spiritual resurrection and a coming together into the land.

3.   THE VISION OF THE TWO STICKS – vs 15-17.

Vs 15.   The Word of the Lord.

Vs 16.   Ezekiel told to take two sticks and write on them.
1. For JUDAH and his companions, i.e. Benjamin, Levi and Judah. The other tribes with the House of Judah. Thus the SCEPTRE House.
2. For JOSEPH or Ephraim (cf. Jeremiah 31:9), and his companions, or tribes. The House of Israel. The BIRTHRIGHT House, cf. Gen 48-49.
Num 17:2; 2 Chronicles 11:12, 13, 16; 15:9; 30:11, 18.

Vs 17.   Join the sticks together and they become ONE in Ezekiel's hand. Vs 22, 24.

4.   THE TWO STICKS INTERPRETED – vs 18-19.

Vs 18.   The children of Israel will ask what is meant by the two sticks. 12:9; 24:19.

Vs 19.   The vision interpreted.
1. The stick of Joseph, Ephraim and his tribes.
2. The stick of Judah and his tribes.
Both of the sticks of the two houses to be one in the hand of the Son of Man. Vs 16, 17; Zech 10:6.
Certainly not Ezekiel but THE Son of Man, Jesus Christ Himself. John 11:47-52; Gather together in ONE ..... John 17. That all may be ONE ......

5.   MESSIANIC PROPHECIES OF THE TWO STICKS – vs 20-28.

Vs 20.   The two sticks written on to be before the eyes of the captives. 12:3.

Vs 21.   God will take the children of Israel from the various countries in which they are scattered and He will gather them back to their own land. 36:24.

Vs 22.   God will bring about a UNITED NATION in due time.

1. ONE NATION in Israel.
2. ONE KING over them. Never been since the times of Saul, David and Solomon.
3. No more two nations, or division into the two kingdoms anymore. 34:22; Isa 11:13; Jeremiah 3:18; Hos 1:11; John 10:16.

Vs 23.
4. Israel no more to defile themselves with idols or detestable Things (36:25) or transgressions.
5. God will save, cleanse them and be their God and they shall be His people. Promises of Messiah and New Covenant. 36:28; Jer 31:31-34; Heb 8:10.

Vs 24.
6. DAVID to be King over them.
7. To have ONE SHEPHERD over them. Then Israel would walk in God's statutes and judgments and do them. Isa 40:11; Jer 23:5; Lk 1:32; John 10:16; Ezek 36:27.

Thus David – type of Messiah, as the Son of David, and Shepherd-King. The ONE Shepherd (as David) would be the Messiah. Psalm 23:1; 80:1-2; 1 Pet 5:4; Heb 13:20.

Vs 25. Israel to dwell in the land again and their children to the 3rd and 4th generations, and for ever.
David to be prince over them and Servant. Vs 24; Isa 60:21; Joel 13:20; Amos 9:15; John 12:34.

Vs 26. A COVENANT OF PEACE (Heb 13:20), the NEW Covenant to be made. An everlasting Covenant. The Noahic, Abrahamic, Davidic and New Covenants are everlasting Covenants. The Old or Mosaic Covenant and Palestinian were not everlasting.
All can only be "everlasting" in and through the NEW Covenant. Psalm 89:3; Isa 55:3; Jeremiah 32:40; Ezekiel 36:10.

Vs 27. The Lord will plant HIS TABERNACLE amongst them and be their God and they shall be His people.
Ultimately can only be in the TABERNACLE OF GOD with men (Rev 21:1-8), and the New Covenant promises. Typically, in the Temple of Solomon, Tabernacles of Moses and David, and/or the restored Temple under Zerubbabel. 11:20; John 1:14-18. The Lord Jesus is THE Tabernacle and THE Temple of God.

Vs 28. The heathen will know that God sanctified (set apart) Israel when His Sanctuary is in the midst of them for evermore. 36:23; 20:12.

The burden of this prophecy can only be when the Lord Jesus comes and unites the TRUE Israel of God as ONE Nation under God, as the One King and One Shepherd (The Shepherd-King).

The Covenant of Peace is the Everlasting Covenant, the New Covenant, and eternal peace was made through the blood of the Cross (Col 1:20; Mt 26:26-28). The Sanctuary or Tabernacle is the City of God in which are the names of the 12 Tribes of Israel in the gates. Rev 21:12.

The Nation of Israel has never been one nation under one king since the times of Saul, David and Solomon, and since the division of the nation into two Houses, two Nations and two Kingdoms.

This united nation can only be under the Davidic King, the LORD JESUS CHRIST, by the blood of the NEW Covenant. It can only be realised in the NEW COVENANT ISRAEL, the true Israel of God who accept the new covenant. Gal 6:16; Rom 9:1-9; Rom 11; Ephesians 2:12-22.

United Nation — Divided Kingdom — House of Israel (Birthright) / House of Judah (Sceptre) — One King, One Nation, One Kingdom, One Shepherd

2000 years   1000 years

EZEKIEL CHAPTER THIRTY-EIGHT

1. **THE NORTHERN ARMIES** – vs 1-7.

Note: Most expositors recognise that Ezekiel 38-39 chapters are speaking of the Latter Day battle between Israel and some Northern Confederacy and in Palestine and that the end result is Divine intervention in behalf of Israel and judgment on the armies of the north. These Northern armies have been interpreted by some to be Russia and its allied armies. Evidence certainly points to the veracity of this proposition, as the following comments show.

Vs 1.   The Word of the Lord.

Vs 2.   Ezekiel is to "set his face against" – i.e. that is the prophetic word of judgment. 35:2-3.
1. Gog – Prince, the Chief Prince,   cf.   Pencils of identification of Gog and Magog.
2. Land of Magog = the Land.
3. Meshech – Tubal = Moscow and Tobolsk.   Cities,   cf. 27:13; 32:6. Gen 10:4.
Uncircumcised nations.   Thus the Prince, the Land and the People here,   cf.   39:1;   Rev 20:8. Tobolsk – Capitol of early Province. Japhetic races here. Gen 10:4.

Vs 3.   God is "against" this nation.   Vs 1, 2, 3. Cf.   Rom 8:31. If God is "against" us, who could be for us? God is against Communist Russia because Communist Russia is against God and His people.

Vs 4.   Northern armies to be brought forth, to turn back, hooks in their jaws, and brought forth. Great Cavalry. Army, men and horses, cf. Vs 9.
Clothed with all sorts of armour (weapons and defence), bucklers, shields and swords, and a great company.
Scofield says "That the primary reference is to the NORTHERN (European) powers, headed by Russia, all agree. The whole passage should be read in connection with Zech 12:1-4; 14:1-9; Mt 24:14-30; 19:17-21. 'Gog' is the 'Prince' and 'Magog' is the 'land' (his land). The reference to Meshech and Tubal (Moscow and Tobolsk) is a clear mark of identification.
Russia and Northern European powers have been the latest persecutors of dispersed Israel, and it is congruous both with

Divine justice and with the Covenants (eg, Gen 15:18; Deut 30:3) that destruction should fall at the climax of the last mad attempt to exterminate the remnant of Israel in Jerusalem.

The whole prophecy belongs to the yet future 'Day of Jehovah' (Isa 2:10-22; Rev 19:11-21;) and the battle of Armageddon (Rev 16:14; 19:19), but also includes the final revolt of the nations at the close of the kingdom age (Rev 20:7-9)."

While the writer here does not fully agree with the above, yet it does agree with the general identification of the Northern powers.

The last War (WW II) showed that Russia had the greatest Cavalry in the whole world. Though snow bound, horses were able to get through. Polish desolations. Since 1934 Russia has 70% of world's horses. Though horses dying out fast around the world, as machines take over, yet Russia increases hers. A great military leader says "The next war may be with horses, and old primitive types of weapons because of the 'death ray' paralysing tanks and other machines of any sort.

Vs 5.   Confederate nations.
    1.   Persia (Modern day Iran – oil nation).
    2.   Ethiopia (Line of Ham).
    3.   Libya (Phut)
Vs 6.   4.   Gomer and all his bands (Line of Japheth). (Some suggest Germany).
    5.   Togomarh of the North quarters and all his bands – 27:14. Many peoples with the Northern armies. Some suggest Turkey/Armenia.

NORTH = symbol of direction of judgment. Thus Assyria, Northern armies; then Babylon, Northern armies, then Syria, the King of the North (Dan 11), and then today, Russia, the northern Kingdom. Judgment from the North (Jeremiah 1).

Note Gen 10 and the origin of these nations, from Shem, Ham and Japheth.
    A.   Vs 2. The 3 sons of Noah.
    B.   Vs 2-5. Gog and Magog, Tubal and Togamarh, of Japheth.
    C.   Vs 6-20. Cush, Canaan, Nimrod and Babel, Nineveh and Asshur – Line of Ham.
    D.   Vs 21-32. Eber – Gen 11:10-32, unto Abraham – Shemite nations.
    E. Vs 15-20. The Canaanite tongues, families and nations. Basically the same nations today, under different names,

and different portions of land, yet basically the same.

Vs 7.   Preparation for Northern armies and others assembled with them, to be a guard unto them.

2.   **THE TIME ELEMENT – THE LATTER DAYS** – vs 8-13

Vs 8.   The Time Element – to be visited in the Latter Years, cf. Isa 29:6.
Note: - Vs 8. In the latter years.
Vs 8. After many days, ie, after many years.
Vs 16. In the latter days.
Vs 17. In those days.
Cf.   Deut 4:30; Gen 49:1; Jeremiah 23:20; Heb 1:1; Joel 2:28-32: Acts 2:17; Isa 2:1-2; 2 Pet 3:1-3; 2 Tim 3:1-6. The Last Days, since the cross. The time element places this battle in the latter days, the times of Messiah's age, and at the close of it.

To come into the land brought back from the sword – gathered out of many people – ie., the mountains of Israel, ie, Palestine. Been wasted, now brought forth out of the nations and the people dwelling carelessly (ie confidently) and safely.

Vs 9.   To ascend and come like a storm, like a cloud to cover the land, all the bands and people with them. Cf. Isa 28:2; Jeremiah 4:13, cf. Notes on vs 15-16 of this chapter also.

Vs 10.   To ascend and come like a storm. The same time that Russia has this THOUGHT come to mind and CONCEIVES this mischievous purpose (Marginal).

Vs 11.   The THOUGHT (seed-sperm), conception (union with egg), and spoken word (birth) all combined here, cf. John 13:2, 27; Luke 22:3; Acts 5:3-4; Jas 1:13-15; Psalm 7:14; Job 15:35.
Thus the Satanic thought conceives in the heart of the Northern armies and is birthed by the mouth. Word spoken is a thought born!
The declaration is to go up to the land of unwalled villages, no bars, no gates, dwelling safely (ie. Confidently). Jeremiah 49:31; Ezekiel 38:8.
The PURPOSE is to take a spoil and prey, to exploit places once desolate and now inhabited by the people (Jewry) gather out of the nations, with cattle and goods, dwelling in the NAVEL (Margin) of the land. Ezekiel 29:19.

163

What more suitable description of the JEWISH people than that "gathered out of the nations" as in vs 12, 8?

Scattered amongst the nations since AD 70 and now since 1914-17 returning to the land and making the desolate places inhabited and fruitful. The SIGN of the House of Judah is certainly inescapable. Not applicable to any other nation in the world but the State of Israel, cf. Lk 19:41-44; 21:20-24. Until the Times of the Gentiles be fulfilled. Note also Zech 12:1-13; Jerusalem to be a burdensome stone and cup of poison to whoever touches it, and whoever drinks of it!

Vs 13. Challenge of the Lions and others.
      1. Sheba – 27:22; Gen 10:7; 1 Kgs 10:1-2; Psa 72:10; Isa 60:6.
      2. Dedan – 27:15; Gen 10:7. Both of these are Hamite races.
      3. Merchants of Tarshish – 27:12; Gen 10:4; 2 Chronicles 20:36. Japheth race and name.
      4. The young Lions thereof – 19:2-3, 5, 6.
         Various nations used the symbol of the Lion, ie. Assyria, Babylon, and now today the British Commonwealth of Nations.
         Films – The Old Lion and her pride of young lions.

Thus there will be challenge of some nations to the Northern armies as to the motive for coming down on Palestine, taking a spoil of silver, gold and goods. Great wealth. Spain and/or Britain formerly known as Tarshish. Ezekiel 38:13; Gen 10:4-5. Tarshish of Noah.
Had a great navy. 1 Kgs 10:22; 22:48.
Great trade by sea. Ezekiel 27:12. Isa 60:9. The ships of Tarshish to bring the Jews to the land. British ships returned Jews to Palestine in 1917.
Jonah 1:1-6. Jonah fled there, far from Palestine. Isa 23:24; 2:16; Psalm 48; Psalm 32. The ships and kingdom of Tarshish.

3. **GOD INTERVENES IN BEHALF OF HIS PEOPLE** – vs 14-23.

Vs 14. God says that they will know that day when Israel dwells safely (vs 8, 11), that is, confidently, that no war can tough them without them winning.

164

Vs 15. Northern armies come down on Palestine when least expected. Out of the NORTH parts with many people, all upon HORSES a great company and mighty army.
Russia has the greatest Cavalry in the world! Horses can go where no armoured warfare can go, cf. Vs 6, 9, 8.

Vs 16. Northern armies comes against God's people of Israel like a cloud covering the land, in the Latter Days.

Thus coming against: 1). The Land, vs 8-13.
2) The People of the Land of Israel –
Vs 14-16.
God will bring them against His land. What for? That the heathen nations will recognise God's sovereignty in the earth and in relation to His people, cf. Rev 17:17. God is sovereign and can put it into the hearts of men and nations to do His will, even though they are doing Satan's will, they think! For the purpose of judgment on them, even as to Babylon, etc. God uses nations against nations.

Vs 17. God foretold His servants the prophets of Israel in past days and many years that He would bring the Northern armies against His people.
Note: Deut 28; Dan 11:36-45.

Vs 18. God's fury to come up in His face at the time they come against the land of Israel.

Vs 19. God's fury, jealousy and fiery wrath causes Him to speak. He is a jealous God, and jealous for His people and His land, cf. 36:5, 6; Psalm 89:46.
In that day there is to be "a great shaking" in the land of Israel.

Vs 20. Fishes/fowls/beasts/creeping things/men – all to SHAKE at God's Presence. Mountains/hills/towers/walls to fall to the ground.
Supernatural intervention here. Hos 4:3; Jer 4:24.
Cf. Isa 64:1-3. The Presence of God makes people and nations tremble.
Ex 19. Presence of God on Mt Sinai shook it. Heb 12:18-21; Judges 5:4-5.

Vs 21. God will call A SWORD against the Northern armies throughout all His mountains – combat of soldiers.

Cf. Jer 25:31-33; 24:10; Ezek 14:17, 21: Psa 105:16; Judges 7:22; 1 Sam 14:20; Ezek 5:17.

Vs 22. God will plead with Gog with pestilence and blood, overflowing rain, great hailstones, fire and brimstone, cf. Isa 66:16; Jeremiah 25:31.
This could be either Atomic or Hydrogen warfare which causes the same phenomena, as in the WW II in Japan, or else supernatural from heaven itself as in Israel's previous history.
Cf. 1. Hailstones – 5:17; Josh 10:11 (Adonizedec); Rev 16:21; Rev 11.19.
2. Fire and Brimstone – Gen 18-19, Sodom and Gomorrah destroyed by such. Psalm 11; Isa 30:30.

Vs 23. God to be magnified (made great) and sanctified (set apart) and be known (recognised) in the eyes of MANY NATIONS, cf. 36:23; 37:28.

Note: - The Great Shaking in the prophets and its progression.
1. Shake the EARTH – Isa 2:10-22.
2. Shake the land of ISRAEL – Ezekiel 38:19-20.
3. Shake the POWERS OF HEAVEN, heavenly bodies and Satanic powers – Mt 24:29; Rev 6:12-14.
4. Shake the heaven and the earth. Hag 2:6-7, 21. Shake the sea, dry land, and ALL NATIONS.
5. Shake EVERYTHING that can be shaken. Heb 12:26-29.

EZEKIEL CHAPTER THIRTY-NINE

1. **NORTHERN ARMIES TO BE JUDGED BY GOD** – Vs 1-7.

Vs 1.   God is against Gog, cf. 38:2-3. Because Gog is against God!
        Communist Russia is anti-God, and anti-Christ. The
        Communist salute is the 'clenched fist raised toward heaven
        in defiance of God'. Godless leaders and rulers. Do not
        believe in God. They hate God and all religion, calling it the
        'opium of the masses.'
        They have blasphemous pictures of the Godhead as two old
        men, and the Holy Spirit as an old hen, plucked.
        They have pictures of the Lord's table, drunken Christ and
        apostles, and also of the cross, and the apostles eating His
        flesh and drinking His blood.
        They have destroyed Bibles, Churches, religion of all sorts.
        The puppet Church preaches what the rulers want taught. It is
        a cover up. All act on the "Trojan horse" principle.
        Millions of Christians have been martyred and slaughtered in
        Siberia, etc.. Millions tortured by 'brain-washing'. Desire to
        get rid of all concepts of God and Christ in the earth and
        destroy the Church. Numerous ministers infiltrate the Church
        to destroy and corrupt it from within with Communistic ideas.
        The 'Red spirit' and philosophy has devoured two-thirds of
        the earth in its reign in the last 50 years or more.

Vs 2.   God will turn the Northern armies back and leave but the
        sixth part of them. Margin = "Strike thee through with six
        plagues; or draw thee back with an hook of six teeth". 38:4.
        To come from the north parts (or sides of the north) against
        the mountains of Israel, cf. 38:15.

Vs 3.   Bow and arrows to be smitten out of their hands by the Lord,
        leave them powerless and weaponless, and defenceless.

Vs 4.   To fall on the mountains of Israel and be given to the birds
        and beasts to be devoured. As war carnage, so do the birds
        and beasts feed on the dead bodies, cf. 38:21; 33:27; Rev
        19:17-18.

Vs 5.   To fall in the open field. God has spoken it.

Vs 6.   God will send a fire on Magog and on those that dwell
        carelessly (confidently) in the ISLES. Know that God is the
        Lord, ie. His sovereignty.

Fire = judgment. Amos 1:4; Psalm 72:10.
The isles – those who dwell in the islands.

Vs 7.   God's holy Name to be known to His people Israel. God's Name not to be polluted. The heathen to know the Lord, the Holy One of Israel.
Note: - His power and Name was known in the plagues on Pharaoh and Egypt in the great deliverance in the Exodus. So here. On the Northern armies.
Ex 3:14-15; Lev 18:21; Ex 9:13-16; 6:1-8; Ezek 39:22; 38:16.

2.   **CLEANSING THE LAND OF WEAPONS** – vs 8-10.

Vs 8.   The day is come and the work is done, cf. Rev 16:17; 21:6. God counts things not done as done when He has spoken it.

Vs 9.   The dwellers in the cities of Israel to burn the weapons of war, enough for 7 years.

Vs 10.   No need to cut down trees as enough weapons for burning the fire. To spoil and rob those that spoiled and robbed them. Isa 14:2.

3.   **CLEANSING THE LAND OF BONES** – vs 11-16.

Vs 11.   Gog and armies to be buried in Israel graves and the valley shall be called "The Valley of the Multitude of Gog." Title of their graveyard!

Vs 12.   Seven months to cleanse the land of burial of the bodies, such as vast host of the dead, cf. Deut 21:23.

Vs 13.   All the people to bury them, cf. 28:22.

Vs 14.   Men continually employed to cleanse the land of the dead bodies over the 7 months, cf. Vs 12.

Vs 15.   A sign to be set up by any bones so that the buriers can bury them.
OT Law of ceremonial defilement to touch the bodies of the dead, or bones, etc. Num 19.

Vs 16.   The city to be called "The multitude" (Margin). Cleanse the land of such. Note the word "cleanse" in vs 12, 14, 16.

4.   THE TABLE OF THE LORD'S SACRIFICE – vs 17-22.

Vs 17.   God tells Ezekiel to call the birds and beasts to assemble and gather to his table of sacrifice of blood and flesh on the mountains of Israel, cf. Vs 4; Rev 19:18.

Vs 18.   To eat the flesh and drink the blood of Princes of the earth, as symbolised under these animals here. Deut 32:14; Psalm 22:12.

Vs 19.   Eat and drink until full and drunken – God's sacrifice. Note the word "sacrifice" in vs 17, 17, 19.

Vs 20.   Filled at MY TABLE with horses and chariots, and men of war. Psalm 76:6; Ezekiel 38:4; Rev 19:18.

Vs 21.   God's glory and hand in judgment will be seen among the heathen. 38:16, 23; Ex 7:4.
          Note: 1.   My sacrifice, vs 19.
                  2.   My table, vs 20.
                  3.   My glory, vs 21.
                  4.   My judgment, vs 21.
                  5.   My hand, vs 21.

Vs 22.   House of Israel to know the Lord from that day forward, vs 7, 28. Interesting to note the increase of vultures in the Middle East in recent years!

5.   THE NATIONS TO SEE GOD'S MERCY ON ISRAEL – vs 23-29

Vs 23.   Heathen will then recognise that God let Israel go to captivity for their iniquities and trespasses. God's face hidden from them and given over to the hands and the sword of their enemies. 36:18-20; Deut 31:17; Isa 59:2; Lev 26:25.

Vs 24.   God judged them according to their uncleanness and transgressions. 36:19.

Vs 25.   Captivity of Jacob to be turned and mercy to be upon the whole House of Israel. God is here jealous for His holy Name. 20:40; 34:13; 36:24; Jeremiah 30:3, 18; Hos 1:11.

Vs 26.   They will have borne their shame and trespass. Dan 9:16; Lev 26:5, 6.

Vs 27. This is to happen when God brings them from the people out of the enemies' land and makes them dwell safely in their own land, unafraid.
God will be sanctified in the eyes of many nations, cf. 28:25-26; 36:23-24; 38:16.

Vs 28. To know the Lod did it, cf. Vs 22; 34:30.

Vs 29. God no longer to hide His face from them but give them an OUTPOURING OF THE SPIRIT on the House of Israel.
Cf. Isa 54:8; Joel 2:28; Zech 12:10; Acts 2:17.

NOTE: Worthy to note that the Jew has suffering mercilessly at the hands of its enemies ever since AD 34 and onwards. But their history over these centuries shows that WAR and/or OUTPOURING of the Spirit are connected.

1. AD 34. Outpouring of the Spirit and first advent of Messiah rejected, and then 40 years later, AD 70. War and siege and destruction of Jerusalem and Temple.
2. Then 1906 Outpouring of the Spirit, and Palestine given to the Jew as home land after 1914-17 WW I. By the British League of Nations.
3. Then 1939-45 WW II, and then 1948 Outpouring of the Spirit, and also Feast of Trumpets and declaration of the Independent State of Israel in 1948. House of Judah. United Nations.
4. Then the 1967 War for 6 days, 50 years (Jubilee) after 1917, and June (Pentecost Feast, and War), and victory. Charismatic movement.
5. Ezekiel 38-39 seems to point to another World War (perhaps WW III), and then closes with an Outpouring of the Spirit on Israel, cf. Joel 2 also. Both Ezekiel and Joel show Northern armies and an Outpouring of the Spirit.
Read also Zech 12-13-14 too as we have Jerusalem in Siege added to an Outpouring of the Spirit and eyes opened. Save Tents of Judah first, opened eyes on them, outpoured Spirit, mourning for only Son, bitterness, and fountain opened. Zech 13:1. Rom 9-10-11. Grafted in again if not abide in unbelief.
Thus they shall:
   1. Know the Lord.
   2. Not hide His face from them any more
   3. Have mercy on them
   4. Gathered them together
   5. Judgment by war

6. Outpoured Spirit of grace and supplication on them.
7. Eyes opened, mourning for the Only Son and then
8. The cleansing fountain of Calvary opened to them.

No doubt this Word War will end with a desire to have a ONE WORLD GOVERNMENT to end all wars. This will no doubt precede the rise of the Antichrist and his World Government. Thus the WHITE horse and the RED horse (Revival and War) ride forth together as the Seals are opened. Rev 6. Jeremiah 25.
Thus Ezekiel and Joel speak of the Northern armies, and close with an Outpouring of the Spirit. Ezekiel 38:15-16; 39:29; Joel 12:20, 28-32; Zech 12:1-14 should be studied together.

AD34

Hide face

Outpoured
Spirit

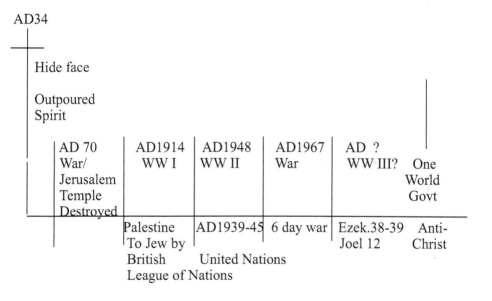

AD 70	AD1914	AD1948	AD1967	AD ?
War/	WW I	WW II	War	WW III? One
Jerusalem				World
Temple				Govt
Destroyed				
	Palestine	AD1939-45	6 day war	Ezek.38-39 Anti-
	To Jew by			Joel 12 Christ
	British	United Nations		
	League of Nations			

| Then 7 years/ | 3 ½ years | Second Advent | Millennium |
| 7 months | | Armageddon | 1000 years |

ADDITIONAL NOTES:

Ezek 38-39. Gog and Magog. TIME:

1. Not at the end of the Millennium.
    a. Here it is certain nations especially from the North. 38:15; 39:2.
    b. There it is all the wicked from the four quarters of the earth.

    a. To take a spoil, silver, gold, cattle and goods.
    b. None of this in the 1000 years.

    a. They will be given to ravenous birds, eating their flesh and drinking their blood. 39:13-20.
    b. These are cast into the Lake of Fire, in their resurrection bodies of damnation.

    a. Their bodies buried and weapons burnt.
    b. Their bodies cast into the Lake of Fire.

2. Not at the end of the Great Tribulation.
    a. That is the Battle of Armageddon.
    b. This is certain nations against Israel.

    a. Christ and His armies against Antichrist and his armies.
    b. This is against Israel.

    a. The ungodly are destroyed by the Word of God, the glory of God revealed. 2 Thess 1:7-10.
    b. Here by brimstone and with blood, overflowing rain, great hailstones, fire and brimstone. 38:21-22.

3. Before the Great Tribulation – in the Last Days. W.W. Patterson.

    1. Distinction between the use of the Name.
        A. Gog and Magog. The origin of the name. Gen 10-11. Japhetic race.
        B. The Northern armies – Russia against Palestine. Prince of Rosh. Ezekiel 38-39.
        C. Seems also applicable to Armageddon at the second advent. Rev 16:12-16; 19:11-21. Christ and Antichrist.
        D. Becomes a representative name for the wicked dead under Prince of the North, Satan, and his hosts. Rev 20:11-15.

172

2.   <u>Time Element Involved.</u>
   A. Not Armageddon at the second advent, although the language is similar and used of both battles. History repeats itself in the prophet's language. Rev 19.
   B. Not after the Millennium, or 1000 years, but used there as a representative name for all the wicked (C.J. McKight suggests it takes place at the close of the Millennium).
   C. It is a World War as the context proves. God uses nations to punish nations.
   D. It must be before Rev 13 and Dan 7 is manifest, for only the feet of the Bear nation remains in the World Kingdom of the Antichrist.
   E. Never been another World Kingdom until Rev 12-13 comes to fulfilment.
   F. The 7 'Heads' of world kingdoms all touch Judah/Israel and/or Jerusalem. It seems then that this is perhaps another or the next (?) World War, and afterwards the One World Government of Antichrist will arise out of it.
   It is in the "latter years" and "latter days" – hence anytime from this period 1980 onwards.

3.   <u>The Cycle of the House of Judah.</u>

3 ½ years	2000 years	3 ½ years	1000 years
Christ	Church Age	Antichrist	Kingdom
Jerusalem		Jerusalem	
Returned from		Return National	
Babylonian Captivity		Captivity	
For Temple		Temple (?)	
First Coming		Second Coming	
Outpouring		Outpouring	

EZEKIEL'S VISION OF THE TEMPLE

INTRODUCTION:

Chapters 40-48 now give a description of A TEMPLE. Interesting to note that Ezekiel's prophecy opens and closes with the vision of the Temple. From the Old Temple the glory departs and it is seen coming into a New Temple. The question is whether this vision is of a material and literal rebuilt Temple, in this age, or a future Millennial Age, or whether it is symbolic of the Church. The following deductions lead us to believe that this Temple is a symbolical Temple and has many lessons for the Church in the present time, and no doubt flows over into eternal truth. By going through the 'process of elimination' we determine whether this speaks of a material or spiritual Temple.

1.   Temples or Habitations in Scripture.
   1. The Tabernacle in Eden. Gen 3.
   2. The Tabernacle of Moses. Ex 25-40.
   3. The Tabernacle of David. 1 Chronicles 15-17.
   4. The Temple of Solomon. 2 Chronicles 1-5.
   5. The Restored Temple under Zerubbabel. Dan 9:24-27.
   6. Herod's Temple or Restored Temple beautified. John 2:18-20.
   7. The Temple of Christ's Body. John 2:20-21.
   8. The Church or the believer as the Temple of God. 1 Cor 3:16; Ephesians 2:20-22.
   9. The Temple to be measured. Rev 11:1-2.
   10. The Temple in heaven. Rev 11:19; Heb 9: Rev 15.
   11. The Temple of Ezekiel's vision. Ezekiel 40-48.
   Each were the habitation of God. The O.T. habitations (material) point to the spiritual.

   Note – It should be remembered that the material habitations of God in the O.T. were symbolic and pointed to the transfer over in N.T. times to the spiritual Temple of Christ and His Church. The cross brings the change from the material to the spiritual.

2.   The Time Element – When?
   1. Not a formerly built Temple.
   2. Not a latterly built Temple under the remnant from Babylon.
   3. Not Herod's Temple.
   4. Jews have had no Temple since AD 70.
   5. Therefore the Temple of Ezekiel must be:
      A. A future material Temple, or a
      B. Spiritual and symbolical Temple, either in
         1. This present age, or
         2. The Millennial age, as such can never be in the Eternal age, for the Lord God and the Lamb are

175

the Temple thereof in the City of God.　Rev 21:22.

A consideration of time element and the context shows that the Temple can only be symbolical and present spiritual truths for the Church in this age.

3.　Three-stage Vision of the Temple.
　1.　Vision – The Cherubim and the glory of the Lord.　Ezekiel 1-3 chapters.
　2.　The Glory of the Lord leaves the material Temple.　Ezekiel 8-11.
　　A.　Image worship by the people.
　　B.　Animal worship by the elders.
　　C.　Sex worship by the women.
　　D.　Sun worship by the priesthood.
　　These corruptions caused the Lord God to leave the Temple to desolation.
　3.　Vision – The NEW Temple and the Glory of God returns.　Ezekiel 40-48;　43:1-3.
　　Ezekiel 40-48 gives a vision of a Temple.　The description of the Land, the Tribal inheritances, the City and the Sanctuary present great difficulties if taken as a material Temple to be built at some future date, such as in the Millennium.　We consider these major difficulties.

4.　Difficulties in a Material Temple, Geographically, Materially, Theologically.

　1.　The Land Area for the 12 Tribes.
　　From Hamath in the north to Kadesh in the south.　The grant of land God gave to Abraham in Gen 15:18.　Boundaries of the land given the same under Moses, unless geographical changes are made.　The distribution of the land in equal portions among the 12 tribes, without respect of numbers, and the parallel sections running from east to west present problems.　The separate tribe existence limits all to a few (about 4-5) miles territory, and 7 tribes were to the north of the south area and 5 tribes to the south. Not much land inheritance if geographically to be so.

　2.　The Sacred Land Area.
　　The Sacred Oblation for the Temple, the Priests and the Levites covers a vast land area.　42:15-20;　45:2;　48:20.　Covers the following area:　It equals 25,000 x 25,000 = (4 square) miles, or about 47-50 sq. miles.　About 20 sq. miles of this is reserved for the priesthood, and again, about 20 square miles of this is also reserved for the Levites.　45:3-4;　48:10;　45:5;　48:13.

3. The Temple Area.
42:15-20; 45:2. Temple area covers all of Ancient Jerusalem; about 3 ½ miles square. Thus about 6 times as large as the circuit of the wall enclosing the old or former Temple and it is also larger than the ancient city of Jerusalem. The Temple therefore is as large as the whole of old Jerusalem. 45:6; 48:15-19. The new Temple is 500 reeds (about 10 miles) away north of 'The City' and about 15 miles from the centre of it, yet the Temple AND the City were always joined in Scripture, the Temple being inside the City. The new Temple would not be on Mt Moriah or Mt Zion either.

4. The City Area,
The city area has between 3-4000 sq. miles, including the Sacred area for the Temple, Priests and Levites and the Prince. This is as large as the whole frame of the land between Jordan and the Mediterranean Sea. The city area reaches to the Dead Sea. 47:19.

5. The River from the Temple.
47:1-12. Problem of having a literal river flowing from literal temple by literal or material altar into the Dead Sea healing their waters. The river parts into two streams and becomes unfordable within 4000 cubits.

6. Materials for the Temple.
In contrast to the Tabernacle of Moses and Temple of Solomon, there is practically nothing mentioned concerning materials. So many chapters, and yet no mention of the materials for the city or Temple.

7. The Mosaic Covenant.
The greatest difficulty of all concerning the VISION is the fact of the RESTORATION of the MOSAIC COVENANT economy, especially in the light of the NEW COVENANT economy as set forth especially in the Book of Hebrews.
We note a list of Old Covenant ceremonials mentioned in the vision.
A. The Temple
Ezekiel, as also Isaiah, points to Christ being a "little Sanctuary" to His people wherever they be scattered. Ezekiel 11:16; Isa 8:14-18; Rev 21:22. The Lord God and the Lamb are the Temple eternally.
Father, Son and Holy Spirit set their seal to the rejection of a material Temple in the Gospels and Acts. Then why go back to the shadow rejected when the real substance is in HIM? Mt 21:12-14; 23:38; 24:1; 27:51; Acts 2:1-4; Isa 66:1-4.

177

B. The Priesthood.
The Melchizedek Priesthood forever abolishes the Aaronic Priesthood and the Levitical system. All believers are now priests unto God. Rev 1:6; 5:9-10; 1 Pet 2:5-9.

C. The Altars.
The Cross of Jesus forever cancelled out all O.T. sacrificial and incense altars made of wood, brass or gold.

D. The Sacrifice and Oblation.
Heb 9-10 show that Christ's one and once-for-all sacrifice and oblation caused all animal sacrifice and oblation to cease, cf. Dan 9:24-27. Neither will it suffice to say that sacrifices will not be offered for sin but only as a "memorial" of Calvary, as the bread and wine of the communion table is a "memorial" of His death and resurrection. The body and blood of Jesus forever repudiates animal body and blood. To have any other is to deny the all-sufficient sacrifice of Christ. "He who sacrificed before confessed Christ, but he who sacrifices now solemnly denies Him."

E. The Feasts of the Lord.
All Feast Days were fulfilled in Christ. He is our Passover, He sends the Holy Spirit and fulfils Pentecost. Hebrews shows that He also fulfilled the Day of Atonement ceremonies.

F. The Sabbaths and New Moons.
The Sabbath will never be the seal of the New Covenant, for it was that of the Old Covenant. Sabbaths, New Moons and other ordinances were nailed to the Cross, and not to be un-nailed again in the future. Col 2:14-17; Heb 8-9-10. We are not to go back to the beggarly elements of the Law again.

G. The Shekinah Glory.
No mention of the Ark, but the Glory in this Temple. The Glory never ever returned even to the material rebuilt Temple under Ezra and Nehemiah, nor to Herod's Temple. It has never returned to a material or literal Temple since it left Solomon's in the time of Ezekiel's vision. The Glory now is 'Christ in you'. Col 1:27.

H. The Mosaic Covenant.
The New Covenant totally and eternally dis-annulled the Old Covenant and the Mosaic system. Jeremiah 31:31-34; Heb 8;

178

2 Cor 3. God does not 'backslide' to the other side of the Cross to reinstate the Old and abolished Covenant.

I. Worship.
John 4:20-26. Jesus said that worship must be "in spirit and in truth" to be accepted of the Father now, not any formalism or ceremonialism. Rev 11:8.

J. No Mention and Mention.
Following is a list of the things specifically mentioned and those not mentioned as in former Temple. These discrepancies make it difficult to accept a material Temple because of their importance to the former.

No Mention	Mentioned
1. Ark of the Covenant	- Jeremiah 3:14-15 – Ark not to be remembered.
2. Pot of Manna	- Jesus is our Manna
3. Aaron's Rod that budded	-
4. Tables of the Law	-
5. Cherubim and Mercy Seat	-
6. Golden candlestick	-
7. Tables and Shewbread	-
8. Altar of Incense	-
9. Veil on Holy of Holies	- Most Holy Place
10. High Priest	- Zadok Priesthood and the Levites
11. Evening Sacrifices	- Burnt, Meal, Drink, Sin, Peace, Trespass
12. Feast of Pentecost	- Passover and Tabernacles
	- The Glory of God.

SUMMARY:
Thus to have all these things in a literal or material Temple, rebuilt now or in the Millennium is to do violence to the teaching and revelation of the N.T. and to insult the work of the cross of Calvary.

The N.T. writers are the infallible interpreters of the O.T. prophets. There is absolutely no mention in the N.T. by the writers of a return to the Old Mosaic economy. Rather, they all see the New Covenant as the fulfilment and abolishment of it. Therefore we cannot use the O.T. to interpret the N.T., since the cross. The N.T. must now interpret the O.T. through the cross. The N.T. is the "time of reformation" (Heb 9:10).

So much of the Book of Ezekiel is in the symbolic manner of communication of spiritual truth.

The things seen are temporal; the things which are not seen are eternal. First the natural, then the spiritual. 2 Cor 3:18; 1 Cor 15:46-47.

It is in the light of thee things that the following chapters on the Temple are used to set forth symbolised truth.

One other of these keys to understanding Ezekiel's Temple is understanding of Solomon's Temple for much is a repeat of things from there.

(Refer to "The Temple of Solomon" by Kevin J. Conner).

EZEKIEL CHAPTER FORTY

SECTION 3 – THE VISION OF THE TEMPLE – EZEKIEL 40-48.

1. **THE VISION OF THE MAN** – vs 1-5.

Vs 1. Date of the vision. The 25th year of the captivity, the 1st month, and 10th day; 14 years after the City was smitten, on the exact same day. The hand of the Lord was upon Ezekiel and brought him to Jerusalem. 33:21; 1:3.

Vs 2. Visions of God brought him to the land of Israel to a very HIGH MOUNTAIN by which was the frame of A CITY on the south.
   Note: 1. Visions of God
   2. The High Mountain, cf. Is 2:1-5; Rev 21:10; Ezekiel 8:3; Rev 21-22 chapters.
   3. The frame of a city of Jerusalem. Note John's vision of the City of God from the high mountain also.

Vs 3. The Man, whose appearance was like brass, with the line of flax and measuring line in his hand, stood at the Gate. THE MAN, ie. The Lord Jesus Christ. Ezekiel 1:7. The appearance of BRASS – symbolic of judgment. 1 Pet 4:17; Rev 1:10-14; Dan 10:6. The flax and measuring reed – Rev 11:1; 21:15. Divine standard of measure of God.

Vs 4. Ezekiel to behold:
   1. With his eyes – insight, vision.
   2. With his ears – hearing, understanding.
   3. With his heart – perception, all that the Lord will show him. This was the reason why the Lord had brought him here in vision. Then he was to declare the vision to the ones of the House of Israel. 44:5; 43:10.

Vs 5. The Man has the measuring line and reed 6 cubits long by 1 cubit and handbreadth wide. He measured the breadth and height of the House and it was one reed both ways, or, in other words, foursquare! 42:20.
   Zech 1-2 also. The Man with the measuring reed to measure Jerusalem. – All must come up to the Divine standards.

2. **MEASURING THE THRESHOLD, PORCH AND CHAMBERS AND GATE** – vs 6-19.

Note the use of the word "measure" in these chapters. Spiritual lessons that the Church and all pertaining to the Kingdom must "measure up" to the Divine standard and measuring rod of the word of God, cf. Rev 11:1-2; 2 Cor 10:12; Ephesians 4:9-16.
All must measure up to the standard of the Son of God.

Vs 6.　Measurement of the threshold of the gate.
Gate looked towards the east. Stairs up to it. Threshold of the gate was one reed square, thus 4 square. A reed was about 10 or 11' as in Ezekiel's vision.

Vs 7.　Measurement of the chambers.
The chambers were one reed long and one reed broad, thus 4 square also, and between them were 5 cubits.
The threshold of the gate within the porch gate was also one reed square.

Vs 8.　Measurement of the Porch.
The porch of the gate within measured one reed.
The porch of the gate, 8 cubits. The posts of the gate were 2 cubits. The porch of the gate was inward.

Vs 10.　The Measurements of the Chambers of the Gate.
Three chambers on one side and three on the other side. All of one measure, as also the posts on both sides.

Vs 11.　Measurements of the Gate and entry.
The breadth of the entry of the gate was 10 cubits and the length of the gate was 13 cubits.

Vs 12.　Measurement of the Chambers.
The space or limit before the little chambers was one cubits on this side and that side. The little chambers were 6 cubits on both sides.

Vs 13.　Measurement of the Gate from the roof of one little chamber to the roof of another one, was, breadth, 25 cubits, door against door.

Vs 14.　Measurements of the Posts were 6 cubits, even to the post of the Court round about the gate.
Cf.　The Posts (Pillars) of the Court of the Tabernacle of Moses.

Vs 15.　Measurement between Court Gate and Porch of the inner gate, 50 cubits. Outer Gate to inner Gate.

Vs 16. The little chambers had narrow (closed) windows and to the posts and to the arches (galleries or porches) windows were within.
The posts were palm trees ornamentation.
Cf. The windows in Solomon's Temple. 1 Kgs 6:4.

Vs 17. The Outward Court   cf. 1 Kgs 6:5; Rev 11:2.
Cf. Solomon's Temple which had inner and outer courts also.
In this court was a pavement and 30 chambers on the pavement.
Cf. Priestly Chambers of Solomon's Temple, cf. Ezekiel 45:5. Priestly Chambers also.
Note also Nehemiah 13:7-9. Tobiah given a Priestly Chamber in the Court of the restored Temple and Nehemiah cast him and his stuff out, cleansing the chamber.

Vs 18. The pavement by the Gates was the lower pavement.

Vs 19. Measurement of the area between lower gate to inner court was 100 cubits eastward and northward, or, square.

3.   **MEASURING THE NORTH GATES OF THE OUTER & INNER COURTS** – vs 20-23

Vs 20. Outward Court Gate facing the North measured in length and breadth.

Vs 21. It had 3 little chambers on each of the posts and arches, the same measurement as the first gate; 50 cubits long and 25 cubits broad.

Vs 22. Windows, arches, palm trees were the same measure as the East Gate. Went up by 7 steps. Arches before them.

Vs 23. Inner Court Gate over against the North and East Gate, and the Gate to Gate was 100 cubits.

4.   **MEASUREMENT OF THE SOUTH GATE** – vs 24-31.

Vs 24. The South Gate, post and arches measured.

Vs 25. Windows and arches, length of Gate 50 cubits and breadth 25 cubits.

Vs 26. There were 7 steps up to it. Arches there. Palm trees on both sides on the posts.

Vs 27. Gate in the Inner Court towards South and from gate to Gate was 100 cubits.

Vs 28. The South Gate in the inner court measured.

Vs 29. Chambers, posts, arches, windows measured; 50 cubits long, 25 cubits broad.

Vs 30. Arches 25 cubits long, 5 cubits broad, cf vs 21, 25, 33, 36.

Vs 31. Arches facing utter (outer court); palm trees on the posts and 8 steps going up to it.

5. **MEASUREMENT OF THE EAST GATE** – vs 32-34.

Vs 32. Inner Court East Gate measured.

Vs 33. Same as vs 25.

Vs 34. Same as vs 29.

6. **MEASUREMENT OF THE NORTH GATE** – vs 35-38.

Vs 35. North Gate measured.

Vs 36. Cf. Vs 25, 33.

Vs 37. Cf. Vs 29, 34.

Vs 38. Chambers and entries of Gate posts where the Burnt Offering was washed.

7. **THE TABLES FOR THE SACRIFICES** – vs 39-43

Vs 39. In the Gate Porch were two tables on each side, for the Burnt, Sin and Trespass offerings, cf. Lev 4:2-3; 5:6; 6:6; 7:1. Thus four tables in all.

Vs 40. Same again going up to the North Gate – 4 tables.

Vs 41. Eight tables in all for the preparation of the sacrifices.

Vs 42. Tables of hewn stone for the Burnt offering. Measurements 1 ½ cubits, thus foursquare.

Instruments for slaying the animals on the tables, cf. Ex 20:24-26 where altars of stone were made for sacrifice before the Brazen Altar was given.

Vs 43. The hooks (or end-irons, or, two hearth-stones) round about the tables. The flesh offering on the table. The Lord's Table is now out 'altar' prepared. Heb 13:8-13.

8.   CHAMBERS FOR THE SINGERS AND PRIESTS – vs 44-47

Vs 44. Chambers of the SINGERS in the inner court, at the side of the North Gate, prospect towards the South. One at East, prospect towards the North.

Vs 45. Chamber facing South for the Priests; keepers of the Charge of the House, cf Lev 8:35; Num 3:27, 28, 32, 38; 18:5; 1 Chronicles 9:33; 2 Chronicles 13:11; Psalm 134:1.

Vs 46. Chamber facing North for the Priests, keepers of the Charge of the Altar. Num 18:5; and the Sons of Zadok, of the sons of Levi, who come near to the Lord who minister unto Him. Cf 44:15; 43:19; 44:15-16; 1 Kgs 2:35.
The Zadok Priesthood!

Vs 47. Court measured 100 x 100 cubits, or foursquare. Also the Altar before the House.

9.   MEASUREMENT OF PORCH AND POSTS – vs 48-49.

Vs 48. Porch of the House, and posts of the Porch, 5 cubits on each side. Gate breadth was 3 cubits on each side.

Vs 49. Porch length was 20 cubits, and breadth 11 cubits. Steps up to the Porches, and Pillars on each side by the posts. 1 Kgs 6:3; 7:21, cf. Pillars of Jachin and Boaz in Solomon's.

EZEKIEL CHAPTER FORTY-ONE

1. **MEASUREMENT OF THE TEMPLE** – vs 1-5
   Vs 1. Temple Posts measured 6 cubits broad on each side, the breadth of the Tabernacle.

   Vs 2. Temple Door measured 10 cubits, 5 cubits on each side. Length 40 cubits and breadth 20 cubits.

   Vs 3. Temple Door Posts, 2 cubits; the Door, 6 cubits and breadth of Door 7 cubits.

   Vs 4. The Most Holy Place; length 20 cubits and breadth 20 cubits, or foursquare, as in Solomon's Temple. There called the Oracle. 1 Kgs 6:20; 2 Chronicles 3:8; 1 Kgs 6:5-6.

   Vs 5. The Wall of the House was 6 cubits. The side Chambers – breadth 4 cubits, round the House on every side.

2. **MEASUREMENTS OF THE CHAMBERS** – vs 6-11.
   Vs 6. The Chambers on sides of the wall 3 stories high and 30 in order (30 and 3 times), entering into the wall of the House, not holding on to the wall but just joined. The same as the Chambers in Solomon's Temple. 1 Kgs 6:5-6. On supports and not part of the wall.

   Vs 7. The winding of side Chambers upward, increasing lowest chamber to the highest. As in Solomon's Temple. 1 Kgs 6:8.

   Vs 8. Side chambers foundations, full reed of 6 cubits round the house. Chamber foundations 6 cubits apart, cf. 40:5.

   Vs 9. Side chamber wall within 5 cubits, leaving other cubit within.

   Vs 10. Chambers 20 cubits wideness all round the House.

   Vs 11. Doors of the Chambers towards the north and south, one on each side, 5 cubits breadth there.

3. **MEASUREMENTS OF THE BUILDING HOUSE** – vs 12-21.
   Vs 12. Building before the separate place at the West end was 70 cubits broad; wall was 5 cubits thick, and the length 90 cubits.

   Vs 13. The House was 100 long. The separate place and building and walls was 100 cubits long.

Vs 14. Breadth of House and place towards east was 100 cubits.

Vs 15. Length of building over against the separate place behind it, and galleries (ceilings of wood) on each side was 100 cubits, with the inner Temple and Court Porches.

Vs 16. Door posts, narrow windows, galleries round about on their stories, all covered. Thus the 3 stories like unto Noah's Ark also. Gen 6-7-8.

Vs 17. To above the door, even to inner house, and without, and wall within and without by measure. Everything measured up.

Vs 18. Cherubim and Palm trees were the ornamentation of the walls, cf. Solomon's Temple which had the same. 1 Kgs 6:29.

Vs 19. Cherubim each had two faces, of the Lion and Man.
1. Face of the Man – towards a Palm tree.
2. Face of the Lion – towards a Palm tree.
Thus the same all about the House, cf. 1:10.
Lion – symbolic of Christ and His saints.
Man – symbolic of Christ and His saints.
Palm – symbolic of uprightness of Christ and His saints.

Vs 20. Cherubim and Palm trees on wall from ground to above door.

Vs 21. Temple Door Posts squared. Sanctuary face also squared. Both appeared the same.

4. **MEASUREMENTS OF THE ALTAR OF WOOD** - vs 22.
Vs 22. The Altar of Wood. The Table before the Lord. Seems to be the Altar of Incense especially, cf. Ex 30:1; Ezekiel 44:16; Ex 30:8; Mal 1:7. Measured 3 cubits high by 2 cubits length.

5. **MEASUREMENTS OF THE TEMPLE DOORS** – vs 23-26.
Vs 23. Temple and Sanctuary had two doors. Same as Solomon's Temple, cf. 1 Kgs 6:31-35.

Vs 24. Two leaves apiece for each door; two turning leaves.

Vs 25. Doors of the Temple had Cherubim and Palm trees as on Temple walls. Thick planks of face of the Porch outside.

Vs 26. Narrow windows and palm trees on the planks of the Porch. Thus Lions = Kingship. Palms = Righteousness. Psalm 92:10-13.

EZEKIEL CHAPTER FORTY-TWO

1. **THE CHAMBERS FOR THE PRIESTS** – vs 1-12.

   Vs 1.   Brought to the utter court, and into chamber over against the place before the building facing north. 41:21.

   Vs 2.   Before the length of the North door was 100 cubits and 50 cubits broad.

   Vs 3.   Court space of 20 cubits between the inner and outer courts, the 3 stories gallery; ie., The Priests chambers. 41:6.

   Vs 4.   A walk-way before the chambers of 10 cubits broad, a way of one cubits; their doors toward the North.

   Vs 5.   Upper Chambers shorter than the other two stories, middle or lower of the three stories. Narrower as getting higher. Margin = Building consisted of the lower and middle-most stories.

   Vs 6.   Three-storied Chambers, not pillars as court pillars; building straitened more than the other two stories.

   Vs 7.   Wall for the Chambers 50 cubits in length.

   Vs 8.   Chambers 50 cubits in length in utter court, before the Temple 100 cubits.

   Vs 9.   Entry to chambers on the east side from the utter court.

   Vs 10. Chambers in the wall thickness of court towards the East, over against the separate place, and over against the building.

   Vs 11. The way before them as the chambers towards the North, same in length, breadth, going out, fashions and doors (vs 4).

   Vs 12. As in vs 4.

2. **THE PRIEST'S USE OF THE CHAMBERS** – vs 13-14.

   These Chambers speak of the 'mansions' or 'resting places' in the Father's House which Jesus spoke of. His Father's House was the earthly Temple, as well as the Heavenly Temple. He was speaking of the Priestly Chambers where the priests went before ministering in the House of the Lord in their respective priestly course.

Vs 13. North and South Chambers, before the separate place, equalled holy chambers for the priests approaching the Lord. They were for:
1. Eating the most holy things.
2. Laying there the most holy things, ie., Meal, Sin and Trespass offerings.
3. The place is holy. Lev 6:16, 26; 24:9; Lev 2:3, 10; 6:14, 7, 17, 25, 29.

Vs 14. Priests also to change their garments after ministering in the Holy Place and put on other garments in their approach to the people.
Thus they were:
1. Garments of approach to the Lord – vs 13. His things.
2. Garments of approach to the People – vs 14. Their things. Thus inward approach – what a Priest is before the Lord. And outward approach – what a Priest is before the People. Cf. 44:19.

3. **MEASURING OF THE AREA BETWEEN THE SANCTUARY AND PROFANE PLACE** – vs 15-20.

Vs 15. When the Inner House was finished being measured, he came to the East Gate and measured around.

Vs 16. The East side measured 500 reeds.

Vs 17. The North side measured 500 reeds.

Vs 18. The South side measured 500 reeds.

Vs 19. The West side measured 500 reeds. Thus foursquare.

Vs 20. Thus the wall was about 500 long by 500 broad, the wall being a separation wall between the Sanctuary and the profane place.
Cf. 40:5; 45:2. Cf. Ephesians 2:14. The wall of separation between Jew and Gentile – the sacred and profane place in Messiah's Times.

Note: - LXX substitutes "cubits" for "reeds" due to the immense size of the whole.
A reed equal about 10' 10", while the cubits was about 1' 6" or 1' 9". Cf. 40:5.

EZEKIEL CHAPTER FORTY-THREE

1. **THE GLORY OF THE LORD RETURNS TO THE NEW TEMPLE** – vs 1-6.

Vs 1.   The prophet brought to the EAST Gate,   cf. 10:19; 40:1.

Vs 2.   The GLORY of the God of Israel came by way of the East, cf. 11:23.
   1. The Glory of the God of Israel – cf. 11:23.
   2. The EAST Gate. 1:14; Gen 3:22-24.
   3. The Voice as many waters – 1:24; Rev 1:15; Dan 10:6; Rev 14:1.
   4. The Earth shined with HIS Glory – 10:4; Rev 18:1.
      The Glory of God of Israel is personified in HIM,   cf. John 1:14-18.

Vs 3.   The vision the same as given in 1:4, 28 when he came to prophesy that the city should be destroyed, and that he had by the river Chebar. Fell on his face. 9:1; Jeremiah 1:10; 3:23.

Vs 4.   Glory came into the HOUSE by way of the east gate,   cf. 10:19. Never ever returned to the restoration Temple under Nehemiah and Ezra.

Vs 5.   The Spirit lifted him up and took him to the inner court and the Glory filled the House, cf. 3:12, 14; 8:3; 1 Kgs 8:10-11.

Vs 6.   The Lord speaks to him out of the House now and the Man of 40:3-4 stands by Him. Thus:
   1. The glory returns the same way as it departed, by way of the East,
   2. By way of the Gate,
   3. By way of the Inner Court,
   4. And into the House filling it – 44:4.

2. **THE WORD OF THE LORD CONCERNING ABOMINATIONS** – vs 7-9.

Vs 7.   The House of the Lord is called:
   1. The Place of My Throne,
   2. The Place of the soles of My feet – ie., His footstool.
   3. The Place where God dwells in the midst of His People.
   4. The Place of His Holy Name.

Not to be defiled any more by the people and things with their whoredoms in the high places.

Cf. Psa 99:1; 1 Chronicles 28:2; Psa 99:5; Ezek 8-10; Ex 29:45; Psa 68:16; 132:14; Joel 13:17; John 1:14; 2 Cor 6:16; Ezek 39:7; Lev 26:30; Jer 16:18; Rev 21:3.

Vs 8.   The setting of:
Their thresholds by My threshold.
Their post by My Post.
The wall between Me and them (Margin).
God's Holy Name defiled by their abominations – God consumed them in His anger.   These abominations caused God to leave the former Temple.
2 Kgs 16:14; 21:4, 5, 7; Ezek 8:3; 23:39; 44:7.

Vs 9.   Called to put away whoredoms and carcasses of their Kings, and God can dwell in their midst forever.
Note: God's Glory cannot dwell in His House with other idolatrous abominations,   cf. Vs 7, 2 Cor 6:14-18.

3.   **THE LAW OF THE HOUSE** – vs 10-12.

Vs 10.   Ezekiel is to show the ouse of the Lord to the House of Israel, to shame them for their iniquities.   They are to measure the pattern, cf 40:4.

Vs 11.   He is to shew them:
1.   The Form –
2.   The Fashion –
3.   The Goings out –
4.   The Comings in –
5.   The Forms thereof –
6.   The Ordinances and Forms thereof –
7.   The Laws thereof –

He is to write it in their sight, so that they might keep the whole things and do them.   Thus the pattern of the house, the approach in and out of God's presence and the ordinances thereof.   Applicable to the House of the Lord and the saints in their approach to the Lord.   Ordinances He has set in the Church as such also applicable here.

Vs 12.   The Law of the House, on the top of the mountain.   The whole summit to be most holy.
Note – The Mountain and the House, cf. Isa 2:1-5; Ezekiel 40:2. The Kingdom and the Church symbolised here also.

4.   **THE MEASUREMENTS OF THE ALTAR OF SACRIFICE** – vs 13-17.

Vs 13.   The higher place of the altar to be a cubit and span. This is the Altar of burnt offering.

Vs 14.
Vs 15.   The Altar to be 4 cubits and to have 4 horns. Note – Margin. The Mountain of God; Ariel, ie., The Lion of God.
Jesus is our Altar, He is the Lion of God, the Lion of the Tribe of Judah. Rev 5:5.

Vs 16.   The Altar to be 12 cubits long by 12 cubits broad, square in the four squares thereof.

Vs 17.   The settle to be 14 cubits long and 14 cubits broad in the four squares thereof.
The border to be a ½ cubit. Bottom to be a cubit about and STAIRS at the Altar to look toward the East.
Cf. Ex 20:24-26. Not to have steps to the Altar of God. Perhaps a slope here, or stairs.

5.   **THE DEDICATION, ORDINANCES AND CONSECRATION OF THE ALTAR AND PRIESTHOOD** – vs 18-27.

Vs 18.   The ordinances of the Altar in the day it is made, to offer Burnt Offerings thereon and to sprinkle the blood, cf. Lev 1:5.

Vs 19.   The Priests, the Levites of the seed of Zadok which approach God, to minister to Him, to be given a young bullock for a Sin offering.
Cf. 44:6; Ex 29:10; Lev 8:14.
Cf. 45:18; (Refer Zadok Priesthood notes).

Vs 20.   Sacrificial blood on the 4 horns of the altar and 4 corners of the settle, and the border, to cleanse it and purge it.

Vs 21.   Bullock of the Sin offering to be burnt in the appointed place of the House, without the Sanctuary.
Cf. Ex 29:14; Heb 13:1. The body burnt "without the camp".

Vs 22.   On the 2nd day to offer the goats without blemish for Sin offering. Cleanse the altar as with the bullock.

Vs 23. After cleansing the Altar, to offer a bullock and ram without blemish.

Vs 24. Offered before the Lord, Priest cast SALT on them and offer as a Burnt offering.
Cf. Lev 2:13. The salt of the Covenant.

Vs 25. Seven days to offer a goat for a Sin offering, a young bullock, and a ram.
Cf. Ex 29:35; Lev 8:33.

Vs 26. Seven days to purge and purify the altar and consecrate (fill the hand) of the Priesthood. Cf Ex 29:24.

Vs 27. On the EIGHTH day and onward, from that time on the PRIESTHOOD can officiate at the Altar, and offer the people's Burnt offering, and Peace and Thank offerings, and God will ACCEPT them.
Cf. Lev 9:1; Ezek 20:40-41; Rom 12:1; 1 Pet 2:5.

Compare this section with Ex 29 and Lev 8-9 chapters.   The Consecration of the Priesthood to minister in behalf of the Israelites.
Also compare this chapter with Num 7 and the Dedication of the Brazen Altar.   And also compare with Lev 1-7 chapters, on the 5 offerings, voluntary and compulsory.
Thus:-
1. Build the Altar first, the foundation of the Gospel.
2. Dedicate and cleanse it by Blood atonement. The Blood alone cleanses from sin.
3. Consecrate the Priesthood.
4. Offer the sacrifices.
5. People are accepted of the Lord.

EZEKIEL CHAPTER FORTY-FOUR

1. **THE GATE FOR THE PRINCE** – vs 1-3.

   Vs 1.   Ezekiel is brought to the gate looking toward the East and it was shut, cf. 43:1.

   Vs 2.   The Gate was to be shut and not opened. None to enter it because it was reserved for the LORD, the God of Israel, because He entered by it. Cf. 43:1-4. The Glory of God came through the East Gate.

   Vs 3.   The Gate reserved for the Prince. He is to SIT in the Gate and eat bread before the Lord. He will enter in and out by the same Gate. Cf. 46:2, 8. Cf. Gen 31:54; 1 Cor 10:18. Jesus is THE PRINCE Messiah; the Prince of Life, the Prince and Saviour and the Prince of the Tribe of Judah. Dan 9:24-27; Rev 1:5; Acts 3:15; 5:31; Mt 2:6.

2. **REPROOF TO THE HOUSE OF ISRAEL** – vs 4-8.

   Vs 4.   He is brought to the North Gate, and sees the Glory of the Lord filling the house and he falls down, cf. 3:23; 1:18.

   Vs 5.   Ezekiel is to mark well the Ordinances and Laws of the Lord's House. As in 43:11; 40:4.

   Vs 6.   There has been enough and suffice of the abominations of the rebellious House of Israel, cf. 2:5; 45:9; 1 Pet 4:13.

   Vs 7.   Strangers (Gentiles, Heathen) brought into the Sanctuary of God to pollute it when offering God's sacrifice to Him. No strangers permitted in House of the Lord.
      1.   Uncircumcised in heart – entered, of the spirit, the true circumcision, internal.
      2.   Uncircumcised in flesh, external, of the flesh, the shadow circumcision, cf. Vs 9; 43:8; Acts 21:28; Lev 22:25; 26:41; Acts 7:51; Lev 21:17; 3:16.
        A. My Sanctuary –
        B. My House –
        C. My Bread –
        D. My Covenant –

   Vs 8.   E. My Holy Things –
        F. My Charge (word, ordinance).

They had not kept such and they set in their own keepers in the Sanctuary, ie. Unconverted people should not minister in the House of the Lord.

3. **THE LEVITES MINISTERING TO THE PEOPLE AND THE HOUSE** – vs 9-14.

Vs 9.   No stranger or uncircumcised in HEART and/or FLESH to enter into the Sanctuary of the Lord, cf. Vs 7 and Gen 17. No heathen or person not in Covenant relationship with the Lord to enter the Sanctuary, cf. Ex 12:43-51. No stranger or uncircumcised could eat the Passover Feast. Only God sees the heart. Man sees the flesh.

Vs 10.   The LEVITES that went astray far from the Lord with the children of Israel are to bear their iniquity. Cf. 2 Kgs 23:8-18; Ezekiel 48:11; Mal 2:1-10. The Levitical tribe to be the priestly tribe to the 12 tribes, to be teaching priests – yet failed to be example to the nation.

Vs 11.   Yet to remain as Ministers of the Sanctuary, doing the following things:
1.   Ministers in My Sanctuary.
2.   Charge of the Gates of the House.
3.   Ministers to the House.
4.   Present the offerings for the people.
5.   Minister unto the people. 1Chron.26:1; 2Chron.29:34; Num 16:9.

Vs 12.   Levites ministered to the people in their idolatry, caused them to fall into iniquity. God's hand against the ministry who cause people to fall – both then and now! 14:3, 4; 22:26; Isa 9:16; Mal 2:8. Failure in the ministry, and become stumbling blocks to the people. Note Margin – "were for a stumbling block of iniquity", Psalm 106:26.

Vs 13.   Not to come near to the Lord or do the office of a priest to Him, or minister in the Most Holy Place. Thus:
1.   Not to come near to Me.
2.   Not to do the office of a priest to Me.
3.   Not to come near any of My holy things.
4.   Not to enter into the Most Holy Place, ie., The Holiest of All, within the veil.
5.   To bear their shame and committed abominations. Num 18:3; 2 Kgs 23:9; Ezekiel 32:30.

Vs 14. To be keepers of the charge and service of God's House. Thus limited ministry here for these Levites, though not put out of the ministry altogether.

DIAGRAM - Tabernacle of Moses, or Temple.

    A. Sons of Zadok – enter within the veil, the Holiest of all.

    B. The Levites – Minister in Outer Court, at the Altar.

4. THE MINISTRY OF THE LEVITES, SONS OF ZADOK – vs 15-16.

Vs 15. The Levitical Priests, the sons of Zadok, kept the charge of God's Sanctuary when Israel went astray and they will have the nearest ministry, as follows:

    1. Come near to Me.
    2. Minister unto Me.
    3. Stand before the Lord, to offer the fat and blood. Cf. 40:46; 1 Sam 2:35; Deut 10:8; 44:7, 10.

Vs 16.

    4. Enter into My Sanctuary.
    5. Come near to My Table.
    6. Minister unto Me.
    7. Keep My charge, cf 41:22.
        (Refer to "The Tabernacle of David" and the Zadok Priesthood, by Kevin J. Conner.)

5. QUALIFICATIONS, INSTRUCTIONS AND DUTIES OF THE PRIESTHOOD MINISTRY – vs 17-31.

This section deals in particular about the qualifications, instructions and duties of the Priesthood. God was very concerned about the standard they would set, and He sets the standard for them in all areas of their life.

1. Their Clothing -

Vs 17. To be clothed with linen garments when entering the Gates of the inner court. Ex 28:40; 39:28. No wool that causes sweat. Sweat speak of the curse of human effort and works.

Vs 18. Linen bonnets, linen breeches on them also. Not to be girded with anything that causes sweat.

Vs 19. Change garments when in the utter court with the people. The "holy garments" to be put in the Priestly Chambers. Thus TWO changes of garments here. Cf. 42:14; 46:20; Ex 30:29;

Lev 6:27; Mt 23:17. Thus LINEN – speaks of purity, righteousness in ministry unto the Lord and people.

2. Their Hair-Style -
Vs 20. Not to shave their heads, or suffer long locks, but poll their heads. Lev 21:5.

3. Their Abstinence –
Vs 21. Not to drink wine when entering the Court, cf. Nadab and Abihu and what they did in drunken presumption. Lev 10:9.

4. Their Marriage –
Vs 22. Not to marry a widow, divorced person, but maidens of the seed of the House of Israel, and/or a Priest's widow. Lev 21:7.

5. Their Ministry –
Vs 23. To teach people the difference between the holy and profane, discern unclean and clean. Cf. 22:26; Mal 2:7.

Vs 24. To judge cases in Israel according to God's standards, laws, statutes. To hallow God's Sabbaths. Cf 22:26; 20:12-20; Deut 17:8; 2 Chronicles 19:8.

6. Their Relatives –
Vs 25. Not to be defiled by dead person unless own relatives.

Vs 26. Cleansing after 7 days if defiled for relatives (Num6:10;19:11

7. Their Cleansing –
Vs 27. To offer a sin offering in the day he goes back into ministry and into the inner court or Sanctuary. Sin and death DEFILE – need cleansing as Priest to minister before the Lord and people. Lev 4:3; Ezekiel 44:17.

8. Their Inheritance –
Vs 28. No possession for the Priest, as the Lord Himself is their inheritance. Num 18:20; Deut 10:9; 18:1-2; Josh 13:14.

9. Their Portions –
Vs 29-31.
The portion for the Priests of the offerings, etc.
1. The Meat offering –
2. The Sin offering –
3. The Trespass offering –
4. The Dedicated things –
5. The First of the First-fruits from all things –

6. The Oblation, of all sorts –
7. The First of the dough –
   Thus 7 things mentioned as the portion of the Priests.
   Lev 7:6; 27:21-28; Num 18:14; Ex 13:2; 22:29; 23:19;
   Num 3:13; 18:12; 15:20; Neh 10:37; Prov 3:9; Mal
   3:10.

The result? The Priest will cause THE BLESSING to rest in
their house. Thus Priestly blessing. Mal 3:10; Num 6:24-27.
The Priest not to eat anything that dies of itself, cf. Ex 22:31;
Lev 22:8.

All good spiritual lessons for the standard of the ministry both then
and today!

EZEKIEL CHAPTER FORTY-FIVE

1. **THE DIVISION OF THE LAND** – vs 1-5.
   The Portion for the Sanctuary and the Priests –
   Vs 1.   The land to be divided by lot and a portion to be offered as an oblation to the Lord. Holy ("Holiness") portion of the land for the Lord to be 25,000 reeds by 10,000 reeds.
   Cf. 47:22; 48:8. Holy in all its borders.

   Vs 2.   Portion of this holy portion to be for the Sanctuary.
   Thus 500 cubits in length, by 500 cubits in breadth, thus foursquare. And 50 cubits round about for suburbs.

   V 3.   Of the 25,000 x 10,000 measurement, in it shall be the Sanctuary and the Most Holy Place, cf. 48:10.

   Vs 4.   The holy portion of the land for the Priest's houses, as well as the Sanctuary, to minister unto the Lord.

   Vs 5.   The same area is also for the Levites, the ministers of the House, and they are to have 20 Chambers, cf. 48:13; 40:17.
   Thus:
          1. Land for the Sanctuary –
          2. Land for the Priests-
          3. Land for the Levites –
          4. Land for the City –

2. **LAND FOR THE CITY** – vs 6.
   Vs 6.   Portion of the City to be 25,000 long x 5,000 broad, over against the oblation of the holy portion. This is for the whole House of Israel, cf. 48:15.

3. **PORTION FOR THE PRINCE** – vs 7-8.
   Vs 7.   Portion for the Prince on each side of the oblation of the holy portion, and city possession, and before them both; westward and eastward borders. Cf. 48:21.

   Vs 8.   His possession to be in the land area.   Princes no more to oppress God's people. Rest of the land given to the House of Israel according to their tribes.

   Cf. 22:27; cf. Jer 22:17; Ezek 22:27; 46:18.
   Closeness of his portion shows closeness to the Sanctuary.

4.   **THE OFFERINGS OF THE PRINCES TO THE PRINCE** – vs 9-17.
Compare this section with Num 7 – Dedication of the altar and offerings of the 12 Princes at the Tabernacle of Moses.

Vs 9. Princes called to remove violence, spoil, and expulsions of God's people and deal in judgment and justice, cf. 44:6; Jeremiah 22:3.

Vs 10. To have JUST balances, Ephah, and Bath. Just weights and measures. Cf. Lev 19:35-36; Prov 11:1.

Vs 11. Ephah and bath to have the same measure, the tenth part of a homer.

Vs 12. The shekel to be 20 gerahs, cf. Ex 30:12. The standard of the Sanctuary. Lev 27:25; Num 3:47.
Thus 20+25+15=60 shekels to be the maneh.
God is JUST in His dealings with His people, and perfectly balanced in His moral attributes. So should His ministers be!

Vs 13. Princes oblation to be offered was the 6th part of an ephah of an homer of wheat and also barley.
Thus:
      1. Wheat, a 6th part.
      2. Barley, a 6th part.

Vs 14.   3. Oil, 10th of bath (10th of a bath = 1 homer). Cf. Lev.2. Meal offering.

Vs 15.   4. One lamb out of 200 lambs for Burnt offering. Lev.1.
      5. Peace offering (Thank). Cf. Lev 3.
      To make reconciliation for the Princes. All VOLUNTARY offerings here by the Princes.

Vs 16. The people of the land to give their oblation to the Princes in Israel. Give to them that they may give! Princes learn the principle of giving to the Lord.

Vs 17. These given things to be for the Princes to give –
      1. Burnt offerings –
      2. Meat and Drink offerings –
      3. For Feasts –
      4. For New Moons –
      5. For Sabbaths –
      6. For Solemn Days –

7. For Sin offerings, Meat and Burnt and Peace offerings —to make reconciliation.

5.   **THE FEASTS OF THE LORD TO BE KEPT** – vs 18-25.
Refer to Lev 16, 23, Num 28-29 chapters on the Festivals.

Vs 18.   Passover Month – Consecration of the Priests to the Sanctuary service. First day of the first month, young blemish-less bullock to be sacrificed to cleanse the Sanctuary. Lev 16:16.

Vs 19.   Priest to take the blood of the Sin offering, put it on the posts of the House, and the 4 corners of the altar settle and on the gate posts of the inner court. Cf. 43:20. As in Ex 12. Posts of the Door and Lintel sprinkled with blood. Passover.

Vs 20.   To be repeated on the 7th day of the month for the erring and simple, reconciling the house. Lev 4:27.
Covering sins of ignorance! Thus 10 days preparation for Passover Lamb.

Vs 21.   Passover – 14th day of the 1st month.
Unleavened Bread for 7 days, cf. Ex 12:18; Lev 23:5-6; Num 9:2,3; 28:16-17; Deut 16:1.

Vs 22.   The Prince to prepare for himself and all the people of the land a bullock for a Sin offering. Lev 4:4.

Vs 23.   For 7 days of the Feast to prepare Burnt offerings.
Thus 7 bullocks, and 7 rams for Burnt offerings, and 1 kid for a Sin offering, for 7 days. Lev 23:8; Num 28:15, 22, 30; 29:5, 11, 15, 19.

Vs 24.   Meal offering – ephah for bullock, ephah for ram, hin of oil per ephah, cf. 46:5,7.

Vs 25.   Feast of Tabernacles – The 7th month, 15th day of the month. Feast of 7 days, 15th-21st. According to Sin, Burnt, Meal, Oil offerings. Lev 23:24; Num 29:12; Deut 16:13.

Note:
1. No mention of Festival day of the Sheaf of First-fruits; 18th day of 1st month.
2. Feast of Pentecost; 50th day and in the 3rd month, not mentioned.
3. No mention of Feast Day of Trumpets; 1st day of the 7th month.

EZEKIEL CHAPTER FORTY-SIX

1. **THE SABBATHS AND NEW MOONS** – vs 1-8.

Vs 1. The Inner courts and its East Gate to be shut for 6 working days; to be opened on the Sabbath Days and New Moons.

Vs 2. The PRINCE to enter by way of the Porch of the Gate, to stand by the Gate post, and the Priest to prepare his Burnt and Peace offerings. To worship in the Gate of the threshold. Gate not to be shut until the evening. Vs 8; 44:3.

Vs 3. People of the land to worship at the Door of this Gate in the Sabbaths and New Moons.

Vs 4. Sabbath Day Princes offering to be:
      1. Six blemish-less lambs –
      2. One blemish-less ram

Vs 5.   3. Ephah for Ram – for Meal offering
         For lambs
         Hin of oil per ephah – cf. Vs 7, 11; 45:24.
         As he is able to give, or the gift of his hand.
         Deut 16:17.

Vs 6. The New Moon offering:
      1. Young blemish-less bullock –
      2. Six lambs blemish-less –
      3. One ram without blemish –

Vs 7.   4. Meal offering ephah per bullock –
         Ephah for ram –
         Ephah for lambs –
         Hin of oil per ephah –

Vs 8. The Prince to enter by way of the porch of the Gate and to leave by the same, as vs 2.

2. **THE SOLEMN FEASTS** – vs 9-12.

Vs 9. The people who gather for the Solemn Feasts (Ex 23:14-17; Deut 16:16), if they enter by the North gate for worship, to leave by the South gate, or visa versa.
Ex 23:14-17; Deut 16:16.

Vs 10. The Prince to be "in the midst" of them they go in and come out, cf. Mt 18:20.

Vs 11. In the Feasts and Solemnities to have the regular Meal offerings of vs 5.

Vs 12. When the Prince prepares the voluntary Burnt or Peace offerings, he is to go in at the East Gate as for the Sabbath Day offerings, cf. Vs 12.
After he leaves the Gate shall be shut. Gate only for him. He alone enters and leaves by the same Gate, the East Gate! Cf 44:3. Because of who he is!

3. **THE DAILY OR CONTINUAL OFFERING** – vs 13-15.

Vs 13. The daily burnt offering to the Lord to be prepared every morning, cf. Ex 29:38; Num 28:3. Daily lamb of the first year without blemish.

Vs 14. The daily Meal offering – 6th part of ephah and 3rd part of oil in fine flour – offered continually with the Burnt offering for perpetual ordinance.
No Burnt offering could be offered without its attendant Meal offering.

Vs 15. The lamb of the Burnt offering; the Meal offering and oil every morning for the daily or continual offering.

4. **THE INHERITANCE OF THE PRINCE** – vs 16-18.

Vs 16. If the Prince gives a gift to any sons, it is to be their inheritance or possession. The sons are always to keep it.

Vs 17. If the Prince gives a gift to any of his servants, it will be theirs until the year of liberty (Jubilee); then it shall return to the Princes.

Vs 18. The Prince not to take any of the peoples inheritance by oppression, nor give it to any of his sons, so that God's people will not be scattered by losing their possessions and Princes becoming the great land-owners! Cf. 45:8; Lev 25:10.

5. **THE COURT PLACE FOR SACRIFICIAL PREPARATION** – vs 19-24.

Vs 19. Ezekiel is brought through the entry at the side of the Gate into the Holy Chambers of the Priests facing the North where he sees a place westward.

Vs 20. This place is where the Priests are to boil the Trespass and Sin Offerings and to bake the Meal offering – not in the utter court.

These offerings were to sanctify the people, cf. 44:19; 2 Chronicles 35:13; Lev 2:4, 5, 7.

Vs 21. Taken then to the utter court and looks at the 4 corners of the court and each corner had a smaller court.

Vs 22. These smaller courts in each corner of the utter court made with chimneys (Margin) and were 40 cubits long by 30 cubits broad; all of one measure.

Vs 23. Each court had a row of buildings round about in them made with boiling places in them.

Vs 24. The purpose was for the ministers of the House to boil the sacrifices of the people, cf. Vs 22.

Thus, probably like this:

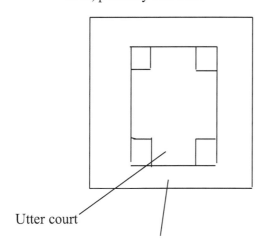

Utter court

Corner Courts for Sacrifices

EZEKIEL CHAPTER FORTY-SEVEN

1. **THE RIVER FROM THE TEMPLE OR HOUSE OF THE LORD** – vs 1-5.

Vs 1.   Ezekiel is brought to the Door of the House and waters issued out from the threshold of the House, Eastward.
The House faced the east.
The waters came down from the right side of the ALTAR of the house and Eastward.
Cf. Joel 3:18; Zech 13:1; 14:8; Rev 22:1.
    1. Gen 2. The River in Eden's Garden – before sin – from a Garden of Delight.
    2. Ezekiel 47. The River in Temple – during sin – from the Altar of Sacrifice.
    3. Rev 22. The River from the Throne in a City – after sin – from a Throne of God.
       The same river of God flows on. Psalm 47; John 7:37-39.
       Always symbolic of the Spirit of God, flowing, moving, refreshing life.

Vs 2.   Taken out of the Northward Gate to the utter gate that looks Eastward where the waters came out.

Vs 3-5. The Man with the measuring line went forward Eastward and he measured the depths of the water.
    1. Waters to the ankles – vs 3 – 1000 cubits.
    2. Waters to the knees – vs 4. – 1000 cubits.
    3. Waters to the loins – vs 4 – 1000 cubits.
    4. Waters to swim in – vs 5 – 1000 cubits.
       The river increases in depth as it flows from the House of God, by way of the Altar.
       Spiritually speaking, the River of God's Spirit can only come out and flow by reason of the Altar of the sacrifice of Jesus. The Rock must be smitten for the waters to flow, cf. Ex 17; Num 20.

2. **THE MINISTRY OF THE RIVER** – vs 6-12.

Vs 6.   Ezekiel caused to come to the brink of the river.

Vs 7.   He sees very many trees on each side of the river, cf. Rev 22:2.

Vs 8. The waters issue out toward the East country and go down to the desert (plain), south of the Jordan and into the sea (Dead Sea).
Result? The waters are healed, cf. Deut 3:17; 4:49; Josh 3:16.

Vs 9. Wherever the river comes there will be:
1. A great multitude of fish -
2. Life wherever it flows –
3. Healing waters wherever it flows –
4. Fruitfulness wherever it flows –
Thus spiritually speaking, wherever the river of the Holy Spirit flows in the Church, as the House of the Lord, there should be souls (fish); life in the Spirit (Spiritual life), and healing (Divine health and healing), and also fruitfulness (fruit of the Spirit, etc).

Jesus called His disciples to be fishers of men. Mark 1; Lk 5.
The early Church had fishing for souls, fruitfulness and healing in the ministry of the Holy Spirit.
The river was divided now into two streams; one to the Mediterranean Sea and the other to the Dead Sea.
Thus the river flows into the seas – ie. Symbolic of peoples, nations, kindreds, and tongues. Rev 17:15-17; Isa 57:21; 17:12-14.

Vs 10. The fishermen to stand on the river from En Gedi ("Fountain of the Kid") to En Eglaim ("The Fountain of the Red Heifer"), to spread forth nets for the fish, all kinds of fish and exceeding many. Cf. Num 34:3; Josh 23:4; Ezekiel 44:28.

Vs 11. The miry places and marshes not healed but given to salt, ie. Such are places that once had an inlet of fresh water, but no outlet now. Thus staleness starts and sets in, in miry places, stagnancy, where there is no river flow, thus no healing.
Marshes = used to get salt for shepherds and sheep. State of barrenness, not healed.

Vs 12. The trees of life on each side of the river. The trees food was good, and the leaf not to fade or whither. Also to bring forth NEW FRUIT, principal fruit during the 12 months of the year, because of the rivers of the Sanctuary.
The fruit to be for medicine and meat; for bruises and for sores, cf. Vs 7; Job 8:16; Psalm 1:3; Jeremiah 17:8; Rev 22:2.

Thus:
1. Tree of Life and River in Eden before sin. Gen 2.
2. Tree of Life and River in Temple during sin. Ezekiel 47.
3. Tree of Life and River in City after sin. Rev 21-22.

3. **THE INHERITANCE OF THE LAND GIVEN TO THE 12 TRIBES** – vs 13-21.

Vs 13. The borders of the inheritance of the land according to the 12 tribes.
1. Joseph – to have two (double) portions, cf. Gen 48:5; 1 Chronicles 5:1; Ezekiel 48:4-5; Gen 15:18-21. Ie. Through his two sons, Ephraim and Manasseh.

Vs 14. The tribes to inherit as God swore to the Fathers for inheritance.
Gen 12:7; 13:15; 15:7; 17:8; 26:3; 20:5-6, 28, 42; Ezek 48:29.

Vs 15. Cf. 48:1; Num 34:8.

Vs 16. Cf. Num 34:8; 2 Sam 8:8.

Vs 17. Cf. Num 34:9; Ezek 48:1.

Vs 18.

Vs 19. Cf. Num 20:13; Deut 32:51; Psa 81:7; Ezek 48:28.

Vs 20.

Vs 21. Land to be divided to the 12 Tribes of Israel.

4. **STRANGERS TO RECEIVE INHERITANCE WITH ISRAEL** – vs 22-23.

Vs 22. To be divided by lots for inheritance to Israel and to strangers amongst them. To be as one born amongst Israel and to have inheritance with Israel. Cf. Ephesians 3:6; Rev 7:9-10; Rom 10:12; Gal 3:28; Col 3:11. Foreshadowing the Gentiles having inheritance with the Israel of God.

Vs 23. Strangers joined to the tribes to be given their inheritance. So in the Gospel Age. Gentile strangers, like Ruth the Moabitess, to be given a place in the tribes, the Commonwealth of Israel, and to receive inheritance with the Israel of God. cf. Ephesians 2:11-22; 1:13-14; 4:30; Jas 1:1-2; 1 Pet 1:1.

EZEKIEL CHAPTER FORTY-EIGHT

1. **THE PORTION FOR THE TRIBES** – vs 1-7, cf. Josh 13:1 – 19:51 also.

Vs 1.	1.	The portion for Dan.
Vs 2.	2.	The portion for Asher.
Vs 3.	3.	The portion for Naphtali.
Vs 4.	4.	The portion for Manasseh} Double portion for Joseph
Vs 5.	5.	The portion for Ephraim } cf. 47:13.
Vs 6.	6.	The portion for Reuben.
Vs 7.	7.	The portion for Judah.

2. **THE PORTION FOR THE SANCTUARY** – vs 8-9.

Vs 8.   On the border of Judah is to be, east to west, the portion for the Sanctuary. 25,000 reeds (about 50 miles), east and west. The Sanctuary to be "in the midst", cf. Vs 10. Tabernacle of Moses also "in the midst" of the Camp of Israel Num 2:17; Ezekiel 45:1-6.

Vs 9.   This portion or oblation is 25,000 reeds long x 10,000 reeds broad.

3. **THE PORTION FOR THE PRIESTS AND LEVITES** – vs 10-14.

A.   The Portion for the Priests of Zadok
Vs 10. Oblation for the Priests, 25,000 north, and 10,000 west.
                          25,000 south, and 10,000 east.
The Sanctuary in the midst, cf. Vs 8.

Vs 11. To be for the Priests, the sons of Zadok, which kept God's charge, when the Levites and Israelites strayed from the Lord. The sanctified portion for the priests (Margin). The Charge = Word, Ordinance, cf. 44:15; 44:10.

Vs 12. This oblation of the land to be a thing most holy by the border of the Levites.

B.   The Portion for the Levites
Vs 13. Cf. 45:1-6. The Priests portion to be divided between the Priests and Levites, 25,000 x 10,000.

Vs 14. Not to be: 1. Sold,
2. Exchanged,
3. Alienated.
This portion is the First-fruits of the land and HOLY to the Lord, cf. Ex 22:29; Lev 27:10, 28, 33.

4. **THE PORTION FOR THE CITY** – vs 15-20.

Vs 15. The 5000 reeds left in the breadth over against the 25,000 to be a profane (or, non-sacred) place for the City, for dwelling and suburbs and the City is to be "in the midst" of this, cf. 45:6; 42:20.

Vs 16. The City measured foursquare; North, South, East and West, 4,500 reeds.

Vs 17. The suburbs to be on the four sides of the City, 250 each side.

Vs 18. The land produce to be on each side, 10,000 east and west side. For the food produce to serve the City.

Vs 19. Those that serve the City to serve out of all the 12 tribes of Israel, cf. 45:6.

Vs 20. The whole oblation to be foursquare with the City in it; thus 25,000 x 25,000.

Thus:

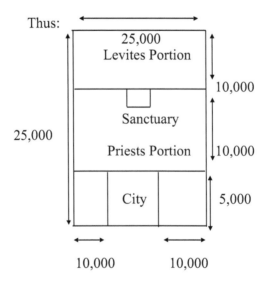

214

Note the foursquare-ness. The Sanctuary "in the midst". The City "in the midst", the land foursquare, the City foursquare. All pointing ultimately to the foursquare City of God, the Eternal Habitation of God with men in Rev 21-22.

5. **THE PORTION FOR THE PRINCE** – vs 21-22.

Vs 21. The remainder on each side of the holy oblation to be for the Prince, over against the City, and the Sanctuary, eastward and westward sides, cf. 45:7-8; 48:8, 10.

Vs 22. This portion of the Levites possession and the City possessions is between the borders of Judah ("Praise") (The Sceptre House), and Benjamin ("Son of the Right Hand").

6. **THE PORTIONS FOR THE OTHER TRIBES** – vs 23-29.

Vs 23. 8.   The portion for Benjamin.
Vs 24. 9.   The portion for Simeon.
Vs25. 10.   The portion of Issachar.
Vs 26. 11.   The portion for Zebulun.
Vs 27. 12.   The portion for Gad.

Vs 28. From Tamar unto Kadesh ("Water of Strife") to the river to the Great (Dead) Sea.

Vs 29. Cf. 47:19; 47:14, 21, 29.
The land divided by lot and given as inheritance to the 12 tribes of Israel.

7. **THE GATES OF THE CITY** – vs 30-35.

Vs 30. The goings out of the City on the North side 4,500 measures. Cf. Vs 16, 32, 33, 34 and the same on the East, South and West sides.

Vs 31-34.
The Gates of the City named after the 12 Tribes of Israel; 3 Gates on each side.
The Gates:
    1.   Three Gates Northward – Rueben, Judah, Levi
    2.   Three Gates Eastward – Joseph, Benjamin, Dan.
    3.   Three Gates Southward – Simeon, Issachar, Zebulun.
    4.   Three Gates Westward – Gad, Asher, Naphtali.

Note that Ephraim and Manasseh (Double Portion) are in Joseph's Gate and Levites have their own Gate.

Compare the 12 Gates of the OLD JERUSALEM and the 12 Gates in the Restoration of the City under Ezra and Nehemiah. Nehemiah 3; 10:39.
Compare the 12 Gates of the NEW JERUSALEM and the 12 Names of the 12 Tribes thereon. Rev 21:12-13, 25.
See "Gates" in Psa 118:19-20; Isa 26:1-4.
Thus all will enter through one of the Gates as the COMMONWEALTH OF ISRAEL of God to worship the Lord.

Vs 35. The goings around the City were 18,000 measures. The name of the City from that forward is JEHOVAH-SHAMMAH, ie. "The LORD is there".
God's presence and Shekinah Glory is there. Mt 18:20. Where two or three .... there I AM in the midst. Redemptive Name revealed in the City.
Cf. Jer 33:16; 3:17; Joel 13:21; Zech 2:10; Rev 21:3; 22:3; Ex 17:15; Judges 6:24.
The redemptive Name of the Lord. Compound redemptive name of Jehovah, meeting the need of His people by His Presence. Ex 3:14-15.

The ultimate revelation is to be found in the foursquare City of God, the New and the heavenly Jerusalem, the eternal city of God. Rev 21-22.

(Refer also to "Dispensational Truth", by Clarence Larkin (p.93-94) "Explore the Book", by J. Sidlow Baxter, on Ezekiel, (p. 32-36) Commentary on the Whole Bible, by Jameson, Fausett, and Brown. "From Eternity to Eternity" by Eric Sauer, (p. 179).

SUMMARY OF SPIRITUAL LESSONS FROM THE TEMPLE OF EZEKIEL

1. The Measurements of the Temple.
   The Church must measure up to the Divine standards. Ephesians 4:1-16; Rev 11:1-2; Ephesians 2:20-22; 1 Cor 3:16; 6:16; 2 Cor 6:16; 2 Cor 10:12.

2. The Man with the Measuring Line.
   The Lord Jesus Christ, the standard Man and His Word.

3.   The Glory of the Lord in the New Temple.
The Holy Spirit as the Shekinah Glory in the spiritual Temple, the
Church. He leaves the material Temple (Ezekiel 1-10) to come to the
new and spiritual Temple (Ezekiel 40-48). God and the Lamb are the
Temple. 1 Cor 3:16; 2 Cor 6:16; Ephesians 2:20-22; 1 Pet 2:5-9.

4.   The Feasts of the Lord.
We enjoy these Feasts spiritually in the Lord, and in the Church.
Spiritual worship. 1 Cor 5; Acts 2; 2 Cor 3; Heb 8-9-10.

5.   The Rivers from the House of the Lord.
The rivers of healing and blessing of the Holy Spirit in the Church,
and on to the world. Fish as souls, and fruitfulness of Christian life,
and healing waters in the Church, the House of the Lord.

6.   The Priesthood and Ordinances.
The ordinances of the priesthood of all believers in the Church.
Church order, and spiritual sacrifices as King-Priests. 1 Pet 2:5-9;
Rev 1:6; 5:9-10. Hebrews Epistle.

7.   Inheritance in the Land.
Ephesians 1:3. Inheritance in Christ Jesus, and spiritual Israel, as
typified in Joshua and Ephesians. Rom 4:13. Saints enter as heirs of
the world and of the kingdom.

8.   The Prince at the East Gate.
The mysterious Prince of the East Gate; Jesus Christ, who is Messiah
the Prince. Dan 9:24-27; Acts 5:31 etc. Prince and Saviour.

9.   The City, Jehovah-Shammah.
The LORD Jesus Christ. The 12 Tribes of spiritual Israel, the
Commonwealth of Israel into which Gentile and Israel may enter by
grace. Mt 18:20. The heavenly and eternal foursquare City of God.
Rev 21-22. The Lord is there. Eternal Presence and Glory.

Thus a measure of fulfilment in the Church here and now, but the ultimate
fulness of it into the Kingdom Age and the Eternal State of the redeemed.

TEMPLE SIZE COMPARISONS

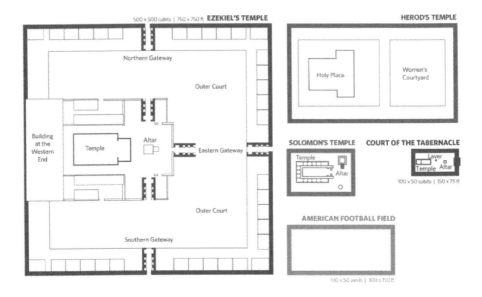

EZEKIEL'S TEMPLE — 500 x 500 cubits | 750 x 750 ft

- Northern Gateway
- Outer Court
- Building at the Western End
- Temple
- Altar
- Eastern Gateway
- Outer Court
- Southern Gateway

HEROD'S TEMPLE

- Holy Place
- Women's Courtyard

SOLOMON'S TEMPLE

- Temple
- Altar

COURT OF THE TABERNACLE — 100 x 50 cubits | 150 x 75 ft

- Laver
- Temple
- Altar

AMERICAN FOOTBALL FIELD — 100 x 50 yards | 300 x 150 ft

SUPPLEMENTARY MATERIAL

EZEKIEL	JESUS
1. Son of Man (93 times)	1. Son of Man (86 times)
2. Prophetic Word	2. The Word made flesh - Prophet
3. A Priest	3. A King and Priest
4. 30 Years of Age	4. 30 Years of Age
5. Opened Heavens - Visions	5. Opened Heavens - Vision
6. Spirit of the Lord	6. Spirit of the Lord in Jordan
7. House of Judah under Babylon	7. House of Judah under Rome
8. Rebellious House - 'Not See and Hear'	8. Rebellious People - Not 'See and Hear'
9. Glory Departs from Material Temple	9. Glory Departs from the Temple
10. The Abominations	10. Abominations in Judah
11. Jerusalem Destroyed by Babylon	11. Jerusalem Destroyed by Rome
12. Spoke of the New Covenant	12. Introduced the New Covenant
13. Visions of the New Temple, Rivers, the Glory	13. The Church the New Temple, Rivers and Glory

EZEKIEL	JOHN
1. Visions of God (Ezek.1)	1. Visions of God (Rev.1)
2. The Throne and the Four Cherubim (Ezek.1)	2. The Throne and the Four Living Creatures (Rev.4-5)
3. Eating the Book (Ezek.3)	3. Eating the Little Book (Rev.10)
4. The Mark in the Foreheads of the Sealed Ones (Ezek.9)	4. Mark in the Forehead of Sealed Ones (Rev.7, 14)
5. Gog and Magog (Ezek.38-39)	5. Gog and Magog (Rev.10)
6. Vision of the New City after the Old City is Destroyed (Ezek.48)	6. Vision of the Bride City when Old City 'As Sodom and Egypt' is Destroyed (Rev.21-22; 11:8)
7. The River of God, Trees of Life (Ezek.47)	7. The River of God, Trees of Life (Rev.22)

EZEKIEL'S CALL AND COMMISSION

There are seven things involved in the call and commission of Ezekiel to ministry to the people of God in this Babylonian situation and condition. These things become Divine equipment for ministry in our times also.

1. The Open Heavens (1:1)

Important expression in the Scripture. The foundation expression for all that follows. The beginning of Ezekiel's call and commission.

In Christ, God has restored "open heavens." Only SIN, not dealt with, will close the heavens to a person, a people, a nation or a leader. Leaders need to maintain "open heavens."

Examples in Old Testament and New Testament of people – believers – who had "open heavens" right here on earth.
a. Moses and the 70 elders - (Ex.24:9-11)
b. Jacob (Gen.32:12). Jacob's ladder.
c. Ezekiel had open heavens (Ezek.1:1; 8:3).
d. Jesus (Matt.3:16; Mrk.1:10; Lke.3:21).
e. Nathaniel (John 1:51).
f. Stephen (Acts 7:56-59).
g. Peter (Acts 10:11,56).
h. Paul (2Cor.12:1-4).
i. John the apostle also experienced "open heavens" as he received the Book of Revelation visions (Rev.4:1; 11:19; 15:5; 19:11).

Everything is clear between you and God, and there is good relationship and fellowship in prayer and consecration to His will.
Otherwise God will "shut up heaven" (1Kgs.8:34-35; Mal.3:8-12). Read again Dt.28:23 and Lev.26:18-19. God wants to "rend the heavens" and allow His Presence to come down and dissolve the mountains (Isa.64).

2. The Visions of God (1:1)

" I saw visions of God…" Arising out "open heavens" come "visions of God" (A vision of God. Margin). No open heavens means no vision from God. The second is totally dependant on the first. Vision comes out of open heavens.

1Sam.3:1. Illustrates.

• Where there is no vision, the people perish - KJV
• Where there is no vision, the people are made naked - KJV. Margin.
• Where there is no vision (no redemptive revelations of God), the people perish - AmpOT.
• Where there is no vision (revelation), the people are unrestrained - NASB
• Where there is no revelation, the people cast off restraint - NIV

- Without prophecy, the people become demoralised - NAB
- Where there is no progressive vision, the people dwell carelessly - Swedish
- Where there are no guidelines, the people run riot.
- Where there is no word from the God, the people are uncontrolled.
- Where there is ignorance of God, the people run wild - LB
- Without revelation, a nation fades, but it prospers in knowing the law - FF
- Where there is no vision, the people cast off restraint –JND

Absolute need of vision. The above are the conditions and results in a nation or person who lacks vision. People perish. Churches perish. People do not want to follow someone who is perishing.

Acts 26:19 Paul could say, I was not disobedient to the heavenly vision. Christ's vision is a victorious church, a glorious church without spot or wrinkle (Matt.16:15-20; Eph.5:23-32).

True vision originates with GOD! Num.12:6-8; Isa.1:1; 6:1-2. Ezekiel had to contend with false prophets whose vision originated out of their own heart and mind and hoped for others "to confirm the word" (Ezek.13:1-8).

Application: What is your vision? For your life, Church, people of God, Missions, evangelism, etc.? Open heavens provide vision!

3. The Word of the Lord (1:3)
"The word of the Lord came expressly to Ezekiel the priest..." Out of "open heavens" comes "visions of God" and with vision comes "the Word of the Lord." Specific Divine order here.

First mention – Gen.15:1,4. "Word of the Lord came to Abram in a vision..." This is the prophetic formula and used numerous times in the OT especially with the Prophets of God. "The word of the Lord came to me, saying..." It is worthy to note:

The word of the Lord" some 253 times in OT., and at least 60 times in Ezekiel, "the word of the Lord"...

It came expressly or specifically
It came an a specific DAY, specific MONTH and specific YEAR. The 30th year, the 4th month, and the 5th day of the month.

Jesus exhorts:
Take heed WHAT you hear" (Mark 4:23,24)
Take heed HOW you hear" (Luke 8:18)
Unto you that hear shall more be given (Mark 4:24)

Have an ear to hear what the Spirit is saying to the Churches (Rev.1,2,3 chapters). To whom is given, more is required. Unto you that hear shall more be given.

To Timothy – "war a good warfare by the prophetic word that went on over you by the presbytery and laying on of the hands..." (1Tim.1:18).
Word may come to us through prophetic word, word of wisdom, word of knowledge, the Written Word, or Jesus the Living Word...

Jer.1:1-3,14. To Jeremiah
The word of the Lord not come to Jesus. HE was THE WORD made flesh or whom all OT Prophets were types (John 1:1-3,14; Heb.1:1-2).

Application: Has the word of the Lord come to you? What are doing about it? Are you warring a good warfare by the prophetic word?

4. The Hand of the Lord (2:1-2)
"The hand of the Lord was there upon him..."
Used seven times in Ezekiel (Ezek.1:3; 2:1-2,9; 3:12,14,24; 8:1; 26:25-29; 33:22; 40:1).
It is wonderful thing when the Lord places His hand upon a person or a fellowship of people; individually or corporately.

- Ezek.3:1
- Ezek.3:14,22
- Ezek.8:1
- Ezek.37:1.
- So for other prophets of God:
- Elijah – 1Kgs.18:46
- Elisha – 2Kgs.3:15
- Nehemiah – Neh.2:8
- Lke.1:66 – John
- Early Church - Acts 4:30; Acts 11:21; Acts 13:11
- The "hand" ministry of the fivefold (Eph.4:9-16).
- John - Laid His hand on me (Rev.1:16-17).
Empowerment, impartation, identification. Laying on of hands.

5. The Spirit of the Lord (2:1)
"...and the Spirit entered me..." Note the three Major Prophets and their emphasis on the Godhead.

Jeremiah – the Prophet of the Father God
Isaiah – the Prophet of the Son, the Messiah
Ezekiel – the Prophet of the Holy Spirit (Also "Son of Man" – 100 times), and most references to the Holy Spirit in Ezekiel (some 25 times at least).
Ezek.2:1-2; 3:12,14,14,24; 1:12,20,20,20,21; 11:1,5,19,24,24; 37:1,14; 43:5.

Absolute necessity of the "the Spirit entering" into us. Born of the Spirit, and filled or baptised in the Spirit (John 3:1-5; Joel 2:28-32 with Acts 2:1-4; John 7:37-39). Make room for the Spirit. Wherever the Spirit went, the wheels went.

- The Prophets (1Pet.1:10-12; 2Pet.1:20-21).
- By My Spirit, says the Lord (Zech.4:6).
- Jesus – John 14,15,16

Application: The leader needs total dependence on the Holy Spirit for ministry, even as Jesus totally depended on the Holy Spirit for all He was, all He said, and all He did.

6. The Scroll of the Book (2:9-10; 3:1-3)
Ezekiel now told to eat the scroll, or eat the book and then speak.

- John (Rev.10:8-10). The Bible is the only book we are told to eat. The Word must become flesh in us first.
- Jesus (Matt.4:8 with Dt.8).
- The Word - Psalms (Psalm 1; Psalm 19; Psalm 119)
The words we speak must be "spirit and life" (John 6:63).

Application: How much time do we give to the reading, study, meditation, and chewing of the Word. Shallow preaching, teaching if shallow attitude to the Word! Bible Research.

7. The Divine Charge (2:6-8; 3:4-27)
The charge and commission now to Ezekiel is to "hear what I say…"and "speak My words to them…" Speak whether they hear or forbear, whether they listen or not.
Divine sovereignty and human responsibility (Jer.1:9-10). My words…your mouth. Mouth not originate the words. God does. Mouth only speak the words God gives. God's mouthpiece. Speak the words of God. Not fear people's faces. Not to compromise the Word, preach to please people, desperate to be accepted. Seeker sensitive or Spirit sensitive?

Application: Preach the Word (Mark. 6:15-20; 2Tim.4:1-5; Matt.28:18-20; Luke 24:46-49). Preach the Gospel to every creature, make disciples of all nations. So that the Lamb will see the fruit of His death (Rev.5:9-10).Seek to be the best communicator of the Word of God that you can be in our generation.

Cannot speak the Word of the Lord without the Spirit empowering, and hearing what God says. We listen, He speaks. When He speaks, we speak. Swift to hear and slow to speak. He has given us His Word. Preach the Word.

This is the message of Ezekiel to us as leaders today and in our generation!

EZEKIEL'S FOURFOLD CALLING

PRIEST	PROPHET	WATCHMAN	SHEPHERD
Inward	Outward	Outward	Inward
Man to God	God to Man	Inward	To Man
Priestly Ministry	Prophetic Ministry	Warn the Wicked Warn the Righteous	Shepherding Ministry
Rev.1:6 Rev.5:9-10 Rev.20:6 Isaiah 61:6	Rev.19:10 1 Cor.12 1 Cor.14 Eph.4:9-16	Col.1:24-29 Acts 20:17-32	John 10 Acts 20 1 Peter 5 Psalm 23
Ezekiel 1	Ezekiel 2	Ezekiel 33	Ezekiel 34

EZEKIEL AND THE MINISTRY OF THE PROPHET

Scriptures: Ezek.2:1-10; 3:1-3
Ezekiel called to be (1) A Priest
(2) A Prophet

Introductory:
Important to understand the ministry of a true prophet in both Old Testament and New Testament times, as well as understanding the distinctions and differences between both.

A. The Word of the Lord
Prophetic formula – "the word of the Lord." The predominant ministry of most of the Old Testament Prophets was receiving and delivering the word of the Lord. Being God's mouthpiece (Jer.1:9-10; 15:16,19).

This expression is used some 240 times in the Old Testament, and 2 times in the New Testament.
• In 1 Kings = 31 times
• In 2 Kings = 15 times
• In Jeremiah = 51 times
• In Ezekiel = 60 times
• None in 13 Old Testament books.
• None in 25 out of 27 New Testament books
• Used 2 times in the New Testament.

1. Prophecy as Forth-telling
This form of prophecy is in the realm of preaching – declaration. It is the outward approach from God to man. Prophets communicating the mind and will of God through the Word of the Lord; exhortation, reproof, warning, comfort or edification.

The Prophet is predominantly A PREACHER and the proclaimer of the Word of God to the people of God, to the people of his generation. The nature of this word is "telling forth" – speaking, or preaching "the word of the Lord."

2. Prophecy as Fore-telling
This aspect of prophecy is in the realm of prediction. It is predominantly speaking of events to take place in the future history of a nation or people. Often the past and the present are woven in context together with the future prophetic words. God reveals His plans and purposes to His servants the Prophets (Amos 3:7-8).

Understanding these two aspects of prophecy, it is seen that prophecy should not be limited by or restricted to predicting the future. A great majority of prophecy is preaching. It is because of this, many expositors only see the gift of prophecy (as in the New Testament) as "preaching." However, true prophecy will sometimes involve both preaching and prediction. Both leaders and God's people need to understand and recogniSe these distinctions.

B. Ezekiel as an Old Testament Prophet

1. Forth-telling – Preaching
In Ezekiel Chapters 12-19 Ezekiel preaches to princes, prophets (false), priests and to elders of the nation of Judah. He reproves them of sin and idolatry and declares the judgments of God upon the evil abominations. He uses parabolic utterances woven into his preaching. He is a preacher of "the word of the Lord."

2. Fore-telling – Prediction
In Ezekiel Chapters 20-24, there are mingled prophecies concerning the judgments of God upon the House of Israel and the House of Judah. Woven throughout there are prophecies of blessing through the coming Messiah.

In Ezekiel Chapters 25-32 there are predictions of judgment on the surrounding Gentile nations. Here the destiny of nations is spoken of. It is mainly prediction. It is similar in the great chapters of Ezekiel 33-39. Here there are prophecies of doom and gloom, yet such are interspersed with prophecies of Messianic blessings.

(Note: Many times there is a blending or over-lapping of preaching and prediction, of forth-telling and fore-telling). Keeping this in mind when reading the Old Testament Prophets will help one's understanding, interpretation and application of things written therein.

C. Distinctions in the Prophetic Realm

1. The Spirit of Prophecy
Rev.19:10
Gen.2:20-25 with Eph.5:23-32
Jude 14-15
2Pet.2:5
Gen.20:7
Heb.11:20,21,24

The Spirit of Prophecy may fall upon a group of people at times –
Num.11:29-30; 1Sam.19:20-24; 10:10; 1Cor.14:25,31

2. The Gift of Prophecy
1Cor.12:10; Rom.12:6; Acts 2:18. All believers may have this gift.

Prophecy – 1Cor.14:3,24,25; 1Thess.5:20
Exhortation – "to stir up"
Edification – "to build up"
Comfort – "to bind up"

3. The Office of a Prophet – Hos.12:10; Heb.1:1
Old Testament – Elijah, Elisha, etc., and the Major and Minor Prophets
Prophetesses = Miriam, Deborah, Huldah, Anna (Ex.15:20; Jud.4:4;
2Chron.34:22; Lke.2:26-38).

4. The Prophecy of Scripture – 2Pet.1:19-21; 2Tim.3:15-17
The infallible Word.
Judges us.
Each judged by the Scripture

D. Ministry of New Testament Prophets

1. For New Covenant Believers
• Guidance, direction and control come from the infallible Word of God, the
  Holy Scriptures.
• Guidance also comes from the indwelling Holy Spirit, always leading in
  harmony with, never contrary to, the infallible Word which He inspired
  (Romans 8:14).
• Guidance and direction may also be confirmed through various ministries
  and counsel in the church, which can include prophets as well as other
  ministries and counsellors.
• As a general rule, the Lord is not going to tell others what you do not know
  yourself, especially as you desire to do the will of God.
• The prophet Agabus confirmed to the Apostle Paul what he already knew to
  be God's will in Acts 21:7-9.

2. New Testament Prophets and Ministry
The ministry of a New Testament prophet may include:
• The spirit of prophecy – Revelation 19:10; 1 Corinthians 12:8.
• Preaching the Word of God – forth-telling – I Peter 1:10-12.
• Fore-telling – predicting future events by the Spirit – Acts11:27-30;
  21:8-14.
• Exhortation and confirmation – Acts 15:22.
• Presbytery gatherings; laying on of hands and prophecy – 1Tim.1:18,19;
  2Tim.1:6-7 (Note: never exalt 'a word' above 'THE Word').
• Conviction by secrets of hearts exposed – I Corinthians 14:24-25.
• Visions and dreams – Numbers 12:6-8.
• Words of wisdom, words of knowledge – 1Cor.12:6-9
• Gifts of the Spirit in operation
• Illumination on the revelation given by inspiration – Eph.3:15

- Working with apostolic ministries for checks and balances – Eph.2:20-22; 1Cor.12:28-29; Luke 11:49

Conclusion/Application:
In this end of the age, the Lord is raising up a prophetic people. This end of the age will reveal it to be the most prophetic generation of all times, prior to the Second Coming of our Lord Jesus Christ. All must be governed by the inspired and infallible Word of the Lord – the Holy Scriptures!

ABOUT THE AUTHOR

Born in Melbourne, Australia in 1927 and saved at the age of 14, Kevin Conner served the Lord in the Salvation Army until the age of 21. At this time he entered into pastoral ministry for a number of years. After that, he was involved in teaching ministry in Australia, New Zealand and for many years at Bible Temple in Portland, Oregon. After serving as Senior Minister of Waverley Christian Fellowship for eight years (1987-1994), he continued to serve the church locally as well as ministering at various conferences and the continued writing of textbooks.

Kevin is recognised internationally as a teaching- apostle after his many years in both church and Bible College ministry. His textbooks have been used by ministers and students throughout the world. He has been in great demand as a teacher and has travelled extensively. Kevin passed away peacefully in Melbourne, Australia in February 2019 at the age of 92.

Visit Kevin's web site at www.kevinconner.org for more details about his life and ministry, as well as information about his 65 books, his video courses, and his audio teaching podcast.

OTHER RESOURCES BY KEVIN J. CONNER

KEVIN CONNER'S AUDIO TEACHING

We are excited to announce a new podcast of Kevin Conner's teaching messages. This podcast is available directly from Podbean (including on their mobile Apps) or from Apple's iTunes (including all iTunes Apps) or from within Spotify (if you are a subscriber).

Every week or so a message will be published, selected from messages Kevin has given over the years at various churches, conferences, and training seminars. Be sure to subscribe so you are notified of recent releases.

The teaching podcast includes a 8 part teaching series on the Book of Ezekiel (released in August 2020).

THE KEY OF KNOWLEDGE SEMINAR

Kevin Conner's popular "Key of Knowledge" Seminar is now available as an online teaching course. Part 1 covers 'Methods and Principles of Bible Research' and includes over 6 hours of video teaching, the required textbooks, extra hand out notes, and a self guided online study program.

Visit the course home page at www.kevinconner.org and select 'Courses' from the Menu for all the details. The first lesson, 'Challenge to Study' is FREE.

The second part of Kevin Conner's popular "Key of Knowledge" Seminar is also available as an online teaching course. While Part 1 covers Methods and Principles of Bible Research, Part 2 covers Interpreting the Bible and includes over 7 hours of video teaching, two downloadable textbooks, extra hand out notes, and a self guided online study program. These two courses can be taken as stand-alone courses, in succession, or simultaneously.

THE FOUNDATIONS OF CHRISTIAN DOCTRINE

Kevin Conner's best-selling book *The Foundations of Christian Doctrine* now has a video teaching course to go along with it, with 67 sessions of Kevin teaching this material in-depth. A self-study guide is included with the course. Visit www.kevinconner.org/courses for details.

KEVIN CONNER'S AUTOBIOGRAPHY

Kevin Conner is known by many people around the world as a theologian, Bible teacher, and best- selling author of over 60 biblical textbooks. Although thousands of people have been impacted by his ministry and his writings, only a few people know his personal story. Kevin took the time to detail his own life journey, including lessons gleaned along the way, in his auto-biography "This is My Story" back in 2007. It is available from www.amazon.com/author/kevinjconner in paperback and eBook formats, from www.word.com.au in Australia in paperback and as an immediate PDF download from www.kevinconner.org/shop

Kevin was an orphan who never met his dad or mum. He grew up in boy's homes before coming to faith in Jesus Christ in the Salvation Army in his teenage years. From there, his life took many turns as he continued to pursue his faith in God and his understanding of the Scriptures and church life. Follow his journey and gain wisdom for your own life and ministry as you read his intriguing life-story.

OTHER BOOKS BY KEVIN CONNER

Are Women Elders Biblical?
Biblical Principles of Leadership
The Book of Acts
The Book of Daniel (An Exposition)
The Book of Deuteronomy
The Book of Hebrews (An Exposition)
The Book of Jude (An Exposition)
The Book of Revelation (An Exposition)
Christian Millennium
The Church in the New Testament
The Church of the Firstborn and the Birthright
The Daily Ministrations
The Day After the Sabbath
The Death-Resurrection Route
An Evaluation of Joseph Prince's 'Destined to Reign'
The Feasts of Israel
Foundations of Christian Doctrine
Foundations of Christian Doctrine (Study Guide) Foundation Principles of Church Membership
Foundation Principles of the Doctrine of Christ
Frequently Asked Questions
Headship, Covering and Hats
The House of God
Interpreting the Book of Revelation
Interpreting the Symbols and Types
Interpreting the Scriptures

Interpreting the Scriptures (Self Study Guide)
The Kingdom Cult of Self
Keep Yourself Pure
Kings of the Kingdom
Law and Grace
The Lord Jesus Christ our Melchizedek Priest
The Manifest Presence
Marriage, Divorce and Remarriage
Methods and Principles of Bible Research
Ministries in the Cluster
The Ministry of Women
Mystery Parables of the Kingdom
The Name of God
New Covenant Realities
Only for Catholics
Passion Week Chart
Psalms - A Commentary
Relevance of Old Testament to a New Testament Church
Restoration Theology
Romans (An Exposition)
Sermon Outlines (3 Volumes)
The Seventy Weeks Prophecy
The Sword and Consequences
The Tabernacle of David
The Tabernacle of Moses
The Temple of Solomon
Table Talks
Tale of Three Trees
This is My Story (Kevin Conner's autobiography)
This We Believe
Three Days and Three Nights (with Chart)
Tithes and Offerings
Today's Prophets
To Drink or Not to Drink
To Smoke or Not to Smoke
Understanding New Birth and Baptism of the Holy Spirit
Vision of an Antioch Church
Water Baptism Thesis
What About Israel?

Visit www.kevinconner.org for more information.

Visit www.amazon.com/author/kevinjconner for a list of other books by Kevin Conner.

Printed in Great Britain
by Amazon